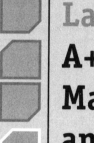

Lab Manual for
A+ Guide to Software: Managing, Maintaining, and Troubleshooting
FIFTH EDITION

Jean Andrews, Ph.D.

Todd Verge

COURSE TECHNOLOGY
CENGAGE Learning

Australia • Canada • Mexico • Singapore • Spain • United Kingdom • United States

COURSE TECHNOLOGY
CENGAGE Learning™

Lab Manual for
A+ Guide to Software: Managing, Maintaining,
and Troubleshooting
Fifth Edition
Jean Andrews/Todd Verge

Vice President, Career and Professional Editorial:
  Dave Garza

Executive Editor: Stephen Helba

Acquisitions Editor: Nick Lombardi

Managing Editor: Marah Bellegarde

Senior Product Manager: Michelle Ruelos Cannistraci

Developmental Editor: Jill Batistick

Editorial Assistant: Sarah Pickering

Vice President, Career and Professional Marketing:
  Jennifer McAvey

Marketing Director: Deborah S. Yarnell

Senior Marketing Manager: Erin Coffin

Marketing Coordinator: Shanna Gibbs

Production Director: Carolyn Miller

Production Manager: Andrew Crouth

Content Project Manager: Andrea Majot

Art Director: Jack Pendleton

Cover photo or illustration: Shutterstock

Manufacturing Coordinator: Julio Esperas

Copyeditor: Katherine A. Orrino

Proofreader: Christine Clark

Compositor: Integra

For product information and technology assistance, contact us at
Cengage Learning Customer & Sales Support, 1-800-354-9706

For permission to use material from this text or product,
submit all requests online at **cengage.com/permissions**
Further permissions questions can be emailed to
permissionrequest@cengage.com

ISBN-13: 978-1-4354-8735-2

ISBN-10: 1-4354-8735-4

Course Technology
25 Channel Center Street
Boston, MA 02210
USA

Some of the product names and company names used in this book have been used for identification purposes only and may be trademarks or registered trademarks of their respective manufacturers and sellers.

Microsoft and the Office logo are either registered trademarks or trademarks of Microsoft Corporation in the United States and/or other countries. Course Technology, a part of Cengage Learning, is an independent entity from the Microsoft Corporation, and not affiliated with Microsoft in any manner.

Any fictional data related to persons or companies or URLs used throughout this book is intended for instructional purposes only. At the time this book was printed, any such data was fictional and not belonging to any real persons or companies.

Course Technology and the Course Technology logo are registered trademarks used under license.

Course Technology, a part of Cengage Learning, reserves the right to revise this publication and make changes from time to time in its content without notice.

The programs in this book are for instructional purposes only. They have been tested with care, but are not guaranteed for any particular intent beyond educational purposes. The author and the publisher do not offer any warranties or representations, nor do they accept any liabilities with respect to the programs.

Cengage Learning is a leading provider of customized learning solutions with office locations around the globe, including Singapore, the United Kingdom, Australia, Mexico, Brazil, and Japan. Locate your local office at: **international.cengage.com/region**

Cengage Learning products are represented in Canada by Nelson Education, Ltd.

For your lifelong learning solutions, visit **course.cengage.com**

Visit our corporate website at **cengage.com**.

Printed in the United States of America
1 2 3 4 5 6 7 12 11 10 09

Table of Contents

Preface

This lab manual is designed to be the best tool on the market to enable you to get the hands-on practical experience you need to learn to troubleshoot and repair personal computers and operating systems. It contains more than 65 labs, each of which targets a practical problem you're likely to face in the real world when troubleshooting PCs. Every attempt has been made to write labs that allow you to use generic hardware devices. A specific hardware configuration isn't necessary to complete the labs. In learning to install, support, and troubleshoot operating systems, you learn to support Windows Vista and Windows XP Professional and to use the command prompt. Each chapter contains labs designed to provide the structure novices need, as well as labs that challenge experienced and inquisitive students.

This book helps prepare you for the new A+ 2009 Certification exams offered through the Computer Technology Industry Association (CompTIA): A+ Essentials (220–701) and A+ Practical Application (220-702). Because the popularity of this certification credential is quickly growing among employers, becoming certified increases your ability to gain employment, improve your salary, and enhance your career. To find more information about A+ Upgrade Certification and its sponsoring organization, CompTIA, go to the CompTIA Web site at *www.comptia.org*.

Whether your goal is to become an A+ certified technician or a PC support technician, the *Lab Manual for A+ Guide to Software, Fifth Edition*, along with Jean Andrews's textbooks, will take you there!

FEATURES

To ensure a successful experience for both instructors and students, this book includes the following pedagogical features:

- ◿ **Objectives**—Every lab opens with learning objectives that set the stage for students to absorb the lab's lessons.
- ◿ **Materials Required**—This feature outlines all the materials students need to complete the lab successfully.
- ◿ **Lab Preparation**—This feature alerts instructors and lab assistants to items to check or set up before the lab begins.
- ◿ **Activity Background**—A brief discussion at the beginning of each lab provides important background information.
- ◿ **Estimated Completion Time**—To help students plan their work, each lab includes an estimate of the total amount of time required to complete it.
- ◿ **Activity**—Detailed, numbered steps walk students through the lab. These steps are divided into manageable sections, with explanatory material between each section.
- ◿ **Figures**—Where appropriate, photographs of hardware or screenshots of software are provided to increase student mastery of the lab topic.
- ◿ **Review Questions**—Questions at the end of each lab help students test their understanding of the lab material.
- ◿ **Web Site**—For updates to this book and information about other A+ and PC Repair products, go to *http://www.cengage.com/coursetechnology/*

ACKNOWLEDGMENTS

Jean and Todd would first like to thank Jill Batistick for her hard work and attention to detail throughout the editorial process. They would also like to extend their sincere appreciation to Michelle Ruelos Cannistraci, Nick Lombardi, Nicole Ashton, Jessica McNavich, Andrea Majot, and all the Course Technology/Cengage staff for their instrumental roles in developing this lab manual. Many thanks to all the instructors who offered great suggestions for new labs and encouraged us to make other changes to the previous editions. Keep those suggestions coming!

Todd gives special thanks to his wife, Janine, and daughters Katie and Ella for their love and support. Finally, he would like to again thank Jean Andrews for her generosity in giving him this opportunity and all the doors it has opened.

Many thanks to the peer reviewers:

Keith Conn, Cleveland Institute of Electronics, Cleveland, OH

Scott Johnson, Crete High School, Crete, NE

Brandon Lehmann, Terra Community College, Fremont, OH

Vincent March, Palomar College, San Marcos, CA

Terry Sadorus, Lewis-Clark State College, Lewiston, ID

Jim Siscoe, Moore Norman Technology Center, Norman, OK

CLASSROOM SETUP

Lab activities have been designed to explore many different hardware setup and troubleshooting problems while attempting to keep the requirements for specific hardware to a minimum. Most labs can be done alone, although a few ask you to work with a partner. If you prefer to work alone, simply do all the steps yourself. Most lab activities have been designed to work in either Windows Vista or Windows XP Professional. In some cases, a particular operating system will be required.

Typical labs take 30 to 45 minutes; a few might take a little longer. For several of the labs, your classroom should be networked and provide access to the Internet. When access to Windows setup files is required, these files can be provided on the Windows installation CD/DVD, a network drive made available to the PC, or some other type of removable storage media.

These are the minimum hardware requirements for Windows Vista:

- 800MHz or better Pentium-compatible computer (1GHz preferred)
- 512MB of RAM (1GB preferred)
- 20GB hard drive (40GB preferred)
- An NTFS partition that can be the partition where Windows Vista is installed
- A user account with administrative privileges

These are the minimum hardware requirements for Windows XP Professional:

- 233MHz or better Pentium-compatible computer (300MHz preferred)
- 64MB of RAM (128MB preferred)
- 1.5GB hard drive (2GB preferred)
- An NTFS partition that can be the partition where Windows XP is installed
- A user account with administrative privileges

When the OS isn't of concern, the minimum hardware requirements are as follows:

- 233MHz or better Pentium-compatible computer
- 64MB of RAM
- 1.5GB hard drive
- A PC toolkit with an antistatic ground bracelet (ESD strap)

A few labs require software that can be freely downloaded from the Internet.

LAB SETUP INSTRUCTIONS

CONFIGURATION TYPE AND OPERATING SYSTEMS

Each lab begins with a list of required materials. Before beginning a lab activity, each student workgroup or individual should verify access to these materials. Then make sure the correct operating system is installed and in good health. Note that in some cases, installing an operating system isn't necessary. When needed, the Windows setup files can be made available on the Windows CD/DVD, a network drive, or some type of removable media storage. In some labs, device drivers are needed. Students can work more efficiently if these drivers are available before beginning the lab.

PROTECT DATA

In several labs, data on the hard drive might get lost or corrupted. For this reason, it's important that valuable data stored on the hard drive is backed up to another medium.

ACCESS TO THE INTERNET

Several labs require access to the Internet. If necessary, you can use one computer to search the Internet and download software or documentation and another computer for performing the lab procedures. If the lab doesn't have Internet access, you can download the required software or documentation before the lab and bring the files to lab on some sort of storage medium.

THE TECHNICIAN'S WORK AREA

When opening a computer case, it's important to have the right tools and to be properly grounded to ensure that you don't cause more damage than you repair. Take a look at the items that should be part of any technician's work area:

- Grounding mat or bench (with grounding wire properly grounded)
- Grounding wrist strap (attached to the grounding mat)
- Non-carpet flooring
- A clean work area (no clutter)
- A set of screwdrivers
- 1/4-inch Torx bit screwdriver
- 1/8-inch Torx bit screwdriver
- Needlenose pliers
- A PLCC (plastic leadless chip carrier)
- Pen light (flashlight)
- Several new antistatic bags (for transporting and storing hardware)

At minimum, you must have at least two key items. The first is a grounding strap. If a grounding mat isn't available, you can attach the grounding strap to the computer's chassis and, in most cases, provide sufficient grounding for handling hardware components inside the computer case. The second key item is, of course, a screwdriver. You won't be able to open most cases without some type of screwdriver.

PROTECT YOURSELF, YOUR HARDWARE, AND YOUR SOFTWARE

When you work on a computer, harming both the computer and yourself is possible. The most common accident when attempting to fix a computer problem is erasing software or data. Experimenting without knowing what you're doing can cause damage. To prevent these sorts of accidents as well as physically dangerous ones, take a few safety precautions. The following sections describe potential sources of damage to computers and explain how to protect against them.

POWER TO THE COMPUTER

To protect yourself and the equipment when working inside a computer, turn off the power, unplug the computer, and always use an antistatic grounding strap. Consider the monitor and the power supply to be "black boxes." Never remove the cover or put your hands inside this equipment unless you know the hazards of charged capacitors. Both the power supply and the monitor can hold a dangerous level of electricity even after they're turned off and disconnected from a power source.

STATIC ELECTRICITY OR ESD

Electrostatic discharge (ESD), commonly known as static electricity, is an electrical charge at rest. A static charge can build up on the surface of a nongrounded conductor and on nonconductive surfaces, such as clothing or plastic. When two objects with dissimilar electrical charges touch, static electricity passes between them until the dissimilar charges are made equal. To see how this works, turn off the lights in a room, scuff your feet on the carpet, and touch another person. Occasionally you see and feel the charge in your fingers. If you can feel the charge, you discharged at least 3000 volts of static electricity. If you hear the discharge, you released at least 6000 volts. If you see the discharge, you released at least 8000 volts of ESD. A charge of less than 3000 volts can damage most electronic components. You can touch a chip on an expansion card or system board and damage the chip with ESD and never feel, hear, or see the discharge.

ESD can cause two types of damage in an electronic component: catastrophic failures and upset failures. A catastrophic failure destroys the component beyond use. An upset failure damages the component so that it doesn't perform well, even though it might still function to some degree. Upset failures are the most difficult to detect because they aren't easily observed.

PROTECT AGAINST ESD

To protect the computer against ESD, always ground yourself before touching electronic components, including the hard drive, system board, expansion cards, processors, and memory modules, by using one or more of the following static control devices or methods:

▴ *Grounding strap or antistatic strap:* A grounding strap is a bracelet you wear around your wrist. The other end is attached to a grounded conductor, such as the computer case or a ground mat, or it can be plugged into a wall outlet. (Only the ground prong makes a connection!)

◿ *Grounding mats:* Grounding mats can come equipped with a cord to plug into a wall outlet to provide a grounded surface on which to work. Remember, if you lift the component off the mat, it's no longer grounded and is susceptible to ESD.

◿ *Static shielding bags:* New components come shipped in static shielding bags. Save the bags to store other devices that aren't currently installed in a PC.

The best way to protect against ESD is to use a grounding strap with a grounding mat. You should consider a grounding strap essential equipment when working on a computer. However, if you're in a situation where you must work without one, touch the computer case before you touch a component. When passing a chip to another person, ground yourself. Leave components inside their protective bags until you're ready to use them. Work on hard floors, not carpet, or use antistatic spray on carpets.

There's an exception to the ground-yourself rule. Inside a monitor case, the electricity stored in capacitors poses a substantial danger. When working inside a monitor, you *don't* want to be grounded, as you would provide a conduit for the voltage to discharge through your body. In this situation, be careful *not* to ground yourself.

When handling system boards and expansion cards, don't touch the chips on the boards. Don't stack boards on top of each other, which could accidentally dislodge a chip. Hold cards by the edges, but don't touch the edge connections on the card.

After you unpack a new device or software that has been wrapped in cellophane, remove the cellophane from the work area quickly. Don't allow anyone who's not properly grounded to touch components. Don't store expansion cards within one foot of a CRT monitor because the monitor can discharge as much as 29,000 volts of ESD from the screen.

Hold an expansion card by the edges. Don't touch any of the soldered components on a card. If you need to put an electronic device down, place it on a grounding mat or a static shielding bag. Keep components away from your hair and clothing.

PROTECT HARD DRIVES AND DISKS

Always turn off a computer before moving it. Doing so protects the hard drive, which is always spinning when the computer is turned on (unless the drive has a sleep mode). Never jar a computer while the hard disk is running. Avoid placing a PC on the floor, where users could accidentally kick it.

Follow the usual precautions to protect CDs and floppy disks. Protect the bottom of CDs from scratches and keep them away from heat and direct sunlight. Keep floppies away from magnetic fields, heat, and extreme cold. Don't open the floppy shuttle window or touch the surface of the disk inside the housing. Treat disks with care, and they'll usually last for years.

CHAPTER 1

Introducing Operating Systems

Labs included in this chapter:

LAB 1.1 EXAMINE FILES AND DIRECTORIES

OBJECTIVES

The goal of this lab is to use different methods to examine files and directories. After completing this lab, you will be able to:

⊿ Use the command line to view information about files and directories

⊿ Use Computer (My Computer in XP) to view information about files and directories

⊿ Display information about files and directories in other ways

MATERIALS REQUIRED

This lab requires the following:

⊿ Windows Vista/XP operating system

LAB PREPARATION

Before the lab begins, the instructor or lab assistant needs to do the following:

⊿ Verify that Windows starts with no errors.

ACTIVITY BACKGROUND

You can access information about a PC's file structure in several ways. At the Windows desktop, you can use Windows Explorer or My Computer to view the files and directories. From the command line, you can use the DIR command to list the same information. In the following lab, you practice using the DIR command and My Computer.

> **ESTIMATED COMPLETION TIME: 30 Minutes**

 Activity

Follow these steps to access file information via the command line:

1. To open a command prompt window, click **Start**, type **cmd** in the Start Search box, and press **Enter**. (In XP, click **Start**, click **Run**, type **cmd**, and press **Enter**.)

2. When the command prompt window opens, type **help** and press **Enter** to view a list of commands that are available. You can get additional information about a command by typing help and the name of the command.

3. Type **help dir** and press **Enter**. Information and parameters (also called "switches" or "options") for the DIR command are displayed. How many different parameters does the command have?

---

4. In a command prompt window, the prompt indicates the current directory. Type **dir** and press **Enter**. A detailed list of files and directories in the current directory is displayed. If there are many files and directories, only the last several are visible on the screen.

5. Use Help to examine the /p and /w switches for the dir command, and then try these variations and explain how the information is displayed:

   dir /p _____

   dir /w _____

6. Examine the results of the DIR command. The results vary with different versions of Windows, but each listing should include the following information:

   ◢ The date and time the file was created

   ◢ The directory markers (directories do not include an extension; instead, they are indicated by a <DIR> marker tag)

   ◢ The file size in bytes

   ◢ The name of a file or directory (most files have an extension)

   ◢ A summary, including the number of files and directories in that directory, the number of bytes those files use, and the number of bytes of free space on the drive

To print this file information, you can copy the contents of the command prompt window to Windows Clipboard, open the Notepad program, paste the file information into Notepad, and then use the Notepad Print command. To try that technique now, follow these steps:

1. On the far left of the command prompt window's title bar, click the **Command Prompt** icon. A drop-down list appears.

2. On the drop-down list, point to **Edit,** and then click **Mark.** A blinking cursor then appears at the top of the command prompt window.

3. Click and drag the cursor over the information you would like to copy to the Clipboard; the information should then be highlighted. You might need to scroll the window to capture all the necessary information.

4. After you have highlighted all the information you want to copy, click the **Command Prompt** icon on the title bar.

5. On the drop-down list, point to **Edit,** and then click **Copy.** The highlighted contents are copied to the Clipboard.

6. To open Notepad, click **Start,** point to **Programs (All Programs** in XP), point to **Accessories,** and click **Notepad.**

7. Click **Edit,** and then click **Paste** from the Notepad menu.

8. Click **File,** and then click **Print** from the Notepad menu. Use the print options to print your document.

9. Close the command prompt window and Notepad without saving the file.

In addition to the command prompt window, you can use Windows Explorer to examine files and directories. Windows Explorer can display information in a variety of ways. Before you view files and directories with this tool, you need to change some settings to control how information is displayed. To change settings in Windows Vista, follow these steps:

1. Click **Start,** and then click **Control Panel.**

2. Click **Appearance and Personalization,** and then click **Folder Options** from the menu. The Folder Options dialog box opens.

3. In the Folder Options dialog box, click the **View** tab, click to select the **Show hidden files and folders** button, and uncheck the **Hide extensions for known file types** check box.

4. Click **Apply,** and then click **OK** to close the Folder Options dialog box.

To change settings in Windows XP, follow these steps:

1. To open the My Computer window, click **Start**, and then click **My Computer**.

2. Click **Tools**, and then click **Folder Options** from the menu. The Folder Options dialog box opens.

3. In the Folder Options dialog box, click the **View** tab (if necessary), click to select the **Show hidden files and folders** button, and click to clear the **Hide extensions for known file types** check box.

4. Click **Apply**, and then click **OK** to close the Folder Options dialog box.

Now that you have changed the way information is displayed, you're ready to use Windows Explorer through Computer (My Computer in XP) to access specific information about your system's files and directories. Complete the following:

1. Click **Start**, and then click **Computer** (**My Computer** in XP). Maximize the Computer window, and click the icon representing drive **C**; you'll see details about the drive displayed in the bottom or left pane.

2. How much free space is available on drive C? What is the total size of the drive?

_____

3. Based on total size and free space, how much space is used on drive C?

_____

4. Double-click the drive C icon. What information about each folder is displayed in this window?

_____

_____

5. Windows uses different icons for different file types. Describe three different icons and the files they represent:

_____

_____

_____

6. From the Computer menu, click **View**, and then click **Details**. Notice that this command displays the same information as the DIR command.

7. Close all open windows.

REVIEW QUESTIONS

1. What command displays a list of files and directories at the command line?

_____

2. Does Windows display all system files by default?

_____

3. How can you change the way Windows displays file extensions?

_____

_____

4. In Computer, what type of graphic displays information about a drive?

_____

5. How does Windows graphically distinguish between different file types?

_____

LAB 1.2 CONVERT BINARY AND HEXADECIMAL NUMBERS

OBJECTIVES

The goal of this lab is to practice converting numbers between decimal, binary, and hexadecimal forms. After completing this lab, you will be able to:

◢ Convert decimal numbers (base 10) to hexadecimal and binary form

◢ Convert hexadecimal numbers (base 16) to binary and decimal form

◢ Convert binary numbers (base 2) to decimal and hexadecimal form

MATERIALS REQUIRED

This lab requires the following:

◢ A pencil and paper and/or Windows Calculator

◢ Access to the online content "The Hexadecimal Number System and Memory Addressing," downloaded from *www.cengage.com/coursetechnology/*

◢ Windows Vista/XP operating system

LAB PREPARATION

Before the lab begins, the instructor or lab assistant needs to do the following:

◢ Announce to students that, before they come to lab, they should read the online content "The Hexadecimal Number System and Memory Addressing." They might like to bring this content to class in printed form.

ACTIVITY BACKGROUND

Sometimes you need to know what resources, such as memory addresses, are being reserved for a device. This information is often displayed on a computer using the binary or hexadecimal (hex) numbering system. Often, you'll want to convert these numbers into more familiar decimal numbers to get a better picture of which resources are reserved for a device.

ESTIMATED COMPLETION TIME: 60 Minutes

🕙 Activity

1. Convert the following decimal numbers to binary numbers using a calculator or by following the instructions in the online content "The Hexadecimal Number System and Memory Addressing." (To access Windows Calculator, click **Start**, point to **All Programs**, point to **Accessories**, and then click **Calculator**. If necessary, click **View**,

and then click **Scientific** from the Calculator menu to perform the conversions in these steps.)

- ◢ 14 = _____
- ◢ 77 = _____
- ◢ 128 = _____
- ◢ 223 = _____
- ◢ 255 = _____

2. Convert the following decimal numbers to hexadecimal notation:

- ◢ 13 = _____
- ◢ 240 = _____
- ◢ 255 = _____
- ◢ 58880 = _____
- ◢ 65535 = _____

3. Convert the following binary numbers to hexadecimal notation:

- ◢ 100 = _____
- ◢ 1011 = _____
- ◢ 111101 = _____
- ◢ 11111000 = _____
- ◢ 10110011 = _____
- ◢ 00000001 = _____

4. Hexadecimal numbers are often preceded with "0x." Convert the following hex numbers to binary numbers:

- ◢ 0x0016 = _____
- ◢ 0x00F8 = _____
- ◢ 0x00B2B = _____
- ◢ 0x005A = _____
- ◢ 0x1234 = _____

5. Convert the following hex numbers to decimal:

- ◢ 0x0013 = _____
- ◢ 0x00AB = _____
- ◢ 0x01CE = _____
- ◢ 0x812A = _____

6. Convert the following binary numbers to decimal:

- ◢ 1011 = _____
- ◢ 11011 = _____
- ◢ 10101010 = _____
- ◢ 111110100 = _____
- ◢ 10111011101 = _____
- ◢ 11111000001111 = _____

A network card, also called a network adapter or NIC, is assigned an address that identifies the card on the network. The address is called the Media Access Control (MAC) or physical address. The address assigned to the network card is expressed in a series of paired hexadecimal numbers separated by dashes. In the following steps, you find out the network address for your network card and then convert the address to a binary number:

1. Open the command prompt window (see Lab 1.1), type **ipconfig /all**, and press **Enter**.

2. Write down the following information for your system:

   ◢ Network adapter address in hexadecimal form: _____

   ◢ Network adapter address in binary pairs: _____

3. Referring to Figure 1-1, convert the numbers in the network adapter's memory range and determine how many bytes, expressed in a decimal number, are in its memory address range.

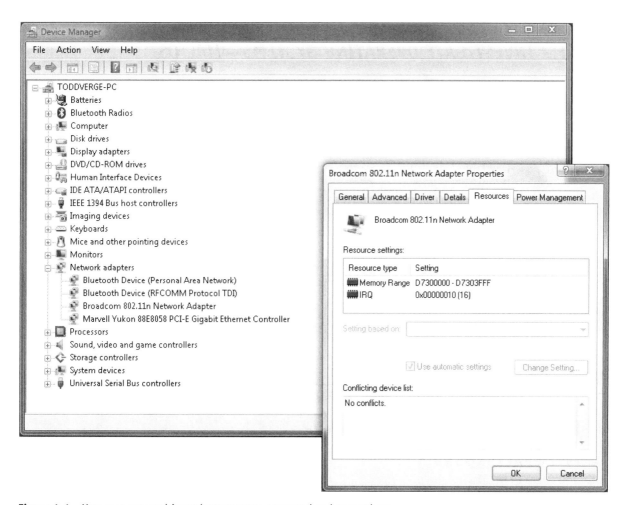

Figure 1-1 Memory range and input/output range expressed as hex numbers
Courtesy: Course Technology/Cengage Learning

CRITICAL THINKING (ADDITIONAL 15 MINUTES)

A typical video card uses a color depth of 8 bits to define the screen color in safe mode. Eight bits can form 256 different numbers from 00000000 to 11111111 in binary (0 to 255 in decimal) so 256 different colors are possible. How many colors are available with a 16-bit color depth? What about a 24-bit or 32-bit depth?

REVIEW QUESTIONS

1. How long, in bits, is a typical MAC address?

   _____

2. Computers often express numbers in _____ format, which is a base 16 numbering system.

3. Most people are more comfortable working with a(n) _____, or base 10, numbering system.

4. In the hexadecimal system, what decimal value does the letter A represent?

   _____

5. Hexadecimal numbers are often preceded by _____ so that a value containing only numerals is not mistaken for a decimal number.

LAB 1.3 INVESTIGATE OPERATING SYSTEMS—MAC OS

OBJECTIVES

The goal of this lab is to familiarize you with Macintosh operating systems and the hardware they support. After completing this lab, you will be able to:

▲ Describe the various Apple operating systems, hardware, and applications

▲ Research Apple technology on the Apple Web site (*www.apple.com*)

MATERIALS REQUIRED

This lab requires the following:

▲ Internet access

LAB PREPARATION

Before the lab begins, the instructor or lab assistant needs to do the following:

▲ Verify that Internet access is available.

> **Notes** If a Macintosh system is available, instructors might want to give a brief demonstration for students.

ACTIVITY BACKGROUND

Macintosh operating systems are designed to be used only on Macintosh (Mac) computers (see Figure 1-2). Many developers (including Apple, the company that created the Macintosh computer) have created Macintosh applications. The Apple Web site (*www.apple.com*) is the best source of information about Macintosh products. In this lab, you investigate Macintosh operating systems, hardware, and applications.

ESTIMATED COMPLETION TIME: 30 Minutes

 Activity

1. Open your browser and go to **www.apple.com**. Explore the site, and when you're done, return to the main page. Use the links on the site to answer the questions in this lab.

Figure 1-2 A typical OS X desktop
Courtesy: Course Technology/Cengage Learning

2. What is the latest version of the Mac operating system available for a new iMac?

_____

3. What is the cost of upgrading your operating system to the latest version of OS X?

_____

4. Compare the iMac, Mac mini, and Mac Pro systems available for sale on the Apple Web site. What are the speeds or frequencies of the processors in each computer?

_____

5. How much does the fastest 24-inch iMac cost?

_____

6. What software comes bundled with an iMac?

_____

7. What is a MacBook?

_____

8. How much does the most expensive MacBook Pro cost?

_____

9. What features are included with the least expensive MacBook?

10. Describe the features of an Apple Mighty Mouse:

11. What is the function of an AirPort Extreme Base Station?

12. What is the difference between the AirPort Extreme and the AirPort Express?

13. What is the purpose of QuickTime software?

14. Describe what the iWork software does:

15. Describe the purposes of iLife software:

REVIEW QUESTIONS

1. What is one advantage of using an Apple computer instead of a PC?

2. What is one disadvantage of using an Apple computer instead of a PC?

3. Why do you think it's easier for Apple to provide compatibility between hardware and the operating system than it is for Microsoft or Linux?

4. Why can't OS X run on a typical PC?

LAB 1.4 INVESTIGATE OPERATING SYSTEMS—LINUX

OBJECTIVES

The goal of this lab is to find information about Linux. After completing this lab, you will be able to:

◢ Research Linux on the Linux Web site (*www.linux.org*)

◢ Compare Linux with other operating systems

◢ Use the Linux tutorial on the Linux Web site

MATERIALS REQUIRED

This lab requires the following:

◢ Internet access

◢ A blank CD

◢ A CD burner and compatible burning software

LAB PREPARATION

Before the lab begins, the instructor or lab assistant needs to do the following:

◢ Verify that Internet access is available.

ACTIVITY BACKGROUND

UNIX is a popular OS used to control networks and support applications on the Internet (see Figure 1-3). Linux is a scaled-down version of UNIX that is provided, in basic form, free of charge and includes open access to the programming code of the OS. Linux can be used as both a server platform and a desktop platform, but its greatest popularity has come in the server market. In this lab, you search the *www.linux.org* site for general information on Linux and survey the Linux tutorial.

ESTIMATED COMPLETION TIME: 45 Minutes

Activity

1. Open your browser and go to **www.linux.org**. Spend a few minutes exploring the site on your own, and then return to the main page.

2. Click the **General Info** link (on the navigation bar). Using the information on the "What is Linux" page, answer the following:

   ◢ What is the current, full-featured version of the Linux kernel?

   _____

   ◢ Who is credited with inventing the Linux kernel?

   _____

   ◢ How is Linux licensed? Read the GNU General Public License. Give a brief description of the terms and conditions of this license:

   _____

   _____

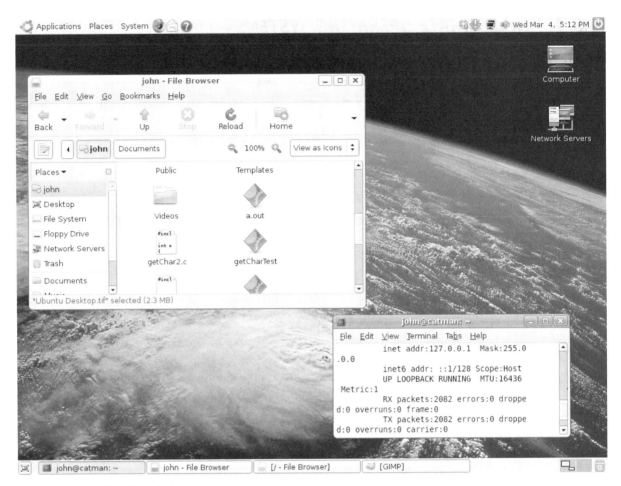

Figure 1-3   A typical Linux desktop
Courtesy: Course Technology/Cengage Learning

◢ How much does Linux cost?

For an operating system to be useful, applications must be written for it. Suppose a small business is interested in using Linux on its desktop computers. Will this business be able to run common business-type applications on its Linux desktops? To find out, click the **Applications** link (on the navigation bar). The types of applications are listed by category. Search this page and its links to answer the following questions:

1. Will the business be able to send faxes from a Linux machine?

2. List two Web browsers suitable for Linux.

3. How many antivirus software packages are available for Linux? List at least two.

4. After searching under Office and Word Processor, list at least three word-processing applications available for Linux.

5. How many accounting applications are available for Linux? List at least two and the URLs where you found them.

_____

_____

Now you can continue exploring the Linux Web site. Follow these steps to compare Linux to other operating systems:

1. Click the **Documentation** link on the navigation bar.

2. Read about the Linux Documentation Project.

3. Use the information on the Linux Web site to answer the following questions:

◢ What is the Linux Documentation Project?

_____

_____

◢ Who is responsible for writing documentation for the Linux operating system?

_____

Next, follow these steps to explore the Web site's Linux tutorial:

1. Return to the home page, scroll down to display the heading **Linux 101**, and then click **more** at the bottom of that section.

2. Scroll down, and then click **Getting Started with Linux – Beginner's Course**. Browse through this tutorial and answer the questions in this lab.

3. What might you consider when deciding which version (distribution) of Linux to install?

_____

_____

4. Can you install Linux on a computer that has another operating system already installed (print the Web page supporting your answer)?

_____

5. If you don't have a high-speed Internet connection or a CD-burner, what is another way you can get a copy of Linux for your home PC?

_____

Continue exploring the Web site by completing the following:

1. Click the **Distributions** link. A link to the source code for Linux kernels is available on this page. Notice the Distribution search area. When searching for a distribution of Linux, if you don't narrow your search, you might get an overwhelming number of returns. The subsequent steps of this lab limit your search.

2. Click **English** in the Language drop-down list.

3. Click **Mainstream/General Public** in the Category drop-down list.

4. Click **Intel compatible** in the Platform list, and then click **Go**. How many distributions do you see listed?

_____

5. Browse through the list, looking for openSUSE, Debian, and Fedora Linux. Which distribution appears to be easiest to use? What is its intended purpose?

_____

6. Can Linux be used on other systems that don't run Intel-compatible processors? Print the Web page supporting your answer.

_____

REVIEW QUESTIONS

1. What are some of the "costs" associated with installing a "free" operating system such as Linux?

_____

2. Why might a company not want to use Linux on its desktop computers?

_____

_____

3. What is one advantage of using Linux rather than a Windows operating system on a desktop?

_____

4. Based on what you learned from the Linux Web site, how do you think companies that provide Linux make the most profit?

_____

CRITICAL THINKING (ADDITIONAL 45 MINUTES)

Many distributions of Linux will run directly off a bootable CD called a Live CD. Go to _www.ubuntu.com_ and download the latest version of the Ubuntu distribution of Linux. Burn the .ISO image you downloaded to a CD and use it to boot your computer. Take some time to explore the interface and then answer the following questions:

1. What does the button in the upper-left corner of the screen allow you to do?

_____

2. Does Ubuntu use the Gnome or KDE graphical interface by default?

_____

3. Name an Internet browser that is included with the operating system.

_____

LAB 1.5 COMPARE OPERATING SYSTEMS

OBJECTIVES

The goal of this lab is to help you learn about the history of PC operating systems and appreciate why many of today's operating systems share similar features. After completing this lab, you will be able to:

◢ Better understand the relationship among operating systems

MATERIALS REQUIRED

This lab requires the following:

◢ Internet access

LAB PREPARATION

Before the lab begins, the instructor or lab assistant needs to do the following:

◢ Verify that Internet access is available.

ACTIVITY BACKGROUND

Modern operating systems, such as Windows, Linux, and Mac OS, have many similar features because they share a common history. Figure 1-4 shows some highlights of this history. The arrows indicate a direct or indirect influence from an earlier operating system.

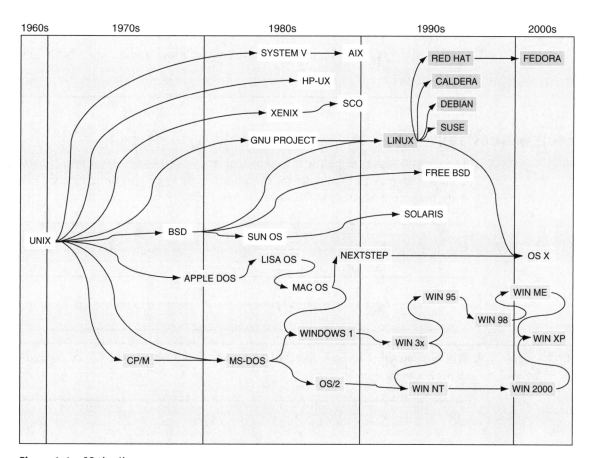

Figure 1-4 OS timeline
Courtesy: Course Technology/Cengage Learning

ESTIMATED COMPLETION TIME: 30 Minutes

 Activity

Use your favorite search engine, such as *www.google.com*, to answer the following questions:

1. Search for the "history of operating systems." List the URLs of three sites that you think do a good job of explaining this history.

2. What are two similarities and two differences between the original Mac OS and Windows?

3. How is OS/2 loosely connected to Windows NT?

4. What is the relationship of QDOS to CP/M and MS-DOS?

5. Modify the timeline by adding any other past operating systems, such as BeOS or VMS, that you think are important.

CHALLENGE ACTIVITY (ADDITIONAL 15 MINUTES)

1. Extend the timeline into the future by adding any new operating systems with their expected release dates.
2. What is the next operating system planned in the Windows line and when will it be released?

REVIEW QUESTIONS

1. Research OS timelines on the Internet (or refer back to Figure 1-4). Then, based on the OS timelines that you find, answer this question: Why do you think Linux and UNIX share more commands than Windows XP and UNIX?

2. Which line of operating systems has recently become more similar to UNIX?

3. Which line of operating systems split into two lines, only to merge again later?

4. Why do you think most versions of Linux and Windows use the CD command to change directories?

LAB 1.6 USE WINDOWS KEYBOARD SHORTCUTS

OBJECTIVES

The goal of this lab is to introduce you to some keyboard shortcuts. After completing this lab, you will be able to use the keyboard to:

⊿ Display the Start menu

⊿ Switch between open applications

⊿ Launch utilities with the Windows logo key

MATERIALS REQUIRED

This lab requires the following:

◢ Windows XP operating system

◢ A keyboard with the Windows logo key

LAB PREPARATION

Before the lab begins, the instructor or lab assistant needs to do the following:

◢ Verify that Windows starts with no errors.

ACTIVITY BACKGROUND

You can use certain keys or key combinations (called keyboard shortcuts) to perform repetitive tasks more efficiently. These shortcuts are also useful when the mouse isn't working. In this lab, you learn to use some common keyboard shortcuts. You can find a full list of keyboard shortcuts by searching for "keyboard shortcuts" in the Windows Help and Support Center.

ESTIMATED COMPLETION TIME: 30 Minutes

 Activity

The F1 key is the universal keyboard shortcut for launching Help. To learn more, follow these steps:

1. Open Paint and then minimize it.

2. Open Notepad and then minimize it.

3. Click the desktop, and then press **F1**. Windows Help and Support opens.

4. Close Windows Help and Support, and restore Paint.

5. Press **F1**. Because Paint is now the active window, Windows Help and Support opens with information on Paint. Close this window.

6. Restore Notepad, and then press **F1**. Windows Help and Support opens with information about Notepad.

You can activate many shortcuts by pressing the Windows logo key in combination with other keys. An enhanced keyboard has two Windows logo keys, usually located between the Ctrl and Alt keys on either side of the spacebar. Try the combinations listed in Table 1-1, and record the result of each key combination in the Result column. (Close each window you open before proceeding to the next key combination.)

Key or Key Combination	Result
Windows logo	
Windows logo+E	
Windows logo+F	
Windows logo+R	
Windows logo+Break	
Windows logo+M	

Table 1-1 Key combinations using the Windows logo key

Suppose for some reason that your mouse isn't working and you have to print a text file. You would have to use the keyboard to find, select, open, and print the document. To learn more, follow these steps:

1. Boot the computer, wait for the Windows desktop to appear, and then unplug the mouse.

2. Press **Tab** a few times until one of the desktop icons is highlighted.

3. Use the arrow keys to highlight **Recycle Bin**.

4. Press **Enter**. The Recycle Bin opens.

5. Press **Tab** a few times and observe all the choices being highlighted. You can use a combination of Tab, arrow keys, and Enter to select almost anything in an open window.

6. Use this method to find, select, and open the Notepad program (from **Start, Programs, Accessories, Notepad**) and type "Have a Nice Day."

7. Notice in the Notepad window that one letter of each menu item becomes underlined after you press **Alt**. You can select menu options by holding down the Alt key while you press this underlined letter. For example, to open the File menu in Notepad, hold down the **Alt** key and press **F**. After the menu is open, you can use the arrow keys to move over the menu and select an option by pressing **Enter**, or you can type the underlined letter of a menu option. With the **Alt** key pressed down, press F. The File menu opens.

8. Press **P** to select Print. The Print dialog box opens.

9. Verify that the correct printer is selected. (To select a different printer, use the arrow keys.)

10. To send the print job to the printer, press **Tab** until the Print button is active, and then press **Enter** (or you can press **Alt+P**).

11. Practice editing text, using the following shortcuts for cutting, copying, and pasting:

    ◢ To delete one or more characters, move your cursor to the beginning of the text you want to delete, hold down the **Shift** key, and use the arrow keys to highlight the text. (If you were using a mouse, you could hold down the left mouse button and drag the mouse until the entire block was highlighted.)

    ◢ With the text highlighted, hold down the **Ctrl** key, press **X**, and then release both keys. This action cuts the highlighted text from its original location and moves it to the Clipboard. You can then paste it in another location.

    ◢ To copy a highlighted block of characters to the Clipboard (without removing it from its original location), hold down the **Ctrl** key, press **C**, and then release both keys. A copy of the highlighted block of characters is placed in the Clipboard. You can then paste it in another location.

    ◢ To paste text from the Clipboard to a new location, move the cursor to the desired location, press and hold the **Ctrl** key, press **V**, and then release both keys.

CRITICAL THINKING (ADDITIONAL 15 MINUTES)

Using the keyboard skills you have learned in this lab, perform the following steps without using the mouse and answer the respective questions:

1. Open Device Manager and view resources for the mouse. What status does Device Manager report about the mouse?

   _____

2. Open the calculator and select the scientific view. How would you express the decimal number 17 in hexadecimal?

   _____

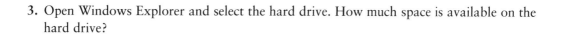

3. Open Windows Explorer and select the hard drive. How much space is available on the hard drive?

REVIEW QUESTIONS

1. What key is universally used to launch Help?

2. How many Windows logo keys are usually included on an enhanced keyboard?

3. What shortcut combination can you use to paste a block of text?

4. What key combination can you use to switch between open applications? (*Hint*: Check Windows Help and Support.)

5. Is it possible to open the Start menu by pressing only one key?

Working with People in a Technical World

Labs included in this chapter:

- **Lab 2.1:** Understand IT Codes of Ethics
- **Lab 2.2:** Provide Customer Service
- **Lab 2.3:** Practice Help Desk Skills
- **Lab 2.4:** Practice Good Communication Skills
- **Lab 2.5:** Understand the Help Desk Procedures for a Company

LAB 2.1 UNDERSTAND IT CODES OF ETHICS

OBJECTIVES

The goal of this lab is to help you become familiar with the concept of a Code of Ethics for IT professionals. After completing this lab, you will be able to:

⊿ Examine a Code of Ethics for IT professionals

⊿ Consider different values when making an ethical decision

MATERIALS REQUIRED

This lab requires the following:

⊿ A workgroup of 2 to 4 students

⊿ Access to the Internet

LAB PREPARATION

Before the lab begins, the instructor or lab assistant needs to do the following:

⊿ Read through the IEEE Code of Ethics and be prepared to discuss it with each group.

ACTIVITY BACKGROUND

Most companies and professional organizations have a *Code of Ethics* or *Code of Conduct* that they expect their employees to uphold. It typically outlines the rights and responsibilities of employees as well as their customers. Certain practices such as respecting confidentially or avoiding conflicts of interest are common to most codes, while other behaviors are industry specific. In addition, many businesses publish a *Statement of Values* that outlines the values or qualities that guide their actions. In this lab, you will examine a Code of Ethics developed by the Institute of Electrical and Electronics Engineers (IEEE) and consider the values it represents.

ESTIMATED COMPLETION TIME: 60 Minutes

Activity

1. Begin by going to **www.ieee.org** and searching for the IEEE Code of Ethics. Print a copy of this code.

   ⊿ Discuss this code among your group. What do you, as a group, consider to be the most important guideline in the list?

   _____

   _____

   _____

   ⊿ Find at least one other technological organization or company that posts a Code of Ethics. Name the organization and respective URL below:

   _____

   _____

◢ Describe any significant similarities or differences between the IEEE code and the code from your one additional organization:

_____

_____

_____

2. Ethical decisions are often constructed around a set of priorities called *values*. These values include fairness, equality, and honesty.

◢ In your group, brainstorm for as many unique values as you can in 10 minutes. You may wish to research "ethical values" on the Internet for inspiration. When you're finished, discuss them with your group and try to agree on what you consider to be the seven most important values. Remember that there are no right or wrong answers; you're just trying to determine what's most important to the members in your group.

◢ List the values below:

1. _____
2. _____
3. _____
4. _____
5. _____
6. _____
7. _____

◢ What values from your brainstormed list are also represented by the IEEE Code of Ethics?

_____

_____

_____

_____

3. Case study: You are working in the IT department of a large company. Your employer has asked you to monitor the e-mail and Internet activity of select individuals in the company and report back at the end of the week.

◢ Does your employer have the right to monitor this information? Does it have a responsibility to do so?

_____

_____

_____

◢ Does your employer have a responsibility to inform its employees that their e-mail and Internet activity are being monitored?

_____

_____

◢ What should you do if you discover an illegal activity during your investigation? What if your employer doesn't agree with your decision?

_____

_____

_____

◢ What would you do if you discovered that your employer was engaged in illegal activity like using pirated software?

_____

_____

_____

◢ If your best friend is found to be using the Internet for job hunting, would you mention it in your report?

_____

_____

_____

REVIEW QUESTIONS

1. Did your groups have any trouble agreeing on the seven most important values?

_____

_____

2. Do you think having a company Code of Ethics makes ethical decisions any easier? Why?

_____

_____

3. Do you think most people share a fundamental set of values?

_____

_____

4. What can you do in cases where your personal values conflict with the values of your employer?

_____

_____

LAB 2.2 PROVIDE CUSTOMER SERVICE

OBJECTIVES

The goal of this lab is to help you appreciate some of the issues involved in providing excellent customer service. After completing this lab, you will be able to:

- Evaluate the service needs of your customers
- Plan for good customer service
- Respond to customer complaints

MATERIALS REQUIRED

This lab requires the following:

- A workgroup of 2 to 4 students

LAB PREPARATION

Before the lab begins, the instructor or lab assistant needs to do the following:

- Read through the customer service scenarios and be prepared to discuss them with each group.

ACTIVITY BACKGROUND

A PC technician needs to be not only technically competent, but also skilled at providing excellent customer service. Acting in a helpful, dependable, and, above all, professional manner is a must, whether the technician deals directly with customers or works with other employees as part of a team.

To complete this lab, work through the following customer service scenarios. When you are done, compare your answers with the rest of your group and see whether you can arrive at a consensus. Keep in mind that there might not be a single right answer to each question.

ESTIMATED COMPLETION TIME: 60 Minutes

Activity

1. A customer returns to your store complaining that the upgraded computer he just picked up doesn't boot. You remember testing the computer yourself before the pickup, and everything was fine.

- What can you do to remedy the situation?

_____

_____

- How can you avoid this kind of problem in the future?

_____

_____

2. You're working in a call center that provides support to customers who are trying to install your product at home. While working with an inexperienced customer over the telephone, you realize that she's having trouble following your directions.

   ◢ What are some ways you can help customers even when they can't see you in a face-to-face environment?

   _____

   _____

   _____

   _____

   _____

   ◢ How can you communicate clearly with your customers while avoiding the impression that you're talking down to them?

   _____

   _____

   _____

3. You arrive on a service call, and the overly confident office supervisor shows you the malfunctioning computer. She begins to explain what she thinks is the problem, but you can tell from the computer's operation that it's something else. You suspect that the office supervisor might have caused the malfunction.

   ◢ How can you troubleshoot the problem without offending your customer?

   _____

   _____

   _____

   ◢ Would it be a mistake to accuse the customer of causing the problem? Why?

   _____

   _____

4. An irate customer calls to complain that he's not satisfied with service he has received from your company and tells you he plans to take his future business elsewhere.

   ◢ Should you apologize even if you don't think your company acted improperly?

   _____

   _____

   ◢ How can you give the customer the impression that you and your company are listening to his complaints?

   _____

   _____

REVIEW QUESTIONS

1. Did the other members of your group come up with any viewpoints you hadn't considered?

   _____

2. Did you have any trouble coming to a consensus about how to deal with each situation?

   _____

3. Why is an understanding of good customer service important for a technician who doesn't work directly with the public?

   _____

   _____

4. How could you go about improving your listening skills with customers?

   _____

   _____

   _____

LAB 2.3: PRACTICE HELP DESK SKILLS

OBJECTIVES

The goal of this lab is to help you learn how to work with a customer using a chat session. After completing this lab, you will be able to:

◢ Use help desk skills in a chat session and on the phone to solve customer problems

MATERIALS REQUIRED

This lab requires the following:

◢ Two or more Windows Vista/XP computers connected by the Internet or a network for each student workgroup

◢ Access to instant messaging software such as MSN Messenger

◢ Phone (or cell phone) for each student

LAB PREPARATION

Before the lab begins, the instructor or lab assistant needs to do the following:

◢ Make available two networked Windows Vista/XP computers for each student workgroup of two or more students.

◢ Verify that messaging software is able to communicate

◢ Tell students to bring their cell phones to the lab, or provide telephones in the lab.

ACTIVITY BACKGROUND

In the past, help desk support was solely by telephone, but more and more companies are offering technical support for their hardware and software products by way of chat sessions between the company help desk and the customer. Help desk personnel need to know how to ask questions, connect with the customer in a friendly and personal tone, and solve the customer's problem using telephone or chat. These chat sessions are typically started by clicking a link on the company's Web site. For example, in Figure 2-1, you can see where to click to start a live chat session with Linksys support.

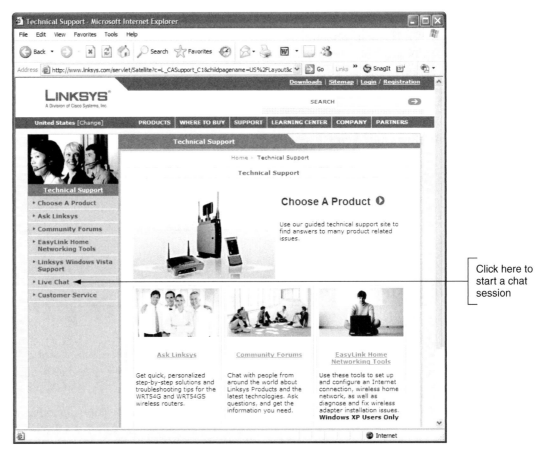

Figure 2-1   Chat sessions for technical support are often available by way of manufacturer Web sites
Courtesy: Course Technology/Cengage Learning

ESTIMATED COMPLETION TIME: 60 Minutes

Activity

Imagine that Jesse is having problems securing his wireless network. The multifunctional router that serves as his wireless access point was giving problems, so he pressed the Reset button on the router to give it a fresh start. The router began working, but he then discovered he had reset the router back to factory default settings, undoing all his wireless security settings. When Jesse tried to reconfigure the router, he could not find the router documentation, which included the username and password to the router firmware utility. After giving up his search for the documentation, he now decides to contact Linksys for help.

TROUBLESHOOTING

Jesse goes to the Linksys Web site and clicks the SUPPORT link, which opens the page shown in Figure 2-1. He clicks the Live Chat link, and on the next page, enters his name, phone number, e-mail address, and product name. After he submits this information, a chat window opens similar to the one in Figure 2-2. Ryan is working the help desk at Linksys and responds.

Figure 2-2 Chat window with technical support
Courtesy: Course Technology/Cengage Learning

Working with a partner in your workgroup, use network and chat software such as MSN Messenger or AIM to do the following:

1. Select one person in your workgroup to play the role of Jesse, the customer. Select another person to play the role of Ryan, the help desk technician.

2. Jesse initiates a chat session with Ryan. What is the first thing Ryan says to Jesse in the chat session?

3. In the chat session between Jesse and Ryan, Ryan does the following:

   Ryan asks Jesse for the serial number of the router. This number is embedded on the bottom of the router.

   Ryan knows the default username and password for this router to be a blank entry for the username and "admin" for the password. Ryan wants Jesse to know it would have been better for him to have reset the router by unplugging it and plugging it back in, rather than using the Reset button. Ryan also suggests to Jesse that for security reasons, he needs to enter a new username and password for the router.

4. Print the chat session. If your chat software does not have the print option, then copy and paste the chat session text into a document and print the document. As a courtesy to their customers, many companies e-mail to the customer a transcription of the chat session with technical support.

5. Critique the chat session with others in your workgroup. Make suggestions that might help Ryan to be more effective, friendly, and helpful. Use telephones to simulate a help desk conversation.

Use the same troubleshooting scenario, but this time reverse roles between Jesse and Ryan. Do the following:

1. Jesse calls Ryan, and Ryan answers, "Hello, this is Ryan Jackson with the Linksys help desk. May I please have your name, the product you need help with, your phone number, and e-mail address?"

2. After the information is collected, Ryan allows Jesse to describe the problem and steps him through the solution.

3. When the problem is solved, Ryan ends the call politely and positively.

4. Make suggestions that might help Ryan to be more effective, friendly, and helpful.

In the next help desk session, Joy contacts technical support for her company, complaining of too many pop-up ads on her desktop. Do the following:

1. Select someone to play the role of Joy and another person to play the role of Sam, the help desk technician.

2. Using chat software, Joy starts a chat session with Sam, and Sam solves the problem. Assume that Joy is a novice user who needs a little extra help with keystrokes.

3. Sam decides to have Joy turn on the IE 6 pop-up blocker, use previously installed antivirus software to scan for viruses, and download, install, and run Windows Defender software from the Microsoft Web site.

4. Print the chat session and discuss it with the workgroup. Do you have any suggestions for Sam to improve his help desk skills?

5. Using telephones, reverse roles for Joy and Sam and solve the same problem. Do you have any suggestions for Sam to improve his help desk skills?

REVIEW QUESTIONS

1. After doing your best, but finding you still cannot solve a customer's problem, what is the appropriate next step?

2. Your cell phone rings while working with a customer. You look at the incoming number and realize it's your sister calling. How do you handle the call?

3. Why is it not a good idea to tell a customer about the time you were able to solve the computer problem of a very important person?

4. A customer is angry and tells you he will never buy another product from your company again. How do you respond?

LAB 2.4: PRACTICE GOOD COMMUNICATION SKILLS

OBJECTIVES

The goal of this lab is to help you learn how to be a better communicator. After completing this lab, you will be able to:

◢ Be a better listener

◢ Work with a customer who is angry

◢ Act with integrity to customers

MATERIALS REQUIRED

This lab requires the following:

◢ Student workgroups of 2 or more students

LAB PREPARATION

No lab preparation is necessary.

ACTIVITY BACKGROUND

PC support technicians are expected to be good communicators. Many times, technical people find this to be a difficult skill, so practice and training are very important. In this lab, you discover some ways to be an active listener and better communicator.

ESTIMATED COMPLETION TIME: 60 Minutes

 Activity

Work with a partner to learn to be a better listener. Do the following:

1. Sit with paper and pencil before another student who will play the role of a customer. As the customer describes a certain computer problem he or she is having, take notes as necessary.

2. Describe the problem back to the customer. Were you able to describe the problem accurately without missing any details? Have the customer rate you from one to ten, ten being the highest rating for good listening skills.

3. Now switch roles as you, the customer, describe a problem to the support technician. Then have the technician repeat the problem and its details. Rate the technician for good listening skills on a scale of one to ten.

4. Now describe an increasingly more difficult problem with more details. Rate the technician on a scale of one to ten for good listening skills.

5. Switch roles and listen to a detailed, difficult problem described. Then repeat the problem and have the customer rate your listening skills.

Being a good communicator requires being able to deal with angry and difficult people. Make suggestions as to the best way to handle these situations:

1. An angry customer calls to tell you that she has left you numerous phone messages that you have not answered. She is not aware that you receive about 25 voice messages a day and are trying hard to keep up with the workload. What do you say?

_____

_____

2. What can you say when an angry customer begins to use abusive language?

_____

_____

3. You have tried for over two hours, but you cannot fix the customer's boot problem. You think the motherboard has failed, but you are not sure. Before you make your conclusions, you want to try a POST diagnostic card. The customer demands that you fix the problem immediately before she leaves the office at 4:45 PM—about 10 minutes from now. What do you say to her?

_____

_____

4. Discuss in your workgroup the ethical thing to do in each situation below. Write down the group consensus to each problem:

  1. You work on commission in a computer retail store, and after working with a very difficult customer for over an hour, he leaves without buying a thing. As he walks out the door, you notice he dropped a twenty-dollar bill near where you were talking. What do you do?

  _____

  _____

  2. A customer is yelling at a coworker in a retail store. You see your coworker does not know how to handle the situation. What do you do?

  _____

  _____

  3. You are working in a corporate office as a technical support person trying to fix a scanner problem at an employee's workstation. You notice the employee has left payroll database information displayed on the screen. You know this employee is not authorized to view this information. What do you do?

  _____

  _____

  4. Your supervisor has asked you to install a game on his computer. The game is on a CD-R and is obviously a pirated copy. What do you do?

  _____

  _____

  5. You work for a retail store that sells a particular brand of computers. A customer asks your opinion of another brand of computer. What do you do?

  _____

  _____

6. You are asked to make a house call to fix a computer problem. When you arrive at the appointed time, a teenage girl answers the door and tells you her mother is not at home, but will return in a half hour. What do you do?

_____

_____

Have a little fun with this one! Working in a group of three, one member of the team plays the role of tech support. A second team member writes down a brief description of a difficult customer and passes the description to a third team member. (The tech support person cannot see this description.) The third team member plays out the described customer role. Use the following scenarios:

1. A customer calls to say his notebook will not start. The LCD panel was broken when the customer dropped the notebook, but he does not willingly disclose the fact that the notebook was dropped.

2. A customer complains that his CD drive does not work. The CD is in the drive upside down, and it is clear that the customer does not want the tech to ask him about such a simple issue.

REVIEW QUESTIONS

1. When working at a retail store that also fixes computers, what five items of information should you request when a customer first brings a computer to your counter?

_____

_____

2. List three things you should not do while at a customer's site:

_____

_____

3. When is it acceptable to ask a customer to refrain from venting?

_____

_____

4. When is it appropriate to answer a cell phone call while working with a customer?

_____

_____

5. When is it appropriate to install pirated software on a computer?

_____

_____

LAB 2.5 UNDERSTAND THE HELP DESK PROCEDURES FOR A COMPANY

OBJECTIVES

The goal of this lab is to demonstrate the process of setting up help desk procedures. After completing this lab, you will be able to:

◢ Identify problems that would prevent users from browsing the network

◢ Decide which types of problems can be solved over the telephone

◢ Decide which types of problems require administrative intervention

◢ Create a support matrix for telephone instruction

MATERIALS REQUIRED

This lab requires the following:

◢ Windows Vista/XP operating system

◢ A PC connected to a working TCP/IP network

◢ Optional: An Internet connection

◢ Two workgroups with 2 to 4 students in each group

LAB PREPARATION

Before the lab begins, the instructor or lab assistant needs to do the following:

◢ Verify that Windows starts with no errors.

◢ Verify that the network connection is available.

ACTIVITY BACKGROUND

When a company sets up a help desk for computer users, it establishes a set of procedures to address common troubleshooting situations. These procedures should include instructions that the average user can be expected to carry out with telephone support. In this lab, you design and create help desk procedures for a common problem: the inability to connect to a network. Assume you're working at the company help desk. If you can't solve the problem, you escalate it to the network administrator or another technician who actually goes to the computer to fix the problem.

ESTIMATED COMPLETION TIME: 60 Minutes

Activity

1. Assume that your company network is designed according to the following parameters. (Note that your instructor might alter these parameters so that they more closely resemble your network's parameters.)

   ◢ Ethernet LAN is using only a single subnet.

   ◢ TCP/IP is the only protocol.

   ◢ The workgroup name is ATLGA.

   ◢ The DHCP server assigns IP information.

2. Assume that all users on your company network use computers with the following parameters. (Note that your instructor might alter these parameters so that they more closely resemble your PC.)

   ◢ Pentium IV 2.8 GHz

   ◢ Windows Vista or XP operating system

   ◢ Internal NIC

   ◢ Category 5e cabling with RJ-45 connectors

3. As a group, discuss the reasons a user might not be able to connect to the network, and then make a list of the four most common reasons. If your group has trouble completing the list, feel free to ask your instructor or search the Internet. List the source of these problems, both hardware and software, on the following lines. In your list, include at least one problem that's difficult to solve over the phone and requires the network administrator or another technician to go to the computer to solve the problem. Order the four problems from the least difficult to solve to the most difficult to solve. Write the one problem that requires administrator intervention at the bottom of the list.

   ◢ Source of Problem 1, which is the least difficult to solve:

   _____

   ◢ Source of Problem 2, which is more difficult to solve:

   _____

   ◢ Source of Problem 3, which is even more difficult to solve:

   _____

   ◢ Source of Problem 4, which is so difficult to solve that it requires an administrator or another technician to get involved:

   _____

For each problem, describe the symptoms as a user would describe them:

   ◢ Symptoms of Problem 1:

   _____

   _____

   ◢ Symptoms of Problem 2:

   _____

   _____

   ◢ Symptoms of Problem 3:

   _____

   _____

   ◢ Symptoms of Problem 4:

   _____

   _____

As a group, decide how to solve each problem by following these steps:

1. On separate sheets of paper, list the steps to verify and solve the problems. (This list of steps is sometimes referred to as a procedure, support matrix, or job aid.)

2. Double-check the steps by testing them on your computer. (In real life, you would test the steps using a computer attached to the network you're supporting.) When making your list of steps, allow for alternatives, based on how the user responds to your questions. For example, you might include one list of steps for situations in which the user says others on the network are visible in My Network Places and another list of steps for situations in which the user says no remote computers can be seen in My Network Places. Well-written help desk procedures ensure that help desk workers know exactly what steps to perform, which results in quicker support and users feeling more confident about getting help.

3. For any problem that can't be solved by the procedure, the last step should be for help desk personnel to notify the administrator. In your procedure, include questions to the user when appropriate. As you work, you might find it helpful to use a diagram or flowchart of the questions asked and decisions made.

Here's an example of one step that involves a question:

⊿ **Question:** Is your computer on?

⊿ **Answer:** Yes, go to Step 3; no, go to Step 2.

Now it is time to test your help desk procedures by using them on another workgroup, as follows:

1. Introduce one of your four problems on a PC connected to a network.

2. Have someone from another workgroup sit at your PC. The remaining steps in this step sequence refer to this person as "the user."

3. Sit with your back to the user so that you can't see what he or she is doing. Place your step-by-step procedures in front of you, on paper or on-screen. (It's helpful if you can sit at a PC connected to the network so that you can perform the same steps you ask the user to perform. However, make sure you can't see the other PC or see what the user is doing.)

4. The user should attempt to access the network and then "call" your help desk for assistance.

5. Follow your procedure to solve the problem.

6. Revise your procedure as necessary.

7. Test all four help desk procedures.

REVIEW QUESTIONS

1. Can all users' computer problems be solved with help desk support? Why or why not?

_____

_____

2. After you design and write your help desk procedures to solve problems, what should you do next?

_____

_____

3. How should help desk procedures address complex problems that require administrative intervention?

_____

_____

_____

4. How should you alter your procedures based on your users' technical experience?

_____

_____

_____

_____

5. Why do you need to consider what the network and computer are like when creating your procedures?

_____

_____

_____

6. What has been your experience when calling a help desk? How well did the technician walk you through the process of solving your problem?

_____

_____

Installing Windows

Labs included in this chapter:

- **Lab 3.1:** Install or Upgrade to Windows 2000
- **Lab 3.2:** Determine Hardware Compatibility with Windows XP
- **Lab 3.3:** Install or Upgrade to Windows XP
- **Lab 3.4:** Install or Upgrade to Windows Vista
- **Lab 3.5:** Critical Thinking: Virtual PC
- **Lab 3.6:** Critical Thinking: Unattended Installation

LAB 3.1 INSTALL OR UPGRADE TO WINDOWS 2000

OBJECTIVES

The goal of this lab is to help you install or upgrade to Windows 2000 Professional. After completing this lab, you will be able to:

⊿ Plan an upgrade or installation

⊿ Identify the benefits of an upgrade or a new installation

⊿ Install or upgrade to Windows 2000 Professional

MATERIALS REQUIRED

This lab requires the following:

⊿ Windows 98 operating system

⊿ Access to drivers or Internet access for downloading drivers

⊿ Windows 2000 Professional installation files or installation CD

⊿ Key from installation CD

LAB PREPARATION

Before the lab begins, the instructor or lab assistant needs to do the following:

⊿ Verify that Windows starts with no errors.

⊿ Provide each student with access to the Windows 2000 installation files or CD and key.

⊿ Verify that any necessary Windows 2000 drivers are available.

ACTIVITY BACKGROUND

Many people are intimidated at the thought of installing or upgrading an operating system. The process doesn't need to be difficult. In fact, if you plan your installation carefully and are prepared to supply required information and device drivers, your main complaint might be that the process is time consuming. Even that annoyance can be minimized, using techniques designed to reduce the total installation time. In this lab, you plan and prepare for an installation or an upgrade to Windows 2000 Professional, and then perform the upgrade or installation.

ESTIMATED COMPLETION TIME: 120 Minutes

 Activity

Follow these steps to plan and prepare for a Windows 2000 Professional installation on your computer:

1. Obtain a list of devices in the system and detailed system specifications, such as processor speed and drive capacity. If no list currently exists, you can use Device Manager to compile one.

2. Make another list of important applications, and check to see whether they are compatible with Windows 2000. If you find any that aren't, check to see whether any patches or upgrades are available to make them compatible.

3. Check each system specification and device against the system requirements list for Windows 2000 on the Microsoft Support site (*http://support.microsoft.com/kb/304297*). Your system will probably be compatible with Windows 2000. However, when working on other systems,

you might discover significant incompatibilities. In that case, you would have to decide whether upgrading to Windows 2000 is really an option. If you decide to go ahead with the upgrade, you would have to decide which applications or hardware you need to upgrade before upgrading the operating system. The Windows 2000 installation CD offers a Check Upgrade Only mode that you can use to check for incompatibility issues in your system before you actually install the OS; however, the information on the Microsoft Web site, which you're using in this step, is often more current and easier to access. Answer the following:

◢ Does your system qualify for Windows 2000?

_____

◢ If not, what hardware or application doesn't qualify?

_____

◢ Will you install using FAT32 or NTFS? Explain your decision:

_____

_____

_____

4. Download or otherwise obtain all necessary drivers, service packs, and application patches from the manufacturer's or Microsoft Web site for installed applications and hardware. Record a summary of the components you were required to install to make your system compatible with Windows 2000:

_____

_____

_____

_____

5. Gather any network-specific information in preparation for the installation. If you're connected to a network, answer the following:

◢ If you're using a TCP/IP network, how is your IP address configured?

_____

◢ For a static IP address, what is the IP address?

_____

◢ What is the workgroup name or domain name of the network?

_____

◢ What is your computer name?

_____

6. Make sure you have the correct CD key for your installation CD. The CD key, provided with the Windows 2000 installation CD, usually consists of a set of alphanumeric characters. You must enter the CD key to complete the installation—even if you're installing the operating system from setup files located somewhere other than on the installation CD.

7. Review the information you have collected so far, and then decide whether to do a fresh installation or an upgrade. For instance, if all the important applications on your system are compatible with Windows 2000, an upgrade will probably save time because it leaves compatible applications in working condition. On the other hand, if you know you'll have to install new applications anyway because of incompatibilities, you might choose to perform a fresh installation. In many ways, a fresh installation is preferable because it ensures that no misconfigured system settings are carried over to the new operating system.

◢ Will you perform a clean install or an upgrade?

_____

◢ Give a brief explanation of why you chose that option:

_____

_____

8. Back up any critical data files (that is, any work you or others have stored on your computer that you can't afford to lose during the installation process).

◢ If you have critical data files on the PC, to what location did you back them up?

_____

You're ready to begin installing Windows 2000 Professional. This lab assumes that you have another version of Windows installed and running such as Windows 98. This is not the only situation in which you would install or even upgrade to Windows 2000, but it's common. Installing the operating system is possible using files on the installation CD, a network drive, or a local hard disk. To speed up the installation process, consider copying the setup files from the installation CD (or from a network drive) to a local hard disk. This method takes extra time at first but is faster overall.

◢ Are you performing the installation from the Windows 2000 CD, files stored on your hard drive, or a network drive?

_____

The following steps are representative of a typical installation. Your installation will probably vary in minor ways, depending on the installation options you choose, your system's hardware configuration, and other factors. The following steps are a general guide to let you know what to expect during the process. Don't become alarmed if your experience differs slightly. Use your knowledge to solve any problems on your own, and ask your instructor for help if you get stuck. You might want to record any differences between these steps and your own experience. Also, record any decisions you make and any information you enter during the installation process.

1. Before you insert the installation CD or run the setup files from a location on your hard drive or network, use antivirus software to scan the computer's memory and hard drive for viruses. After the scan is finished, make sure to disable any automatic scans and close the antivirus program before beginning installation.

2. The Setup program starts after the setup CD has been inserted. This program guides you through the actual installation. If it doesn't begin automatically, click **Start, Run**, and run WINNT32.exe from the \I386 folder.

◢ Did Setup start automatically for you, or did you have to use the Run command?

_____

3. Setup informs you that you're running an older version of Windows and asks whether you want to upgrade to Windows 2000. Click **Yes** to continue and follow the instructions in the Setup program. Note that although Setup initially uses the word "upgrade," you're then given the option of doing an upgrade or a fresh installation of Windows 2000.

4. Accept the end user license agreement (EULA) and click **Next**.

5. When prompted, enter the CD key and click **Next**.

6. Setup examines your system and reports any situations that could cause problems during installation. You're given the opportunity to print the report and exit Setup to correct the problems. Even if some problems are reported, you have done your homework during planning and probably have the solution, so continue the installation.

7. You're given the opportunity to review the Hardware Compatibility List. If you want to review it again, do so and click **Next** to continue.

8. Specify your file system as NTFS and click **Next**. The system begins to copy files for the installation. Then the text portion of the installation, which has a command-line interface rather than a Windows GUI, begins. The text portion includes the following:

   ◢ Examining hardware

   ◢ Deleting old Windows files, if applicable

   ◢ Copying Windows 2000 operating system files

   ◢ Rebooting your computer automatically

> **Notes** Windows 98 doesn't support NTFS, so if you were setting up a dual-boot system that used that operating system, you should choose FAT32 as the file system.

After your computer reboots, the Windows 2000 Setup portion begins, which includes the following:

   ◢ Verifying the file system

   ◢ Checking the file structure

   ◢ Converting the file system to NTFS

   ◢ Rebooting automatically

1. Select **Windows 2000 Professional** in the startup menu. Because you converted your file system to NTFS, you should see a message indicating that the conversion was successful.

2. The system installs software for detected devices. When prompted, enter the requested network information. After you have specified how your network is configured, Setup performs some final setup tasks, including the following:

   ◢ Configuring the startup menu

   ◢ Registering components

   ◢ Upgrading programs and system settings

   ◢ Saving settings

   ◢ Removing temporary files

3. The computer reboots one more time. Now you can log on as an administrator and install any new applications or devices.

4. Verify that the system is working correctly.

On the following lines, record any differences you noted between these installation steps and your own experience. Also, record any decisions you made and any information you entered during the installation process:

_____

_____

_____

_____

_____

_____

_____

REVIEW QUESTIONS

1. List five things you should do before starting the installation process:

   _____

   _____

   _____

   _____

   _____

2. How can you find out whether your video card will work with Windows 2000?

   _____

3. What type of installation can save time because it usually retains system settings and leaves applications in working condition?

   _____

4. What step is critical to ensure that you don't lose important data during installation?

   _____

5. What step can you take to speed up the actual installation process?

   _____

CHALLENGE ACTIVITY (ADDITIONAL 15 MINUTES)

Another alternative for upgrading the operating systems on an older Windows 98 machine is Microsoft Windows Fundamentals for Legacy PCs (FLP), which is optimized for older computers. Use the Internet to find answers to the following questions:

1. What are the minimum and recommended requirements for installing FLP?

   _____

   _____

2. Will FLP support most Windows XP applications? Is there anything it doesn't support?

_____

_____

3. What would be some advantages and disadvantages of upgrading a Windows 98 machine to FLP?

_____

_____

_____

LAB 3.2 DETERMINE HARDWARE COMPATIBILITY WITH WINDOWS XP

OBJECTIVES

The goal of this lab is to help you determine whether your hardware is compatible with Windows XP. After completing this lab, you will be able to:

◢ Use Windows to identify system components

◢ Find and use the Microsoft Hardware Compatibility List (HCL)

MATERIALS REQUIRED

This lab requires the following:

◢ Windows 9x or Windows 2000 operating system

◢ Internet access

LAB PREPARATION

Before the lab begins, the instructor or lab assistant needs to do the following:

◢ Verify that Windows starts with no errors.

◢ Verify that Internet access is available.

ACTIVITY BACKGROUND

You can't assume that an operating system will support your hardware, especially with older devices, because software developers focus on supporting the most capable and popular devices. To verify that Microsoft operating systems support your hardware, you can check the Windows Logo'd Product List, formerly called the Microsoft Hardware Compatibility List (HCL), at *http://winqual.microsoft.com/HCL/Default.aspx?m=x*. The HCL includes devices that have drivers written by Microsoft or devices that have drivers tested and approved by Microsoft. In this lab, you use Device Manager to inventory devices in a system. Then you check the HCL to see whether Windows XP Professional supports the system's devices.

ESTIMATED COMPLETION TIME: 30 Minutes

 Activity

To use Device Manager to inventory your system, follow these steps:

1. Open Control Panel and double-click the **System** icon.

2. In Windows 2000, click the **Hardware** tab, and then click the **Device Manager** button. In Windows 9x, click the **Device Manager** tab. The Device Manager window opens.

3. In Device Manager, devices are arranged by category. To see what kind of video adapter is installed on your system, click the + (plus sign) to the left of Display Adapters.

4. Click your video adapter and click the **Properties** button. Record the information about the model and manufacturer that's displayed:

_____

_____

_____

5. Use Device Manager to find similar information for your network adapter, modem card, or sound card, and record that information here:

_____

_____

_____

Now that you have a list of devices installed on your system, check the Windows Logo'd Product List to see whether Windows XP supports these devices. Web sites change often, so the following steps might have to be adjusted to accommodate changes. If you have difficulty following these steps because of Web site changes, see your instructor for help.

1. Open your browser and go to **www.microsoft.com/whdc/hcl/default.mspx**. Click the **Windows XP Hardware Compatibility List** link.

2. At the left under **Devices**, point to **Components** and then click **Video Cards**. Using the information about your video adapter you recorded previously in Step 4, find your video card by scrolling the list or using the drop-down lists across the top.

3. Confirm that you have found your device by verifying that the correct manufacturer and model are listed.

4. Add a note to your list of devices indicating whether the device is compatible with Windows XP Professional.

5. Check the other devices in your list, and note whether they are compatible with Windows XP Professional.

6. If a device isn't listed in the HCL, what are your options when installing Windows XP? List at least two possibilities:

_____

_____

_____

7. Does the hardware in your system qualify for Windows XP? If it doesn't, explain why:

_____

_____

REVIEW QUESTIONS

1. Explain how to compile a list of devices installed on your system:

   _____

   _____

   _____

2. How are devices grouped in Device Manager?

   _____

3. Where can you find the HCL?

   _____

4. If a device isn't listed in the HCL, is there still a chance it will work in your machine?

   _____

   _____

5. Why might it be a bad idea to use a device that's not listed in the HCL?

   _____

   _____

LAB 3.3 INSTALL OR UPGRADE TO WINDOWS XP

OBJECTIVES

The goal of this lab is to help you install or upgrade to Windows XP Professional. After completing this lab, you will be able to:

◢ Plan an upgrade or installation

◢ Identify the benefits of an upgrade or new installation

◢ Install or upgrade to Windows XP Professional

MATERIALS REQUIRED

This lab requires the following:

◢ Windows 9x or Windows 2000 operating system

◢ Access to drivers or Internet access for downloading drivers

◢ Windows XP Professional installation CD or installation files

◢ Product Key from installation CD

◢ A storage medium for updated device drivers

LAB PREPARATION

Before the lab begins, the instructor or lab assistant needs to do the following:

◢ Verify that Windows starts with no errors.

◢ Provide each student with access to the Windows XP installation files and key.

◢ Verify that any necessary Windows XP drivers are available.

ACTIVITY BACKGROUND

Windows XP is designed to be reliable and has a different user interface from Windows 9x to give you a more personalized computing experience. The operating system's updated look uses more graphics to simplify the user interface. It has a task-oriented design, which gives you options specifically associated with the task or file you're working on. You can upgrade your computer's operating system to Windows XP Professional from Windows 98/98SE, Windows Me, Windows NT Workstation 4.0, Windows 2000, or Windows XP Home Edition. Installing or upgrading an operating system isn't difficult. Careful planning can minimize or eliminate many of the headaches some users have experienced when upgrading to Windows XP.

ESTIMATED COMPLETION TIME: 90-120 Minutes

Activity

Your lab system will likely be compatible with Windows XP. However, when working on other systems, you might discover significant incompatibilities. In that case, you have to decide whether upgrading to Windows XP Professional is really an option. Many users have problems with device drivers when upgrading to a new version of Windows. For this reason, it's essential to do your research and download device drivers that are compatible with Windows XP Professional before you install the upgrade. You might need to visit the manufacturer Web sites for all your devices, such as scanners, printers, modems, keyboards, mouse, camera, and so on, to see whether they are compatible with Windows XP Professional. If the manufacturer provides an updated device driver to support Windows XP Professional, you need to download the files to a storage medium. Also, when planning an upgrade, recording information in a table, such as Table 3-1, is helpful. Follow these steps to create a plan and prepare for a Windows XP Professional upgrade on your computer:

1. Use Device Manager to compile the information and fill in Table 3-1 as you complete the following steps.

Things to Do	Further Information
Does the PC meet the minimum or recommended hardware requirements?	CPU: RAM: Hard drive size: Free space on the hard drive:
Have you checked all your applications to verify that they qualify for Windows XP or if they need patches to qualify?	Applications that need to be upgraded:
Have you checked the Microsoft Web site to verify that all your hardware qualifies?	Hardware that needs to be upgraded:
Have you decided how you will join a network?	Workgroup name: Domain name: Computer name:
Can you find the product key?	Product key:
Have you backed up critical data?	Location of backup files:
Is your hard drive ready?	Size of the hard drive partition: Free space on the partition: File system you plan to use:

Table 3-1   Things to do and information to collect when planning a Windows upgrade

2. Compare your information to the Windows XP requirements in Table 3-2.

   ◢ Does your system meet the minimum requirements?

   _____

   ◢ Does your system meet the recommended requirements?

   _____

Component or Device	Minimum Requirement	Recommended Requirement
One or two CPUs	Pentium II 233 MHz or better	Pentium II 300 MHz or better
RAM	64 MB	128 MB up to 4 GB
Hard drive partition	2 GB	2 GB or more
Free space on the hard drive partition	640 MB (bare bones)	2 GB or more
CD-ROM drive	12×	12× or faster
Accessories	Keyboard and mouse or other pointing device	Keyboard and mouse or other pointing device

Table 3-2 Minimum and recommended requirements for Windows XP Professional

3. Make a list of important applications on your system and verify whether they are compatible with Windows XP Professional. If you find any that aren't, check to see whether patches or upgrades are available to make them compatible. List in Table 3-1 any applications that don't qualify or that need patches to qualify. List any software upgrades or patches you downloaded to prepare your applications for Windows XP:

   _____

   _____

   _____

4. Install any application upgrades or patches you have downloaded.

5. Start with the list compiled in Lab 3.2 and list in Table 3-1 any hardware devices that need updated drivers.

6. Download or otherwise obtain all necessary drivers from the manufacturers' Web sites or the Microsoft site for your hardware. List any drivers you were required to install to make your hardware compatible with Windows XP Professional:

   _____

   _____

7. Gather any network-specific information in preparation for the installation. If you're connected to a network, answer the following:

   ◢ If you're using a TCP/IP network, how is your IP address configured?

   _____

   ◢ For a static IP address, what is the IP address?

   _____

   ◢ What is the workgroup name or domain name of the network?

   _____

   ◢ What is your computer name?

   _____

Record the workgroup or domain name and the computer name in Table 3-1.

8. Make sure you have the correct CD key for your installation CD and record it in Table 3-1. The CD key, provided with the Windows XP Professional installation CD, usually consists of a set of alphanumeric characters. You must enter the CD key to complete the installation, even if you're installing the operating system from setup files located somewhere other than the installation CD.

9. Review the information you've collected so far, and answer the following:

   ◢ Does your system qualify for Windows XP Professional?

   _____

   ◢ If not, what hardware or application doesn't qualify?

   _____

10. Now decide whether to do a fresh installation or an upgrade. For instance, if all the important applications on your system are compatible with Windows XP Professional, an upgrade will probably save time because it leaves compatible applications in working condition. On the other hand, if you know you have to install new applications because of incompatibilities, you might choose to perform a fresh installation. In many ways, a fresh installation is preferable because it ensures that no misconfigured system settings are carried over to the new operating system.

11. Back up critical data files (that is, any work you or others have stored on your computer that you can't afford to lose during the installation process).

12. If you have critical files on the PC, to what location did you back them up? Record that information in Table 3-1.

13. The hard drive partition that is to be the active partition for Windows XP must be at least 2 GB and have at least 2 GB free. Record the size of the hard drive partition and the amount of free space on that partition in Table 3-1. Answer these questions:

   ◢ What Windows utilities or commands did you use to determine the size of the active partition?

   _____

   _____

◢ What Windows utilities or commands did you use to determine how much free space is on that partition?

_____

_____

14. When installing Windows XP, you have a choice of using the FAT or NTFS file system. For this installation, use the NTFS file system. Record that information in Table 3-1.

You're ready to begin installing Windows XP Professional. This lab assumes that you have another version of Windows installed and running. This is not the only situation in which you would install or upgrade to Windows XP Professional, but it's common. Installing Windows XP is possible using setup files stored on the installation CD, a network drive, or a local hard disk.

The following steps are representative of a typical upgrade. Your installation will probably vary in minor ways, depending on the installation options you choose, your system's hardware configuration, and other factors. The following steps are a general guide to let you know what to expect during the process. Don't become alarmed if your experience differs slightly. Use your knowledge to solve any problems on your own, and ask your instructor for help if you get stuck. You might want to record any differences between these steps and your own experience. Also, record any decisions you make and any information you enter during the installation process.

1. Before you insert the installation CD or run the installation files from a location on your hard drive or network, use antivirus software to scan the computer's memory and hard drive for viruses. After the scan is finished, make sure you disable any automatic scans and close the antivirus program before beginning the installation.

2. Insert the Windows XP Professional CD. The Setup program starts. This program guides you through the actual installation. If it doesn't begin automatically, click **Start, Run** and browse for the Setup.exe file to begin the installation.

3. The Welcome to Microsoft Windows XP window opens with some options. What options do you see?

_____

_____

_____

_____

_____

4. Click **Install Windows XP**. The Setup program begins collecting information, and the Welcome to Windows Setup window opens with Installation Type: Upgrade (Recommended) in the text box. Click **Next**.

5. Accept the EULA, and then click **Next**.

6. When prompted, enter the CD key, and then click **Next**.

7. If the Windows Setup Upgrade Report window opens, click the **Show me hardware issues and a limited set of software issues (Recommended)** option, and then click **Next**.

8. The Windows Setup Get Updated Setup Files window opens. Because you can check for updates later and are focusing on upgrading for now, click **No, skip this step and continue installing Windows**, and click **Next**.

9. Windows is now preparing the installation of Windows XP Professional by analyzing your computer. This setup takes approximately 60 minutes. Read the informational screens as they're displayed. You can gain a lot of knowledge of Windows XP through this minitutorial. Your computer restarts several times during the installation and setup process.

10. When the installation is finished and Windows XP has restarted for the last time, the Welcome to Microsoft Windows window opens. Click **Next** to continue.

11. If you see a Help Protect your PC screen, select **Help protect my PC by turning on Automatic Updates now** and click **Next**.

    In the Ready to activate windows screen, click **No, remind me every few days** and then click **Next**.

12. Now you may have an option to enter your user information. You can type the name of each person who will use this computer. Windows creates a separate user account for each person, so you can personalize the way you want Windows to organize and display information, protect your files and computer settings, and customize the desktop. The user names you enter appear in the Welcome window in alphabetical order. When you start Windows, you simply click your name in the Welcome window to begin working in Windows XP Professional. For now, enter only your first name, and then click **Next**.

13. When you see a Thank you! message, click **Finish** to continue.

14. You may also have the option to set a password for all Windows XP accounts. Enter a password to be used for all the listed accounts. If you want to change the passwords later, go to the User Accounts applet in Control Panel.

15. To begin using Windows XP, click your user name and enter your password. A Welcome window appears. Wait while Windows XP loads your personal settings. The first time you start Windows XP, the Start menu is displayed until you click something else. Thereafter, you open the Start menu by clicking the Start button at the left of the taskbar.

16. Remove the installation CD from the drive and return it to your instructor.

17. The basic installation is complete. The next steps would be to install a virus checker, check the operating system for updates, and upgrade any necessary drivers and applications.

18. Was the Windows XP upgrade a success? If so, what did you find to be most challenging about the upgrade process?

    _____

    _____

19. Describe the Windows XP desktop:

    _____

    _____

    _____

REVIEW QUESTIONS

1. By default, which icon appears on the Windows XP desktop?

    _____

2. Where did you find the Windows product key?

    _____

3. Why will an upgrade save time over a fresh installation?

_____

4. What possible locations can be used to store the setup files?

_____

5. Which should you do first, install a virus checker or check for updates to the operating system? Why?

_____

_____

LAB 3.4 INSTALL OR UPGRADE TO WINDOWS VISTA

OBJECTIVES

The goal of this lab is to help you install or upgrade to Windows Vista. After completing this lab, you will be able to:

◢ Plan an upgrade or installation

◢ Identify the benefits of an upgrade or new installation

◢ Install or upgrade to Windows Vista

MATERIALS REQUIRED

This lab requires the following:

◢ Windows 2000/XP operating system

◢ Access to drivers or Internet access for downloading drivers

◢ Windows Vista installation DVD or installation files

◢ Key from installation DVD

◢ A storage medium for updated device drivers

LAB PREPARATION

Before the lab begins, the instructor or lab assistant needs to do the following:

◢ Verify that Windows starts with no errors.

◢ Provide each student with access to the Windows Vista installation files and key.

◢ Verify that any necessary Windows Vista drivers are available.

ACTIVITY BACKGROUND

Windows Vista was designed to replace XP with a new line of operating systems that offer improved reliability, security, and ease of use. Some of the key new features in Vista include:

◢ A new 3D look known as the Aero glass interface

◢ A new version of Internet Explorer

◢ A sidebar full of small applications called gadgets

◢ Faster startup and shutdown

◢ A new spyware monitor called Windows Defender

Activity

The most common problem people have when installing Windows Vista is with incompatible hardware drivers. Therefore, it is important to research and download device drivers that are compatible with Windows Vista before you begin the install. Sometimes manufacturers of older products provide drivers for new operating systems, but usually they don't. Follow these steps to install Windows Vista:

1. Go online and research the minimum and recommended requirements for the version of Windows Vista that you will be using and enter them in the space below:

   _____

   _____

   _____

   _____

   _____

   _____

2. Gather the necessary information about your computer to answer the following questions (see Lab 3.3):

   ◢ Does your system meet the minimum requirements?

   _____

   ◢ Does your system meet the recommended requirements?

   _____

3. Make a list of important applications on your system and verify whether they are compatible with Windows Vista. If you find any that aren't, check to see whether patches or upgrades are available to make them compatible. List any software upgrades or patches you downloaded to prepare your applications for Windows Vista:

   _____

   _____

   _____

   _____

4. Install any application upgrades or patches you have downloaded.

5. Download or otherwise obtain all necessary drivers from the manufacturers' Web sites or the Microsoft site for your hardware. List any drivers you were required to install to make your hardware compatible with Windows Vista:

   _____

   _____

6. Gather any network-specific information in preparation for the installation. If you're connected to a network, answer the following:

◢ If you're using a TCP/IP network, how is your IP address configured?

_____

◢ For a static IP address, what is the IP address?

_____

◢ What is the workgroup name or domain name of the network?

_____

◢ What is your computer name?

_____

7. The product key, provided with the Windows Vista installation DVD, usually consists of a set of alphanumeric characters and determines the edition of Vista being installed. You must enter the key to complete the installation, even if you're installing the operating system from setup files located somewhere other than the installation DVD. Make sure you have the correct product key for your installation DVD and record it below:

_____

8. Review the information you've collected so far, and then decide whether to do a fresh installation or an upgrade. For instance, if all the important applications on your system are compatible with Windows Vista, an upgrade will probably save time because it leaves compatible applications in working condition. On the other hand, if you know you have to install new applications because of incompatibilities, you might choose to perform a fresh installation. In many ways, a fresh installation is preferable because it ensures that no misconfigured system settings are carried over to the new operating system.

9. Back up critical data files (that is, any work you or others have stored on your computer that you can't afford to lose during the installation process).

The following steps are representative of a typical installation. Steps for both an upgrade and a clean installation are included. Your installation will probably vary in minor ways, depending on the installation options you choose, your system's hardware configuration, and other factors. The following steps are a general guide to let you know what to expect during the process. Don't become alarmed if your experience differs slightly. Use your knowledge to solve any problems on your own, and ask your instructor for help if you get stuck. You might want to record any differences between these steps and your own experience. Also, record any decisions you make and any information you enter during the installation process.

If you are performing an in-place upgrade to Vista, follow these steps:

1. Close any open applications that might interfere with the installation such as antivirus or boot management software.

2. From the Windows desktop, launch the Vista DVD. When the Setup program starts, click **Install now**. This program guides you through the actual installation. If it doesn't begin automatically, click **Start, Run** and browse for the Setup.exe file to begin the installation.

3. On the next screen, choose to allow the setup program to download updates. Click **Go online to get the latest updates for installation (recommended)**.

4. Enter the product key and click **Next**.

5. Accept the EULA, and then click **Next**.

6. Click **Upgrade**.

7. As the installation continues, the computer may reboot several times and you may be asked to enter some information about your location and hardware setup or whether you want to help protect Windows automatically.

8. Next, you may be asked to enter a username, password, computer name, date, and time. Record all of your answers below:

_____

_____

_____

_____

9. At the end of the setup process, a logon screen appears.

If you are performing a clean install of Vista, follow these steps:

1. Insert the Windows Vista installation DVD and reboot your computer. If you receive a "Press any key to boot from CD/DVD" message, press a key. If your system is not configured to boot from the DVD drive, you will need to change the boot order in the BIOS.

2. When the Install Windows window appears, you may have to select some configuration information such as your preferred language and keyboard type. When you're finished, click **Next**.

3. When the opening menu appears, click **Install now**.

4. Enter the product key and click **Next**.

5. Accept the EULA and click **Next**.

6. Click **Custom** (**advanced**).

7. The next screen shows the list of partitions where you can install Vista. Copy this list below:

_____

_____

8. Since this is a clean install, you want to replace the old operating system by installing Vista on top of the old Windows partition. Make your selection and click **Next**.

9. As the installation continues, the computer may reboot several times and you may be asked to enter some information about your location and hardware setup.

10. Next, you will be asked to enter a username, password, computer name, date, and time. Record all of your answers below:

_____

_____

_____

_____

11. At the end of the setup process, a logon screen appears.

12. At this point, you would log on and start installing the application, starting with your antivirus program, followed by Windows updates.

13. Remove the installation DVD from the drive and return it to your instructor.

14. Was the Windows Vista installation a success? If so, what did you find to be most challenging about the installation process?

_____

_____

15. Describe the Windows Vista desktop:

_____

_____

_____

REVIEW QUESTIONS

1. How does the Windows Vista user interface differ from Windows XP?

_____

_____

_____

2. When would a clean install be preferable to an in-place upgrade?

_____

_____

3. When would an in-place upgrade be preferable to a clean install?

_____

_____

4. Why do you need to close applications before performing an in-place upgrade to Vista?

_____

_____

5. Where did you go to find the computer name while you were gathering information?

_____

_____

LAB 3.5 CRITICAL THINKING: VIRTUAL PC

OBJECTIVES

The goal of this lab is to help you do an installation of Windows in a virtual environment. After completing this lab, you will be able to:

◢ Download and install Virtual PC

◢ Perform an installation of Windows XP on a virtual machine

MATERIALS REQUIRED

This lab requires the following:

◢ Windows Vista/XP operating system

◢ Internet access or access to the Virtual PC executable file

◢ Windows XP installation files or installation CD

◢ Key from installation CD

LAB PREPARATION

Before the lab begins, the instructor or lab assistant needs to do the following:

◢ Verify that Windows starts with no errors.

◢ Provide each student with access to the Windows installation files or CD and key.

◢ Verify that any necessary Windows drivers are available.

◢ For labs that don't have Internet access, provide the Virtual PC executable file from *www.microsoft.com/downloads*.

ACTIVITY BACKGROUND

A virtual computer or virtual machine is software that simulates the hardware of a physical computer. Using this software, you can install and run multiple operating systems on a single PC. The two most popular virtual machine programs are Virtual PC by Microsoft and VMware by VMware, Inc. In this lab, you will install Windows on a virtual machine that you set up using Virtual PC.

ESTIMATED COMPLETION TIME: 90 Minutes

 Activity

Follow these steps to download and use Microsoft Virtual PC 2007 onto your computer:

1. Open your browser, go to **www.microsoft.com/downloads,** and search for Virtual PC 2007.

2. Click the **download** link and download the latest version of the Virtual PC installer for your machine.

3. Run the setup program by double-clicking the executable file. Accept the License Agreement and install the program.

4. Once the installation is complete, run the program. When the **New Virtual Machine Wizard** appears, click **Next.**

5. Select **Create a virtual machine** and click **Next.**

6. Enter a name and location for your virtual machine and record this information below:

_____

_____

7. Click **Next** to continue. The next screen allows you to choose which operating system will be installed and then allocates the appropriate resources. Choose **Windows XP** and then click **Next**.

8. The Memory screen allows you to choose how much RAM is reserved for the virtual machine. Generally, no more than half of your system's memory should be used for all of the virtual machines you plan to run at once. Stick with the recommended amount and click **Next**.

9. In the **Virtual Hard Disk Options** screen, select **A new virtual hard disk** and click **Next**.

10. Pick a location and size for the virtual hard drive and click **Next**.

11. Finally, click **Finish** to close the wizard.

12. In the **Virtual PC Console** window, select your virtual machine and click **Start**.

13. As the virtual machine attempts to boot (see Figure 3-1), note which version of BIOS it uses:

_____

14. Examine the **Settings** under the **Edit** drop-down menu and confirm how much memory is running on your virtual machine.

_____

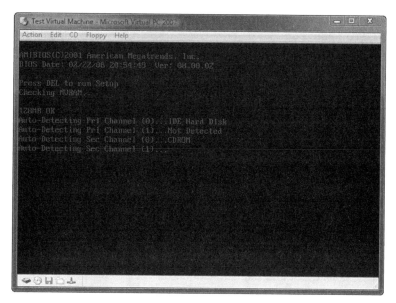

Figure 3-1 Virtual machine during boot up
Courtesy: Course Technology/Cengage Learning

15. To install an operating system, add the installation CD to the virtual machine by selecting **Use Physical Drive D:** from the **CD** drop-down menu. (*Note:* The letter assigned to your CD drive may vary depending on your system's configuration.)

16. Insert the Windows XP installation CD and restart the virtual machine to install Windows (see Lab 3.3).

REVIEW QUESTIONS

1. Why might an operating system on a virtual drive run slower than one installed directly on a PC?

   _____

   _____

2. Describe a situation where you might want to install several different virtual machines on a system.

   _____

   _____

   _____

3. Why can't you use all of your system memory to run a virtual machine?

   _____

   _____

4. Why do you think you can't change the amount of RAM on your virtual machine while it's running?

   _____

   _____

5. Why might it be important to set up a shared folder between the virtual machine and the physical computer?

   _____

   _____

LAB 3.6 CRITICAL THINKING: UNATTENDED INSTALLATION

OBJECTIVES

The goal of this lab is to help you do an unattended installation of Windows. After completing this lab, you will be able to:

◢ Use nLite to create an answer file for an unattended installation of Windows

◢ Identify the benefits of an unattended installation

◢ Perform an unattended installation of Windows XP

MATERIALS REQUIRED

This lab requires the following:

◢ Windows Vista/XP operating system with a burnable CD-ROM

◢ Internet access (optional)

◢ Windows XP installation files or installation CD

◢ Key from installation CD

LAB PREPARATION

Before the lab begins, the instructor or lab assistant needs to do the following:

◢ Verify that Windows starts with no errors.

◢ Provide each student with access to the Windows installation files or CD and key.

◢ Verify that any necessary Windows drivers are available.

◢ For labs that don't have Internet access, provide the nLite executable file from *www.nliteos.com*.

ACTIVITY BACKGROUND

System administrators may not have time to install Windows on dozens or even hundreds of machines. Instead, they can choose to perform an unattended installation where all the questions about the installation are answered ahead of time and stored in an answer file. Unattended installations work for both upgrades and clean installs. In this lab, an unattended installation will be performed with the help of a Freeware preinstallation tool called nLite.

ESTIMATED COMPLETION TIME: 90 Minutes

Activity

Follow these steps to download nLite onto your computer:

1. Open your browser and go to **www.nliteos.com**.

2. Click the **download** link and download the latest version of the nLite installer.

3. Run the setup program by double-clicking the executable file and accept the License Agreement.

4. Accept all the defaults to finish the installation. Once the installation is complete, run nLite. The screen in Figure 3-2 should appear.

Figure 3-2 The nLite custom Windows installation wizard
Courtesy: Course Technology/Cengage Learning

5. Select your preferred language and click **Next**.

6. Select the location of your installation files or CD and click **Next**.

7. Choose a location where you want to save the installation files and wait while nLite copies the files. Click **Next** to continue.

8. The **Presets** screen allows you to load previous settings. Click **Next** to continue.

9. In the **Task Selection** screen, users can decide which features they would like to include in their installation, such as service packs or additional drivers. Take a moment to explore each of these options shown in Figure 3-3 and then select **Unattended** and **Bootable ISO** and click **Next** to continue.

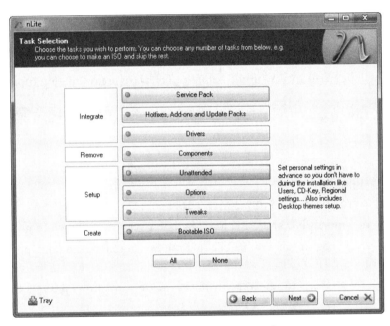

Figure 3-3 Choose which tasks you would like to perform
Courtesy: Course Technology/Cengage Learning

10. The **Unattended** screen presents all of the configuration questions that are usually resolved during the installation, such as the product key or the user name (see Figure 3-4). Take some time to review these options and then fill out the form with the same information that you used to install Windows XP (see Lab 3.3). When you are finished, click **Next** to continue.

11. Click **Yes** to begin the process and click **Next**.

12. At the **Bootable ISO** screen, in the **Mode** section, select **Direct Burn** and choose the device that will be used to burn the installation CD. Click **Burn**, then **Next**, and then **Finish**.

13. Once the new installation CD has been created, use it to perform an unattended installation of Windows XP.

14. Describe the installation process from the unattended installation CD you created.

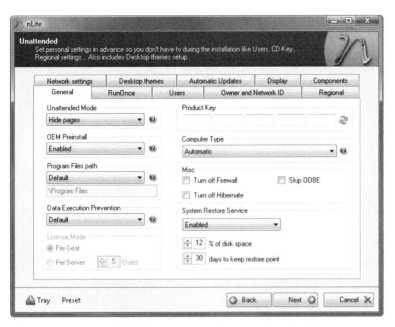

Figure 3-4 Unattended allows you to configure settings in advance
Courtesy: Course Technology/Cengage Learning

REVIEW QUESTIONS

1. Could the same unattended installation file be used on two different computers? Why or why not?

   _____

   _____

   _____

2. Describe a situation where you might want to remove a windows component before the installation:

   _____

   _____

   _____

3. Why does nLite also allow you to save the installation image as an .ISO file?

   _____

   _____

4. When might an unattended installation not save any time?

   _____

   _____

5. When might you choose to use nLite even if you're only doing a single installation?

   _____

   _____

CHAPTER 4

Maintaining Windows

Labs included in this chapter:

LAB 4.1 PERFORM HARD DRIVE ROUTINE MAINTENANCE

OBJECTIVES

The goal of this lab is to help you perform routine maintenance on a hard drive. After completing this lab, you will be able to:

◢ Delete unneeded files on a hard drive

◢ Defragment a hard drive

◢ Scan a hard drive for errors

MATERIALS REQUIRED

This lab requires the following:

◢ Windows Vista/XP operating system

LAB PREPARATION

Before the lab begins, the instructor or lab assistant needs to do the following:

◢ Verify that Windows starts with no errors.

ACTIVITY BACKGROUND

To ensure that your hard drive operates in peak condition, you should perform some routine maintenance tasks regularly. For starters, you need to ensure that your hard drive includes enough unused space (which it requires to operate efficiently). In other words, you should remove unnecessary files from the drive.

In addition, files on a hard drive sometimes become fragmented over time; defragmenting the drive can improve performance because files can be read sequentially without jumping around on the drive. Other routine maintenance tasks include scanning the hard drive for errors and repairing them. In this lab, you learn about three tools you can use for important disk maintenance tasks. You should use these tools on a scheduled basis to keep your hard drive error free and performing well.

ESTIMATED COMPLETION TIME: 30-45 Minutes

 Activity

Follow these steps to delete unnecessary files on your hard drive:

1. Close all open applications.

2. Click **Start**, click **All Programs**, click **Accessories**, click **System Tools**, and then click **Disk Cleanup**. If Windows asks you to choose which files to clean up, select **Files from all users on this computer**. If Vista opens a UAC box, click **Continue**.

3. If the Disk Cleanup Drive Selection (Select Drive in XP) dialog box opens, select the drive you want to clean up in the drop-down list, and click **OK** to close the Disk Cleanup Drive Selection dialog box.

4. The Disk Cleanup dialog box opens. You need to select the types of files you want Disk Cleanup to delete. Select all possible options. Depending on your system, these options might include Downloaded Program Files, Recycle Bin, Temporary files, and Temporary Internet files.

◢ How much disk space does each group of files take up?

_____

_____

_____

_____

◢ Based on information in the Disk Cleanup dialog box, what is the purpose of each group of files?

_____

_____

_____

_____

◢ What is the total amount of disk space you would gain by deleting these files?

_____

◢ What types of files might you not want to delete during Disk Cleanup? Why?

_____

_____

5. Click **OK** to delete the selected groups of files.

6. When asked to confirm the deletion, click **Delete Files** (or **Yes** in XP). The Disk Cleanup dialog box closes, and a progress indicator appears while the cleanup is under way. The progress indicator closes when the cleanup is finished, returning you to the desktop.

The next step in routine maintenance is to use Windows Chkdsk to examine the hard drive and repair errors.

Follow these steps:

1. Close any open applications so they aren't trying to write to the hard drive while it's being repaired.

2. Click **Start** and type **cmd** in the Start Search box (in XP, click **Start, Run** and type **cmd** in the Run dialog box) and press **Enter**. The command prompt window opens.

3. Several switches (options) are associated with the Chkdsk utility. To show all available switches, type **chkdsk /?** at the command prompt and press **Enter**. Answer the following:

   ◢ What are two switches used to fix errors that Chkdsk finds?

   _____

   ◢ Why do the /I and /C switches in Chkdsk reduce the amount of time needed to run the defragmentation?

   _____

4. To use the Chkdsk utility to scan the C: hard drive for errors and repair them, type **chkdsk C: /R** and press **Enter**. (_Note:_ You may have to substitute a different drive letter depending on your computer's configuration.)

5. When Chkdsk is finished, close the command prompt window.

The last step in routine hard drive maintenance is to use the Disk Defragmenter tool to locate fragmented files and rewrite them to the hard drive in contiguous segments. You should do the defragmentation last because other actions, like cleaning up files, will further fragment the files on the disk.

Follow these steps:

1. Close all open applications.

2. Click **Start**, click **All Programs**, click **Accessories**, click **System Tools**, and then click **Disk Defragmenter**. If Vista opens a UAC box, click **Continue**. The Disk Defragmenter window opens.

3. In Windows Vista, click **Defragment now...** (click **Defragment** in Windows XP). If prompted, select the drive you want to defragment. Disk Defragmenter begins defragmenting the drive, displaying a progress indicator of estimated fragmentation before and after it works.

> **Notes** Fully defragmenting your hard drive can take a few hours, depending on how fragmented it is. If you don't have time to wait, you can stop the process by clicking **Cancel defragmentation** (click **Stop** in Windows XP).

4. In Windows XP, you can observe a graphical representation of the defragmentation process.

5. To see what happens in XP when you open an application while the hard drive is defragmenting, open Microsoft Word or another program. Use the program for a moment and then close it. Answer the following:

   ◢ What happened to Disk Defragmenter when you opened another application?

   _____

6. When defragmentation is completed, close the Disk Defragmenter window.

REVIEW QUESTIONS

1. Why should you run Disk Cleanup before running Disk Defragmenter?

   _____

   _____

2. How does defragmentation improve performance?

   _____

   _____

3. Why shouldn't you attempt to use other programs while Chkdsk is running?

   _____

   _____

4. Which type of files removed by Disk Cleanup took up the most space? Do you think this will usually be the case?

   _____

   _____

LAB 4.2 SCHEDULE MAINTENANCE TASKS

OBJECTIVES

The goal of this lab is to help you schedule automatic maintenance on your computer. After completing this lab, you will be able to:

⊿ Open the Windows Task Scheduler and view scheduled tasks

⊿ Use the Windows Task Scheduler to schedule weekly hard drive defragmentation

MATERIALS REQUIRED

This lab requires the following:

⊿ Windows Vista/XP operating system

LAB PREPARATION

Before the lab begins, the instructor or lab assistant needs to do the following:

⊿ Verify that Windows starts with no errors.

ACTIVITY BACKGROUND

Windows includes a tool called the Task Scheduler that can be used to automate some of the routine maintenance on your PC. Tasks like file defragmentation, virus scanning, or checking your hard drive for errors can be set to run automatically at times that do not interfere with your day-to-day activities, like weekends or evenings. In Vista, many of these tasks are already scheduled to run when needed.

ESTIMATED COMPLETION TIME: 30 Minutes

Activity

Follow these steps to open the Task Scheduler and schedule a weekly defragmentation of your hard drive:

1. Log in as an administrator and close all open applications. (*Note:* Some tasks may require that the administrator account have a password.)

2. Click **Start** and open the Control Panel.

3. Click **System and Maintenance** (**Performance and Maintenance** in XP).

4. Scroll down to **Administrative Tools** and click **Schedule tasks** (in XP, click **Scheduled Tasks**). If Windows needs your permission to continue, click **Continue**.

In Windows XP, follow these steps:

1. Double-click **Add Scheduled Task**. When The Scheduled Task Wizard opens, click **Next**.

2. Click **Browse**, locate defrag.exe in the windows\system32 folder, and then click **Open**.

3. Name the task WeeklyDefrag and click the **Weekly** radio button. Click **Next** to continue.

4. Choose to schedule the task for every Wednesday at 1:00 AM and click **Next**.

5. If prompted, enter your password and click **Next**.

6. Select **Open advanced properties for this task when I click Finish** and click **Finish**.

7. Add the volume letter of the hard drive you want to defrag (i.e., defrag C:) in the Run box after the existing command and click **OK**.

8. Again, enter your password and click **OK**.

9. Finally, close the Scheduled Tasks window.

Windows Vista already schedules most of the routine maintenance your computer will need. To view the tasks that have already been scheduled, follow these steps:

1. In the Task Status section of the Task Scheduler window, determine how many tasks have been started in the past 24 hours.

2. Scroll down to a group of tasks called ManualDefrag and click the + to expand the category.

3. Select the most recent ManualDefrag task and determine when it was last run.

4. The automatically scheduled defragmentation is labeled ScheduledDefrag in the Vista Task Scheduler. You can determine more information about the ScheduledDefrag task in the Task Scheduler Library (shown in the left column of Figure 4-1). Use the Task Scheduler Library to answer the following questions:

   ◢ Which user account is used to run this task?

   ◢ When does this task run?

   ◢ Will the Task Scheduler wake the computer to start this task?

5. When you're finished, close the Scheduled Tasks window.

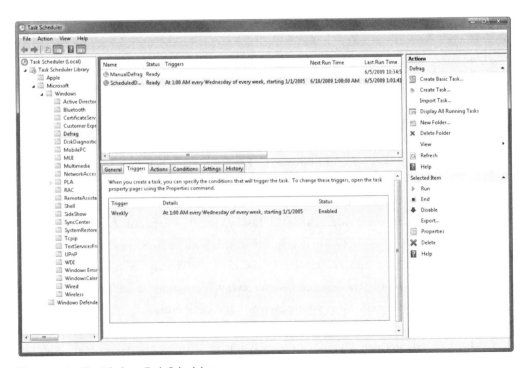

Figure 4-1   The Windows Task Scheduler
Courtesy: Course Technology/Cengage Learning

6. Next, use the Task Scheduler Library to determine when Windows Defender runs an MP Scheduled Scan.

   _____

7. When you are finished, close the Task Scheduler.

REVIEW QUESTIONS

1. Why are some tasks scheduled in the middle of the night?

   _____

   _____

2. Besides defragmentation, what are some other tasks you might choose to automate?

   _____

   _____

3. Why are some tasks set to run whether the user is logged in or not?

   _____

   _____

4. Why might you want to disable some of the automatic tasks set up in Vista?

   _____

   _____

5. Why do you think some tasks are set to run only if a network connection is available?

   _____

   _____

LAB 4.3 BACK UP AND RESTORE FILES IN WINDOWS XP

OBJECTIVES

The goal of this lab is to help you use the Windows XP Backup and Recovery Tools to back up and recover lost files. After completing this lab, you will be able to:

◢ Back up files

◢ Delete files

◢ Recover deleted files

MATERIALS REQUIRED

This lab requires the following:

◢ Windows XP operating system

LAB PREPARATION

Before the lab begins, the instructor or lab assistant needs to do the following:

⊿ Verify that Windows starts with no errors.

⊿ Ensure access to an Administrator and User account

ACTIVITY BACKGROUND

Windows provides the Backup and Recovery Tools to help you safeguard data in Windows system files. Using these tools, you can back up a single file or even an entire drive from the local or remote computer. Backups, compressed into a single file, can be saved to a location of your choice, without the need for a dedicated backup device, such as a tape drive. In this lab, you back up, delete, and restore data files using the Backup and Recovery Tools.

ESTIMATED COMPLETION TIME: 45 Minutes

 Activity

Follow these steps to select the files or folders you want to back up:

1. Log on as an Administrator.

2. Create folders called **C:\Backups** and **C:\BackMeUp**.

3. Create a text file on the root of the C: drive called singlefile.txt. Also create several text files in the C:\BackMeUp folder called file1.txt, file2.txt, and file3.txt.

4. Click **Start**, point to **All Programs**, point to **Accessories**, point to **System Tools**, and then click **Backup**. Click **Advanced Mode**. The Windows Backup and Recovery Tools utility opens. What three options are available on the Welcome tab?

_____

_____

_____

5. Click the **Backup** tab. In the left pane, click the + (plus sign) next to drive C and then select the drive itself. The right pane displays all the items you can back up.

6. First, you back up an entire folder. Click the check box next to the **BackMeUp** folder in the right pane; doing so indicates that you want to back up the entire contents of that folder.

7. Also, instruct the system to back up the entire contents of the Documents and Settings folder. Explain how you performed this task:

_____

_____

_____

8. In addition to the folders you just selected for backup, you'll select a single file, singlefile.txt, for backup.

9. Click the **singlefile.txt** check box to specify that you want to back up this file.

10. In the Backup media or file name text box, type **C:\Backups\Lab4.bkf**, which specifies the name and location of the backup file you're creating.

Follow these steps to start the backup process:

1. In the Backup tab, click **Start Backup**. The Backup Job Information dialog box opens. The Backup description text box displays date and time information about this backup. This information is displayed later to help you identify the backup during a recovery process. If you need to perform many backup operations (and, therefore, have to keep track of multiple backup sets), you should always use this text box to describe the files in this set. Alternatively, you might want to keep a backup log book and refer to an entry number that describes in detail what's in this backup set. Because this is your initial backup, you can ignore the other sections of the dialog box and click **Start Backup**.

2. The Backup Job Information dialog box opens. Click **Start Backup** in this dialog box.

3. The Backup begins and displays information about its progress. Answer these questions:

   ◢ What three items give you an idea of how the backup is progressing?

   _____

   _____

   _____

   ◢ Can you tell how many files must be backed up?

   _____

   ◢ Can you tell which files have already been completed or are currently being processed?

   _____

   ◢ What information continues to change even when the backup process is paused?

   _____

4. When the backup is finished, click **Report** in the Backup Progress dialog box to open the Backup log in Notepad.

5. Print and examine the report. What errors and causes are reported?

   _____

   _____

   _____

6. When you're finished, close Notepad and click **Close** in the Backup Progress dialog box.

Follow these steps to delete files and observe the effects:

1. Log off and log on as a different user. Ensure the Recycle Bin is empty. Right-click **Recycle Bin** on the desktop, and click **Empty Recycle Bin** in the shortcut menu. Click **Yes** to confirm that you want to empty the Recycle Bin.

2. Open a command prompt window. At the command prompt, type **DEL C:\BackMeUp*.*** and press **Enter** to delete all files in the C:\BackMeUp directory. Confirm the deletion when prompted. Close the command prompt window.

3. In Windows Explorer, delete C:\singlefile.txt.

4. Double-click **Recycle Bin** and note which files are displayed:

_____

_____

_____

5. Empty the Recycle Bin again and then, in Windows Explorer, look for your text files in C:\ and C:\BackMeUp to confirm that they are gone.

Follow these steps to restore the deleted files:

1. Log off and log on as an administrator.

2. Click **Start**, point to **All Programs**, point to **Accessories**, point to **System Tools**, and then click **Backup**. The Backup window opens.

3. Click **Advanced Mode** and click the **Restore and Manage Media** tab. In the left pane, click the + (plus sign) to expand the File symbol, and then click to expand **Lab4.bkf created** _Date at Time_.

4. Select **Lab4.bkf** in the C:\Backups folder. Your backup is displayed in the left pane of the Restore and Manage Media tab.

5. To restore files and folders, click the necessary check boxes, and then click **Start Restore**. Do you think you could choose to restore only part of the information? If so, how?

_____

_____

6. The Confirm Restore dialog box opens. Click **OK** to continue.

7. The Restore Progress dialog box opens. When the restore operation is finished, click **Close** to close the Restore Progress dialog box and then close the Backup utility.

8. To confirm that the restore is complete, look for your text files using Explorer.

REVIEW QUESTIONS

1. Is it more important to back up Windows system files or data files? Why?

_____

_____

2. What is the Start menu path for launching Windows Backup and Restore Tools?

_____

3. What features of Windows Backup and Restore Tools can you use if you're unfamiliar with the backup and restore process?

_____

_____

4. What does the Backup Job Information dialog box allow you to define? Why is this function useful?

_____

_____

_____

5. If you forgot the name of your backup file, how else might you identify it?

_____

_____

LAB 4.4 MANAGE USER ACCOUNTS IN WINDOWS VISTA/XP

OBJECTIVES

The goal of this lab is to give you experience adding and modifying user accounts by using Computer Management. After completing this lab, you will be able to:

⊿ Add users

⊿ Reset passwords

⊿ Control password policies

MATERIALS REQUIRED

This lab requires the following:

⊿ Windows Vista/XP Professional operating system

⊿ An administrator account and password

LAB PREPARATION

Before the lab begins, the instructor or lab assistant needs to do the following:

⊿ Verify that Windows starts with no errors.

ACTIVITY BACKGROUND

Maintaining Windows involves more than just managing physical resources like hard drives; you also sometimes need to manage users and their access to these resources. Windows needs just a few pieces of information to set up a user account: a unique user name, the user's full name, a description of the user (typically title and department), and a password. Managing users can take quite a bit of administrative time, however. Much of this time is spent helping users who have forgotten their passwords or entered their passwords incorrectly multiple times, causing Windows to lock their accounts. In this lab, you practice managing user accounts and passwords in Computer Management.

ESTIMATED COMPLETION TIME: 30 Minutes

 Activity

To examine the user account information available via Computer Management, follow these steps:

1. Log on as an administrator.

2. Click **Start, Control Panel,** and then click **System and Maintenance (Performance** and **Maintenance** in XP).

3. Click **Administrative Tools** and double-click **Computer Management.** If you are presented with a UAC dialog box, click **Continue.** The Computer Management window opens, and is similar to the one in Figure 4-2.

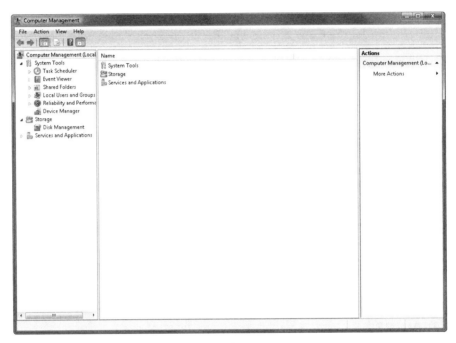

Figure 4-2 The Computer Management console
Courtesy: Course Technology/Cengage Learning

4. Click the arrow (+ sign in XP) next to Local Users and Groups to expand the category and select the **Users** folder. Examine the Computer Management window and answer the following questions:

◢ Based on your knowledge of Windows, what two user accounts are included on a Windows system by default?

_____

◢ Does your system contain any personal user accounts? If so, list them here:

_____

◢ What user groups are included on your Windows system?

_____

In Computer Management, you can add and configure users on a local computer by following these steps:

1. In the left pane under Local Users and Groups, if necessary, click the **Users** folder to display a list of current user names.

2. Right-click **Users** and click **New User** in the shortcut menu. The New User dialog box opens.

3. In the User name text box, type **James.**

4. In the Full name text box, type **James Clark**.

5. In the Description text box, type **Supervisor**.

6. In the Password text box, type **newuser**.

7. Confirm the password, make sure the **User must change password at next logon** and **Account is disabled** check boxes are cleared.

   ◢ What other check box could you select?

   _____

   _____

8. Click **Create** and close all open windows.

When Windows creates a new user, that user is added only to the Users group, which means the account can't create, delete, or change other accounts; make system-wide changes; or install software. To give the account administrative privileges, do the following:

1. Open Computer Management and select the **James Clark** account.

2. Double-click the **James Clark** account to open the test Properties window, and then click the **Member Of** tab.

3. To what group(s) does James Clark currently belong?

   _____

4. Click **Add** to open the Select Groups window.

5. Click **Advanced** and click **Find Now**.

6. Select the **Administrators** group and click **OK** and **OK** again to close the Select Groups window. To what groups does the James Clark account now belong?

   _____

7. Log off your computer and log on as James Clark. List the steps you took to accomplish that task:

   _____

   _____

   _____

Occasionally, administrators have to reset user passwords. To reset a user's password, do the following:

1. Log on with the original administrator account.

2. Open Computer Management and select the **James Clark** account.

3. Right-click the **James Clark** account and select **Set Password**. If a user knows his or her password and wants to change it, what can he or she do?

   _____

   _____

4. Click **Proceed** and enter a password called **newpass**.

5. Confirm the password and click **OK**.

6. Click **OK** again to acknowledge that the password has been changed.

7. Try to log on with the James Clark account using the old password. What error do you get?

_____

_____

8. Now test the new password by logging on successfully.

9. Finally, log back on as the administrator and delete the James Clark account. List the steps that you used:

_____

_____

_____

_____

REVIEW QUESTIONS

1. Besides adding and deleting users, what other tasks can you perform with Computer Management in the Local Users and Groups category?

_____

2. List three of the differences between User and Administrator accounts:

_____

_____

_____

3. List the steps to change the group to which an account belongs:

_____

_____

_____

_____

4. Why do you think new users are not automatically members of the Administrators group?

_____

_____

_____

5. Why is it a good idea to have users change their passwords the first time they log on?

_____

_____

LAB 4.5 SET DISK QUOTAS

OBJECTIVES

The goal of this lab is to show you how to set and monitor disk quotas. After completing this lab, you will be able to:

◢ Convert a logical drive from FAT to NTFS

◢ Set disk quotas for new users

◢ Monitor quota logs

◢ Identify when quotas have been exceeded

MATERIALS REQUIRED

This lab requires the following:

◢ Windows Vista/XP Professional operating system

◢ A computer containing a partition (which can be the partition where Windows is installed) that has no important information

LAB PREPARATION

Before the lab begins, the instructor or lab assistant needs to do the following:

◢ Verify that Windows starts with no errors.

ACTIVITY BACKGROUND

When a system is used by more than one account or when server storage space is limited, setting storage limits for each user is often a good idea. No one account should monopolize storage space by filling up the server and preventing other users from storing data. Note, however, that you can impose disk quotas only on drives formatted with NTFS. In this lab, you use disk quotas to limit user storage space.

ESTIMATED COMPLETION TIME: 30 Minutes

 Activity

In the following steps, you set very small disk quotas for all users. That way, you can easily exceed the disk quota limit later and observe the results. Do the following to verify that you're using the NTFS file system:

1. Log on as an administrator.

2. Open Windows Explorer, right-click drive **C** (or another logical drive designated by your instructor), and click **Properties** in the shortcut menu. The Local Disk (C:) Properties dialog box opens. (If you selected another drive letter, the dialog box name will be different.) On the General tab, verify that the drive is using the NTFS file system.

If you currently have the FAT32 file system and need to convert to NTFS, use the following steps, and then open the Local Disk (C:) Properties dialog box again. If you already have NTFS, skip the next three steps.

1. Open a command prompt window.

2. At the command prompt, type **convert C: /fs:ntfs** and press **Enter**. (If necessary, substitute the drive letter for another logical drive in the command, as specified by your instructor.)

3. After the command runs, reboot your computer to complete the conversion to NTFS.

To enable disk quotas, do the following:

1. In the Local Disk (C:) Properties dialog box, click the **Quota** tab.

2. Click **Show Quota Settings** and click the **Enable quota management** check box. If Windows presents you with a UAC box, click **Continue**. This option allows you to set and change quotas.

3. Click the **Deny disk space to users exceeding quota limit** check box. This option prevents users from using more disk space after reaching their quota.

4. Verify that the **Limit disk space to** option button is selected and that **1** appears in the text box to the right. Then click **MB** in the drop-down list to set the disk quota to 1 MB of storage space.

5. In the Set warning level to text box, type **500**, and then verify that **KB** is displayed in the text box to the right. This setting ensures that users receive warnings after they have used 500 KB of disk space.

6. Click **Log event when a user exceeds their quota limit**. This option ensures that a record is made when a user exceeds the quota limit.

7. Click **Log event when a user exceeds their warning level**. This option ensures that a record is made when users reach their warning limit. (You can view these records in the Local Disk (C:) Properties dialog box.)

8. Click **OK** to apply the new settings, and click **OK** to close the Local Disk (C:) Properties dialog box.

Follow these steps to exceed the quota limits you have just set:

1. Using what you learned in Lab 4.4, create a new restricted user called **Quota Test**.

2. Create a directory called **Quota** in the root of the NTFS drive.

3. Log off as an administrator, and log on as **Quota Test**.

4. In Windows Explorer, open the Windows or WINNT folder, and click the **Show the contents of this folder** link. One at a time, copy (*do not cut*) all .gif and .bmp files in the Windows or WINNT folder, and paste them into the Quota folder.

◢ What happens when you exceed the warning level and then the storage quota?

_____

_____

5. Log off as the Quota Test user.

Because of the options you selected when you created the disk quota, logs were created when you exceeded the warning level and the storage quota. To view these quota logs, follow these steps:

1. Log on as an administrator.

2. Open the Local Disk (C:) Properties dialog box, and then click the **Quota** tab. Click the **Show Quota Settings** button, and then click the **Quota Entries** button. The Quota Entries window opens, displaying the log of quota entries for certain events.

◢ What types of information are displayed for each entry?

_____

_____

3. Double-click an entry for Quota Test. The Quota Settings dialog box for that user opens. Note that you can raise or lower the user's disk quotas.

4. Check the quota settings for each entry, and record any entry for which you were unable to adjust settings:

_____

_____

Because disk quotas may interfere with future labs, it is important to remove the quotas. To disable disk quotas, do the following:

1. In the Local Disk (C:) Properties dialog box, click the **Quota** tab.

2. Click **Show Quota Settings** and deselect the **Enable quota management** check box.

3. Click **OK** and close any open windows.

REVIEW QUESTIONS

1. How would you set up disk quotas on a drive formatted with FAT32?

_____

_____

2. Why might you want to impose disk quotas?

_____

3. What option must be selected to specify a warning level?

_____

_____

4. What options must be selected to prevent users from exceeding their quotas?

_____

_____

5. Explain how to monitor and change disk quotas:

_____

_____

LAB 4.6 MANAGE VIRTUAL MEMORY

OBJECTIVES

The goal of this lab is to learn to manage virtual memory. After completing this lab, you will be able to:

◢ Locate the Windows tool for adjusting virtual memory settings

◢ Change the size of the paging file

MATERIALS REQUIRED

This lab requires the following:

◢ Windows Vista/XP Professional operating system

◢ Internet access

◢ A printer

LAB PREPARATION

Before the lab begins, the instructor or lab assistant needs to do the following:

◢ Verify that Windows starts with no errors.

◢ Verify that Internet access is available.

ACTIVITY BACKGROUND

Virtual memory allows the OS to make use of an HDD (hard drive) to simulate RAM. This option can be useful when, for instance, the OS is running a number of applications, and each requires an allocation of RAM reserved for its use. Ideally, the Virtual Memory Manager protects actual RAM for the most active applications by moving the data other applications use to a swap file on the hard drive. In Windows Vista/XP, the swap file is called a "paging file." The virtual memory default settings allow Windows to manage the paging file, increasing or decreasing the size as needed.

In most situations, allowing Windows to manage virtual memory with default settings works fine, but this practice can cause pauses in application response time when the OS switches to an application with data stored in the paging file. This delay is caused by longer access time when reading from a drive instead of reading from RAM. The access time increases especially if the file is on the boot partition or any other partition subject to heavy use. If performance has become a problem, you might want to specify virtual memory settings manually.

ESTIMATED COMPLETION TIME: 30 Minutes

 Activity

Log on to your computer using an account with administrative privileges. Complete the following steps to gather information about your system:

1. Click **Start, Control Panel**. The Control Panel window opens.

2. Click **System and Maintenance** (**Performance and Maintenance** in XP). The Control Panel window changes to System and Maintenance.

3. Click **System** and the System window opens (System Properties in XP).

4. Note how much RAM is installed (in the General tab in XP) and then click **Back** in the System window (**Close** in the System Properties window in XP).

5. Click **Administrative Tools** and double-click the **Computer Management** shortcut. The Computer Management console opens.

6. In the left pane, click **Disk Management**, and review the information in the right pane. List the required information on the following lines, and then close the Computer Management console and Administrative Tools window.

   ◢ Disks installed:

◢ Partitions and letters assigned:

_____

◢ Partition designated as the system partition:

_____

◢ Disk with unallocated space:

_____

    7. Close any open windows.

It's unlikely that you would ever have to make changes to the paging file in Vista. You won't be making the changes because Vista does a much better job managing memory than earlier versions of Windows did with the same task. Visit the Microsoft Web site at *http://support.microsoft.com* and search the Knowledge Base for the following articles on managing the XP paging file:

    ◢ Article 314482: How to Configure Paging Files for Optimization and Recovery in Windows XP

    ◢ Article 307886: How to Move the Paging File in Windows XP

Print and read these articles, and then answer the following questions:

    1. What is the paging file's default or recommended size?

_____

    2. What is a disadvantage of totally removing the paging file from the boot partition?

_____

_____

    3. What performance-degrading issue is the paging file subject to if it's moved to a partition containing data?

_____

_____

    4. What additional benefit is there to setting up a paging file on multiple hard drives?

_____

_____

    5. According to Article 307886, how do you select the partition on which you want to modify paging file settings?

_____

_____

Next, you work with the Virtual Memory dialog box to view and record paging file settings. The information about the paging file's recommended maximum size might not be clear. As you record your settings, notice that the maximum size is the same as the recommended size.

Follow these steps:

    1. Click **Start, Control Panel**. The Control Panel window opens.

    2. Click **System and Maintenance**. Control Panel changes to the System and Maintenance window.

3. Click the **System** icon in System and Maintenance (Performance and Maintenance in XP).

4. Click **Advanced system settings** (the **Advanced** tab in XP). If a UAC box opens, click **Continue**.

5. In the Performance section of the Advanced tab, click **Settings**. The Performance Options dialog box opens.

6. In the Performance Options dialog box, click the **Advanced** tab, shown in Figure 4-3.

Figure 4-3   Use the Performance Options dialog box to access
information on your computer's paging file
Courtesy: Course Technology/Cengage Learning

7. In the Virtual memory section, click the **Change** button. The Virtual Memory dialog box opens (see Figure 4-4). List the current settings on the following lines.

◢ Does your computer have multiple paging files?

_____

◢ Drive(s) where a paging file is located:

_____

◢ Current size of the paging file:

_____

◢ Recommended size:

_____

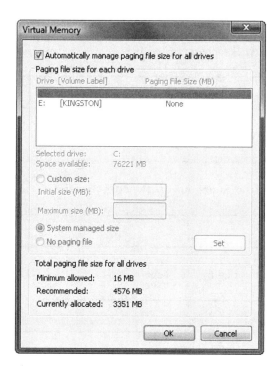

Figure 4-4 The Virtual Memory dialog box
Courtesy: Course Technology/Cengage Learning

Based on information in the Knowledge Base articles and the data you have collected about your computer, answer the following questions:

1. Given your computer's current physical configuration, is the paging file set for optimal performance? Explain:

   _____

   _____

2. What actions and paging file settings do you recommend to maximize performance? Explain:

   _____

   _____

3. Consider a 32-bit Windows computer with the following configuration:

   ◢ 512 MB RAM

   ◢ HDD0 C: (system) 17 GB NTFS with 2.8 GB unallocated disk space

   ◢ HDD1 D: (general storage) 20 GB NTFS with no unallocated disk space

   ◢ Paging file on the C drive with a custom size of 384 MB initial and 786 MB maximum

Based on what you've learned so far, what is your recommendation to maximize virtual memory performance while allowing the use of debugging information?

   _____

   _____

   _____

   _____

REVIEW QUESTIONS

1. What is meant by the term "virtual memory"?

   _____

   _____

2. What is the swap file called in Windows Vista/XP?

   _____

3. Why would you want to move the paging file off the boot partition?

   _____

   _____

4. When could fragmentation of the paging file occur?

   _____

   _____

5. What is the main reason for slight pauses in an application when retrieving information from the paging file?

   _____

   _____

6. *Bonus*: Because Microsoft acknowledges a performance advantage in locating the paging file off the boot partition, what's the main reason the boot partition is its default location?

   _____

   _____

LAB 4.7 LEARN TO WORK FROM THE COMMAND LINE

OBJECTIVES

The goal of this lab is to introduce you to some commands used when working from the command line. You change and examine directories and drives, and then perform a copy operation. You also learn to use the command-line Help feature and how to read Help information. After completing this lab, you will be able to:

◢ Create a file and folder with Notepad and Computer (My Computer in XP)

◢ Examine directories

◢ Switch drives and directories

◢ Use various commands at the command prompt

MATERIALS REQUIRED

This lab requires the following:

◢ Windows Vista/XP operating system

◢ A blank formatted floppy disk (optional)

LAB PREPARATION

Before the lab begins, the instructor or lab assistant needs to do the following:

◢ Verify that Windows starts with no errors.

ACTIVITY BACKGROUND

In Lab 1.1, you used the DIR command to explore file structure. Experienced technicians can use the command line for tasks that just can't be done in a graphical interface, especially when troubleshooting a system. For most tasks, however, you'll rely on a graphical interface, such as Windows Explorer. In this lab, you use Windows Explorer (Computer) to create a new folder and a new file. Then you use the command line to delete that file. In this lab, it's assumed that Windows is installed on the C drive. If your installation is on a different drive, substitute that drive letter in the following steps.

> **ESTIMATED COMPLETION TIME: 30 Minutes**

4

 Activity

To create a new folder and text file in My Computer, follow these steps:

1. Click **Start,** and then click **Computer** (**My Computer** in XP).

2. Right-click anywhere in the blank area of the drive C window, point to **New** on the shortcut menu, and then click **Folder**. A new folder icon appears with "New Folder" highlighted as the default name, ready for you to rename it.

3. To rename the folder Tools, type **Tools** and press **Enter**.

4. To create a file in the Tools folder, double-click the **Tools** folder icon, and then right-click anywhere in the blank area of the Tools window. Point to **New**, and then click **Text Document**. A new file icon appears in the Tools window with "New Text Document.txt" highlighted to indicate it's ready for renaming.

5. Double-click the **New Text Document.txt** icon to open the file in Notepad.

6. On the Notepad menu, click **File, Save As**.

7. In the Save As dialog box, name the file **Deleteme**, and make sure the selection in the Save as type drop-down list is **Text Documents**. Click the **Save** button.

8. Close Notepad.

9. In Computer, right-click **New Text Document.txt** and click **Delete** in the shortcut menu. Click **Yes** to confirm the deletion.

10. Close all open windows.

To practice using the command-line environment, follow these steps:

1. To open a command prompt window, click **Start, Run**, type **cmd**, and press **Enter**. The command prompt window opens, and the cursor is flashing at the command prompt.

2. The title bar of the command prompt window varies with different versions of Windows and depends on the user name of the person currently logged in, for example:

C:\Documents and Settings\James Clark>

The command prompt indicates the working drive (drive C) and working directory (the \Windows directory, the root directory indicated by the backslash, or the current user's Documents and Settings directory). Commands issued from this prompt apply to this folder unless you indicate otherwise.

3. Type **DIR** and press **Enter**. Remember that DIR is the command used to list a directory's contents. If the list of files and directories DIR displays is too large to fit on one screen, you see only the last few entries. Entries with the <DIR> label indicate that they are directories (folders), which can contain files or other directories. Also listed for each entry are the time and date it was created and the number of bytes it contains. (This information is displayed differently depending on which version of Windows you're using.) The last two lines in the list summarize the number of files and directories in the current directory, the space they consume, and the free space available on the drive.

As you'll see in the next set of steps, there are two ways to view any files that aren't displayed because of the length of the list and the window size. To learn more about displaying lists of files in the command-line environment, perform the following steps:

1. Type **DIR /?** and press **Enter** to display Help information for the directory command. You can view Help information for any command by entering the command followed by the /? parameter (also called a "switch").

2. Type **DIR /W** and press **Enter**. What happened?

3. Type **DIR /P** and press **Enter**. What happened?

4. Type **DIR /OS** and press **Enter**. What happened?

5. Type **DIR /O-S** and press **Enter**. What happened? What do you think the hyphen between O and S accomplishes?

6. Insert a blank disk in the floppy drive (if available). Type **A:** and press **Enter**. The resulting prompt should look like this: A:\>. What does the A: indicate?

7. What do you think you would see if you issued the DIR command at this prompt?

8. Type **DIR** and press **Enter**. Did you see what you were expecting?

9. Change back to the C: drive by typing **C:** and pressing **Enter**.

10. Type **DIR C:\Tools** and press **Enter**. This command tells the computer to list the contents of a specific directory without actually changing to that directory. In the resulting file list, you should see the file you created earlier, Deleteme.txt.

File attributes are managed by using the Attrib command. Follow these steps to learn how to view and manage file attributes:

1. To make C:\Tools the default directory, type **CD C:\Tools** and press **Enter**.

2. To view the attributes of the Deleteme.txt file, type **Attrib Deleteme.txt** and press **Enter**.

3. To change the file to a hidden file, type **Attrib +H Deleteme.txt** and press **Enter**.

4. View the attributes of the Deleteme.txt file again.

   ◢ What command did you use?

   _____

   ◢ How have the attributes changed?

   _____

5. To view the contents of the C:\Tools directory, type **DIR** and press **Enter**. Why doesn't the Deleteme.txt file show in the directory list?

   _____

6. To change the attributes so that the file is a system file, type **Attrib +S Deleteme.txt** and press **Enter**. What error message did you get?

   _____

7. Because you can't change the attributes of a hidden file, first remove the hidden attribute by typing **Attrib -H Deleteme.txt** and pressing **Enter**.

8. Now try to make the file a system file. What command did you use?

   _____

9. Use the DIR command to list the contents of the C:\Tools directory. Are system files listed?

10. To remove the file's system attribute, type **Attrib -S Deleteme.txt** and press **Enter**.

11. Move to the root directory, type **CD C:** and press **Enter**.

To learn how to delete a file from the command prompt, follow these steps:

1. Type **DEL Deleteme.txt** and press **Enter** to instruct the computer to delete that file. You'll see a message stating that the file couldn't be found because the system assumes that commands refer to the working directory unless a specific path is given. What command could you use to delete the file without changing to that directory?

   _____

2. The current prompt should be C:\>. The \ in the command you typed indicates the root directory.

3. Type **CD Tools** and press **Enter**. The prompt now ends with "Tools>" (indicating that Tools is the current working directory).

4. Now type **DEL Deleteme.txt /p** and press **Enter**. You're prompted to type **Y** for Yes or **N** for No to confirm the deletion. If you don't enter the /p switch (which means "prompt for verification"), the file is deleted automatically without a confirmation message. It's a good practice to use this /p switch, especially when deleting multiple files with wildcard characters. Also, when you delete a file from the command line, the file doesn't go to the Recycle Bin, as it would if you deleted it in Windows Explorer or Computer (My Computer in XP). Because deletion from the command line bypasses the Recycle Bin, recovering accidentally deleted files is more difficult.

5. Type **Y** and press **Enter** to delete the Deleteme.txt file. You're returned to the Tools directory.

To display certain files in a directory, you can use an asterisk (*) or a question mark (?) as wildcard characters. Wildcard characters are placeholders that represent other unspecified characters. The asterisk can represent one or more characters, and the question mark represents any single character. The asterisk is the most useful wildcard, so it's the one you'll encounter most often. To learn more, follow these steps:

1. Return to the root directory. What command did you use?

   _____

2. Type **DIR *.*** and press **Enter**. How many files are displayed?

   _____

3. Type **DIR C*.*** and press **Enter**. How many files are displayed?

   _____

4. Explain why the results differed in the previous two commands:

   _____

   _____

CRITICAL THINKING (ADDITIONAL 30 MINUTES)

Follow these steps to practice using additional commands at the command prompt:

1. Copy the program file Notepad.exe from the \Windows to the \Tools directory. What command did you use?

   _____

2. Rename the file in the \Tools directory as **Newfile.exe**. What command did you use?

   _____

3. Change the attributes of Newfile.exe to make it a hidden file. What command did you use?

   _____

4. Type **DIR** and press **Enter**. Is the Newfile.exe file displayed?

   _____

5. Unhide **Newfile.exe**. What command did you use?

   _____

6. List all files in the \Windows directory that have an .exe file extension. What command did you use?

   _____

   _____

7. Create a new directory named **\New** in \Windows and then copy **Newfile.exe** to the \New directory. What commands did you use?

   _____

   _____

8. Using the /p switch to prompt for verification, delete the **\New** directory. What commands did you use?

   _____

   _____

9. Open the Help and Support Center. Use the Search text box or the Internet to answer the following questions:

   ◢ What is the purpose of the Recover command?

   _____

   _____

   ◢ What is the purpose of the Assoc command?

   _____

   _____

REVIEW QUESTIONS

1. What command/switch do you use to view Help information for the DIR command?

   _____

2. What do you add to the DIR command to list the contents of a directory that's not the current working directory?

   _____

3. What command do you use to change directories?

   _____

4. What command do you use to delete a file?

   _____

5. What command do you use to switch from drive A to drive C?

   _____

LAB 4.8 USE THE XCOPY AND ROBOCOPY COMMANDS

OBJECTIVES

The goal of this lab is to help you observe differences in the Xcopy and Robocopy commands. After completing this lab, you will be able to:

⊿ Copy files and folders with the Xcopy or Robocopy command

MATERIALS REQUIRED

This lab requires the following:

⊿ Windows Vista/XP operating system

⊿ Floppy drive and formatted floppy disk or another form of removable media such as a USB drive

LAB PREPARATION

Before the lab begins, the instructor or lab assistant needs to do the following:

⊿ Verify that Windows starts with no errors.

ACTIVITY BACKGROUND

The Copy command allows you to copy files from one folder to another folder. Using a single Xcopy command, you can copy files from multiple folders, duplicating an entire file structure in another location. The Robocopy command (Vista only) is basically a new version of Xcopy with a few more features, such as the ability to schedule copying to run automatically or delete the source files when the copying is finished. In this lab, you learn to copy files using either of these commands.

> **ESTIMATED COMPLETION TIME: 30 Minutes**

Activity

Before you begin using the Xcopy and Robocopy commands, you need to create a test directory to use when copying files. Follow these steps:

1. Open a command prompt window, and make the root of drive C the current directory. The quickest way to change to the root of a drive is to type **X:** (where *X* is the drive letter) and press **Enter**.

2. Make a directory in the drive C root called **copytest**.

Now you can begin experimenting with the Xcopy command. Follow these steps:

1. Type **Xcopy /?** and press **Enter**. Xcopy Help information is displayed. Notice all the switches you can use to modify the Xcopy command. In particular, you can use the /e switch to instruct Xcopy to copy all files and subdirectories in a directory, including any empty subdirectories, to a new location.

2. If you are using a Windows Vista machine, type **Robocopy /?** and press **Enter**. What are some new features unique to Robocopy?

_____

_____

_____

_____

3. Type **Xcopy C:\"program files"\"internet explorer" C:\copytest /e** and press **Enter**. (You must use quotation marks in the command line to surround a folder name containing spaces.) You'll see a list of files scroll by as they are copied from the C:\program files\internet explorer folder to the C:\copytest folder.

4. When the copy operation is finished, check the copytest folder to see that the files have been copied and the subdirectories created.

5. Insert a blank floppy disk into drive A or attach an equivalent removable device, type **md A:\copytest**, and then press **Enter**. This command creates a directory named copytest on the A drive. (*Note:* You may have to substitute A: with the drive letter associated with your storage device.)

6. To copy all files in the copytest directory on the hard drive to the copytest directory on drive A, type **Xcopy C:\"program files"\ "internet explorer" A:\copytest** and press **Enter**.

7. The system begins copying files, but the floppy disk lacks the capacity to hold the entire \internet explorer directory. As a result, the system displays a message stating that the disk is out of space and asking you to insert another disk. What is the exact error message?

_____

_____

8. In this case, you don't want to copy the entire directory to the floppy disk, so you need to stop the copying process. To do that, press **Ctrl+Pause/Break**. You're returned to the command prompt.

CRITICAL THINKING (ADDITIONAL 15 MINUTES)

Do the following to create and use a Windows Vista/XP bootable floppy disk:

1. Using Windows Explorer on a Windows Vista/XP computer, format a floppy disk.

2. Copy **Ntldr, Ntdetect.com,** and **Boot.ini** from the root of drive C to the root of the floppy disk.

3. Use the bootable floppy disk to boot the system. What appears on your screen after the boot?

_____

4. How might this bootable floppy disk be useful in troubleshooting?

_____

_____

REVIEW QUESTIONS

1. Can a single Copy command copy files from more than one directory?

2. What switch do you use with Xcopy or Robocopy to copy subdirectories?

3. Why might you want to schedule a Robocopy command to occur at a later time?

4. Which Xcopy switch suppresses overwrite confirmation?

CHAPTER 5

Optimizing Windows

Labs included in this chapter:

- **Lab 5.1:** Customize Windows Vista
- **Lab 5.2:** Use the Microsoft Management Console
- **Lab 5.3:** Analyze a System with Event Viewer
- **Lab 5.4:** Use Task Manager
- **Lab 5.5:** Edit the Registry with Regedit
- **Lab 5.6:** Critical Thinking: Use Windows Utilities to Speed Up a System

LAB 5.1 CUSTOMIZE WINDOWS VISTA

OBJECTIVES

The goal of this lab is to help you become familiar with customizing the Windows Vista user interface. After completing this lab, you will be able to:

◢ Customize the taskbar

◢ Work with a program shortcut

◢ Customize the Start menu

◢ Clean up the Windows desktop

◢ Locate essential system information

MATERIALS REQUIRED

This lab requires the following:

◢ Windows Vista operating system

LAB PREPARATION

Before the lab begins, the instructor or lab assistant needs to do the following:

◢ Verify that Windows starts with no errors.

ACTIVITY BACKGROUND

Becoming proficient at navigating a new operating system can require some time and effort. Upgrading from Windows XP to Windows Vista is a big step, especially after you look at the differences in the user interface. From the redesigned Start menu to the new Windows Sidebar, just about everything looks a bit different in Windows Vista, and locating previously used utilities might prove a challenge. In this lab, you explore how Windows Vista handles some routine tasks.

ESTIMATED COMPLETION TIME: 30 Minutes

 Activity

To work with the taskbar, follow these steps:

1. Place the mouse pointer over an empty part of the taskbar, and drag the taskbar to the right side of the screen.

   ◢ Were you able to move the taskbar? If not, what do you think the problem might be?

   _____

   _____

2. Right-click an empty area of the taskbar. Click **Lock the Taskbar** to deselect this option. Now try to move the taskbar to the right side of the screen. Return the taskbar to its default position.

   ◢ Were you able to move the taskbar?

   _____

You can create shortcuts and place them on the desktop to provide quick access to programs. You can also rename and delete a shortcut on your desktop. To create, rename, and delete a desktop shortcut, follow these steps:

1. Click **Start,** click **All Programs,** and click **Accessories.**

2. Right-click **Calculator.** In the menu that opens, point to **Send To,** and then click **Desktop (create shortcut).** Windows adds the shortcut to your desktop. (You might need to close the Start menu by clicking the desktop to see it.)

3. Right-click the shortcut, and click **Rename** in the shortcut menu.

4. Type a new name for the shortcut, and press **Enter.**

5. To delete a shortcut icon from the desktop, right-click it, and click **Delete** in the shortcut menu. In the Confirm Delete File dialog box that opens, click **Yes.** The shortcut is deleted from the desktop.

The Start menu has been reorganized in Windows Vista to give you easy access to programs. When you install most programs, they are added automatically to the Start menu. If a program isn't added during installation, you can add it yourself. Windows Vista enables you to "pin" a program to your Start menu. To customize the Start menu, follow these steps:

1. First, you need to find a program to pin to the Start menu. In this case, you'll pin the Calculator applet to the Start menu. Click **Start,** point to **All Programs,** and click **Accessories.**

2. Right-click **Calculator,** and click **Pin to Start Menu** in the shortcut menu. The program is added to your Start menu. Write the steps you would take to unpin the Calculator from the Start menu:

   _____

   _____

   _____

If you're accustomed to the older Windows Start menu style, now called the Classic menu, you might find that changes to the Start menu take some getting used to. Giving the new Start menu a try is recommended, however, because it was designed to increase efficiency. If you're unable to adjust, you can revert to the Classic version of the Start menu by following these steps:

1. Right-click **Start** and click **Properties** in the shortcut menu. If necessary, click the **Start Menu** tab.

2. Click the **Classic Start menu** option button, and then click **Apply.** Click **OK** and take some time to explore the Classic start menu.

3. Which Start menu version do you prefer, and why?

   _____

   _____

4. Return to the new Start menu. List the steps you performed to do this:

   _____

   _____

In the next steps, you locate essential system information using Computer and Control Panel. Remember, however, with the new interface, locating some items might not be as easy.

1. Click **Start**, and then click **Computer**.

◢ Click the **Views** pull-down menu. List all the views that are available:

_____

_____

◢ What additional information is displayed with the Details view that isn't shown with the List view?

_____

_____

◢ What happens at the bottom of the Computer window when you click the drive C: icon?

_____

_____

2. Double-click the drive **C:** icon.

◢ Describe how Windows Vista displays information about your hard drive:

_____

_____

◢ What happens when you click the **Date modified** column header?

_____

_____

3. Click the **Back** button and close the Computer window.
4. Click **Start**, and click **Control Panel**. Make sure **Control Panel Home** is selected.

◢ What categories of information are displayed in Control Panel?

_____

_____

_____

◢ List the steps you would take to view information or make changes to your mouse settings:

_____

_____

_____

_____

◢ Do you prefer the categories listed in the Classic view? Why or why not?

_____

_____

_____

5. Close Control Panel and return to the Windows desktop.

REVIEW QUESTIONS

1. What steps must you take to locate Computer?

_____

2. Why might it be important to view files sorted by the date they were modified?

_____

_____

_____

3. What Windows control panel category would you use to change your mouse settings?

_____

4. Why does Windows allow you to change to a Classic Start menu?

_____

5. Why does Windows allow you to lock your taskbar?

_____

LAB 5.2 USE THE MICROSOFT MANAGEMENT CONSOLE

OBJECTIVES

The goal of this lab is to help you add snap-ins and save settings using the Microsoft Management Console (MMC) to create a customized console. After completing this lab, you will be able to:

◢ Use the MMC to add snap-ins

◢ Save a customized console

◢ Identify how to launch a console from the Start menu

MATERIALS REQUIRED

This lab requires the following:

◢ Windows Vista/XP Professional operating system

LAB PREPARATION

Before the lab begins, the instructor or lab assistant needs to do the following:

◢ Verify that Windows starts with no errors.

ACTIVITY BACKGROUND

The Microsoft Management Console (MMC) is a standard management tool you can use to create a customized console by adding administrative tools called snap-ins. You can use snap-ins provided by Microsoft or other vendors. Many of the administrative tools you have already used (such as Device Manager) can be added to a console as a snap-in. The console itself serves as a convenient interface that helps you organize and manage the administrative tools you use most often. In this lab, you use the MMC to create a customized console.

ESTIMATED COMPLETION TIME: 30 Minutes

 Activity

Follow these steps to build a customized console:

1. If necessary, log on as an administrator.

2. Click **Start**.

3. In the Start Search box, type **mmc** and then press **Enter**. If Windows needs your permission to continue, click **Continue**. (In XP, click **Run**, type **mmc**, and then click **OK**.) An MMC window named Console1 opens, and within it is another window named Console Root, which is used to display the console's contents.

4. From the Console1 menu, click **File, Add/Remove Snap-in . . . .** The Add or Remove Snap-ins dialog box opens. Console1 is currently empty—that is, it doesn't contain any snap-ins yet. As you can see in the Selected snap-ins list box, any new snap-ins are added to the Console Root folder.

5. The Selected snap-ins list box opens, displaying a list of available snap-ins, as pictured in Figure 5-1. Note that this list includes some administrative tools you have already used, such as Device Manager and Event Viewer.

6. Click **Device Manager**, and then click **Add**.

7. The Device Manager dialog box opens, where you specify which computer you want this Device Manager snap-in to manage. You want it to manage the computer you're currently working on, so verify that the **Local computer** option button is selected, and then click **Finish**.

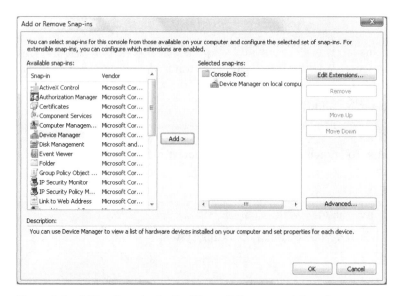

Figure 5-1 Adding Snap-ins to the Microsoft Management Console
Courtesy: Course Technology/Cengage Learning

8. Next, you add Event Viewer as a snap-in. Click **Event Viewer** in the Available Snap-ins list, and then click **Add**. The Select Computer dialog box opens.

9. Verify that the **Local computer** option button is selected, and then click **OK**.

10. Click **OK** to close the Add or Remove Snap-ins dialog box.

You have finished adding snap-ins for the local computer to your console. Next, you add another Event Viewer snap-in to be used on a network computer. If your computer isn't connected to a network, you can read the following set of steps, but don't attempt to perform them. If your computer is connected to a network, follow these steps:

1. Add another Event Viewer snap-in, and then click the **Another computer** option button in the Select Computer dialog box. Now you need to specify the name of the computer to which you want this Event Viewer snap-in to apply. You could type the name of the computer, but it's easier to select the computer by using the Browse button.

2. Click the **Browse** button. A different Select Computer dialog box opens. Click **Advanced** and click **Find Now** to begin searching the network for eligible computers. Eventually, it displays a list of eligible computers.

3. Click the name of the computer to which you want to apply this Event Viewer snap-in, and then click **OK**. The second Select Computer dialog box closes, and you return to the first Select Computer dialog box.

4. Click **OK** to close all three Select Computer dialog boxes, and a second Event Viewer snap-in is added below the first. The new Event Viewer listing is followed by the name of the remote computer in parentheses.

At this point, regardless of whether your computer is connected to a network, the Add or Remove Snap-ins dialog box should be open. You're finished adding snap-ins and are ready to return to the Console1 window and save your new, customized console so that you can use it whenever you need it. Follow these steps:

1. Click **OK**. The Add or Remove Snap-ins dialog box closes, and you return to the Console1 window. The left pane of the Console Root window (within the Console1 window) now contains the following items: Device Manager on local computer, Event Viewer (Local), and Event Viewer (*remote computer name*).

2. In the Console1 window, click **File, Save As** from the menu. The Save As dialog box opens with the default location set to the Administrative Tools folder. If you save your customized console in this location, Administrative Tools is also added to the Start menu. Instead, use the Save in drop-down list box to choose the Programs folder for the save location.

3. Name the console **Custom.msc**, and then click **Save**. The Save As dialog box closes.

4. Close the Custom window.

Follow these steps to open and use your customized console:

1. Click **Start**, point to **All Programs**, and click **Custom**. If a UAC dialog box opens, click **Continue**. Your customized console opens in a window named Custom - [Console Root].

2. Maximize the console window, if necessary.

3. In the left pane, click **Device Manager on local computer** and observe the options in the middle pane.

4. In the left pane, click the arrow next to Event Viewer (Local). Subcategories are displayed below Event Viewer (Local). List the subcategories you see:

_____

_____

_____

5. Click **Event Viewer** (*remote computer name*), and observe that the events displayed are events occurring on the remote computer.

6. From the Custom - [Console Root] menu, click **File, Exit**. A message box opens, asking if you want to save the current settings.

7. Click **Yes**. The console closes.

8. Launch the customized console from the Start menu again, and record the type of information displayed in the middle pane when the console opens:

_____

REVIEW QUESTIONS

1. What term is used to refer to the specialized tools you can add to a console with the MMC? What are they used for?

_____

_____

2. Suppose you haven't created a customized MMC yet. How would you start the MMC?

_____

_____

3. How can a customized console be used to manage many computers from a single machine?

_____

_____

4. Why might you want the ability to manage a remote computer through a network?

_____

_____

5. How do you add a customized console to the Start menu?

_____

_____

LAB 5.3 ANALYZE A SYSTEM WITH EVENT VIEWER

OBJECTIVES

The goal of this lab is to help you learn to work with Windows Vista/XP Event Viewer. After completing this lab, you will be able to use Event Viewer to:

◢ View Windows events

◢ Save events

◢ View events logs

◢ Compare recent events to logged events

MATERIALS REQUIRED

This lab requires the following:

◢ Windows Vista/XP Professional operating system

◢ Network access using the TCP/IP protocol suite

◢ An administrator account and password

LAB PREPARATION

Before the lab begins, the instructor or lab assistant needs to do the following:

◢ Verify that Windows starts with no errors.

ACTIVITY BACKGROUND

Most of the things that happen to your computer while running Windows Vista/XP are recorded in a log. In this lab, you will take another look at a tool called Event Viewer, an application that provides information on various operations and tasks (known as events) in Windows. Event Viewer notes the occurrence of various events, lists them chronologically, and gives you the option of saving the list so that you can compare it to a future list. You can use Event Viewer to find out how healthy your system is and to diagnose nonfatal startup problems. Fatal startup problems don't allow you into Windows far enough to use Event Viewer.

ESTIMATED COMPLETION TIME: 30 Minutes

 Activity

Follow these steps to begin using Event Viewer:

1. If necessary, boot the system and log on as an administrator.

2. Click **Start, Control Panel** to open the Control Panel window.

3. Click **System and Maintenance** (**Performance and Maintenance** in XP), and then click **Administrative Tools**. The Administrative Tools applet opens.

4. Double-click **Event Viewer** to open the Event Viewer window. If Windows opens a UAC dialog box, click **Continue**. The latest events of each type are displayed in chronological order from most recent to oldest (see Figure 5-2).

5. Locate the listings for the four most recent events on your system by double-clicking **Windows Log** and then choosing **System** (choose **System** in XP). The symbols to the left of each event indicate important information about the event. For example, a lowercase "i" in a circle indicates an event providing information about the system, and an exclamation mark in a triangle indicates a warning, such as a disk being near its capacity. The listing for each event includes a brief description and the time and date it occurred.

For each event, list the source (what triggered the event), time, and date:

_____

_____

_____

_____

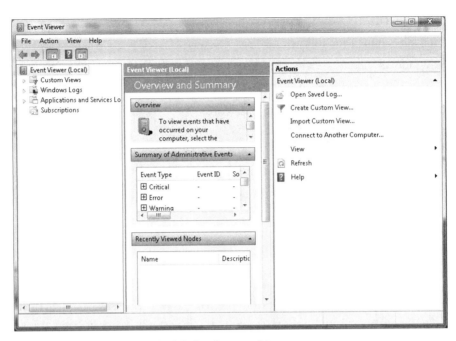

Figure 5-2   Event Viewer tracks failed and successful events
Courtesy: Course Technology/Cengage Learning

6. Double-click the top (most recent) event. The Event Properties dialog box opens. What additional information does this dialog box provide? Note that you can also see an event's properties by clicking an event to select it, and then clicking **Action, Event Properties** from the menu.

_____

_____

_____

7. Close the Event Properties dialog box.

You can save the list of events shown in Event Viewer as a special file called a log file. When naming a log file, it's helpful to use the following format: EV*mm-dd-yy*.evt (*mm* = month, *dd* = day, and *yy* = year). For example, you would name a log file saved on January 13, 2009 as EV01-13-09.evtx. After you create a log file, you can delete the current list of events from Event Viewer, allowing the utility to begin creating an entirely new list of events. Follow these steps to save the currently displayed events as a log file, and then clear the current events:

1. Open Windows Explorer, and create a folder called **Logs** in the root directory of drive C.

2. Leaving Windows Explorer open, return to Event Viewer and click somewhere on the Event Viewer window so that no event is selected. Then click **Action, Save Event As** from the menu.

3. Navigate to the **Logs** folder created in Step 1, name the file **EV*mm-dd-yy*.evtx,** and then click **Save** and click **OK.** Now you're ready to clear the current list of events from Event Viewer.

4. Click **Action, Clear Log** from the menu.

5. When asked if you want to save the System log, click **Clear.** The Event Viewer window no longer displays any events.

6. Close Event Viewer.

Next, you try to create an intentional problem by attempting to remove a system file. Recall that the Windows Resource Protection (Windows File Protection in XP) feature doesn't allow you to delete or rename a system file. If you try to do that, the event is recorded in Event Viewer. To attempt to delete a system file, do the following:

1. Return to Windows Explorer, and locate the Tcpip.sys file in the \windows\system32\drivers folder.

2. Click **tcpip.sys** and press **Delete**. When you're asked to confirm sending this file to the Recycle Bin, click **Yes**. Would Windows allow you to delete this file? How do you know?

_____

_____

3. The file makes it possible for the computer to communicate over the network and is a protected system file, so Windows protects the file.

4. Close Windows Explorer and open Event Viewer. Open **Windows Logs**, click **Security**, and find the event you just caused. Answer these questions:

   ◢ What is the description of the event?

   _____

   _____

   _____

   ◢ What is the type assigned to this event?

   _____

5. Close the Event Properties dialog box.

6. Open Windows Explorer. Is Tcpip.sys in the \WINNT\system32\drivers folder?

   _____

Next, you create an intentional problem by disconnecting the network cable from your PC, and then see how the resulting errors are recorded in Event Viewer. Do the following:

1. Carefully disconnect the network cable from the network port on the back of your PC.

2. Restart the computer and log on as an administrator. Record the messages you receive, if any:

   _____

   _____

3. Open Network (My Network Places in XP). Are you able to browse the network?

   _____

4. Close Network, and then open Event Viewer. How many new events are displayed?

   _____

5. List the source, date, and time for any error events (indicated by a red icon) you see:

   _____

   _____

   _____

   _____

   _____

6. Click each error or warning event, and read the details. How does Event Viewer describe what happened when you unplugged the network port?

When troubleshooting a system, comparing current events with a list of events you previously stored in a log file is often helpful because you can spot the time when a particular problem occurred. Follow these steps to compare the current list of events to the log you saved earlier:

1. Open another instance of Event Viewer (that is, open a second Event Viewer window without closing the first one).

2. In the new Event Viewer window, click a blank area of the window so that no event is selected. Then click **Action, Open Saved Log** from the menu.

3. If necessary, open the **Logs** folder, click the log file you created earlier, and click **OK**.

4. To position the two instances of Event Viewer on your desktop so that you can compare them, right-click a blank spot on the taskbar. A shortcut menu opens, giving you options for how to arrange all open windows. Click **Show Windows Side by Side** to position the two open windows side by side.

5. You might notice that the current list of events contains one more successful event than the log of previous events. One of these successful events might be the cause of a failed event. For instance, a service starting and allocating resources that another component was previously using would be listed as a successful event. However, allocating resources currently in use would cause the component that had been using the resources to fail, thereby resulting in a failed event. Judging by the log file you created earlier, how many events occur in a normal startup?

To restore the network connection and verify that the connection is working, follow these steps:

1. Reconnect the network cable to the network port on the back of your computer, restart your computer, and log on. Did you receive any messages after you started Windows this time?

---

2. Open Event Viewer and verify that no errors occurred during startup.

3. Open another instance of Event Viewer, open the log you saved earlier (in the Logs folder), and verify that the same events occurred in both windows.

4. Close both Event Viewer windows.

CRITICAL THINKING (ADDITIONAL 30 MINUTES)

Using the Internet for research, find answers to the following questions. Be sure to list the URLs that support your answers.

1. Which version of Windows introduced Windows Resource Protection? Explain what Windows File Resource does:

_____

_____

2. How could Windows event viewer be used to determine the health of your system?

_____

_____

3. How might Event Viewer be used to diagnose a Windows Startup problem?

_____

_____

4. What are the key differences between Windows File Protection used in XP and Windows Resource Protection used in Vista?

_____

_____

REVIEW QUESTIONS

1. Judging by the path to Event Viewer using the Start menu, what type of tool is Event Viewer?

_____

2. Based on what you learned in this lab, what might be your first indication that a problem occurred after startup?

_____

3. How can you examine events after you have cleared them from Event Viewer?

_____

_____

4. Explain how to compare a log file with the current set of listed events:

_____

_____

5. Why might you like to keep a log file of events that occurred when your computer started correctly? List the steps to create this log of a successful startup:

_____

_____

_____

_____

_____

LAB 5.4 USE TASK MANAGER

OBJECTIVES

The goal of this lab is to help you use Task Manager to examine your system. After completing this lab, you will be able to:

- Identify applications that are currently running
- Launch an application
- Display general system performance and process information in Task Manager

MATERIALS REQUIRED

This lab requires the following:

- Windows Vista/XP Professional operating system
- Installed CD/DVD drive, installed/on-board sound card, and an audio CD

LAB PREPARATION

Before the lab begins, the instructor or lab assistant needs to do the following:

- Verify that Windows starts with no errors.
- Verify that a CD drive and sound card have been installed on student computers.

ACTIVITY BACKGROUND

Task Manager is a useful tool that allows you to switch between tasks, end tasks, and observe system use and performance. In this lab, you use Task Manager to manage applications and observe system performance.

ESTIMATED COMPLETION TIME: 30 Minutes

 Activity

Follow these steps to use Task Manager:

1. If necessary, log on as an administrator.
2. Press **Ctrl+Alt+Del** and click **Start Task Manager**, or right-click any blank area on the taskbar and click **Task Manager** in the shortcut menu. The Task Manager

dialog box opens, with tabs you can use to find information about applications, processes, and programs running on the computer and information on system performance.

3. If necessary, click the **Applications** tab. What information is currently listed in the Task list box?

_____

_____

_____

4. Use the Start menu to open Windows Help and Support and then observe the change to the Task list in the Applications tab. What change occurred in the Task list?

_____

5. Right-click the new task and click **Go To Process**. What process is associated with this task?

_____

6. On the Applications tab, click the **New Task** button. The Create New Task dialog box opens, which is almost identical to the Run dialog box you open from the Start menu in Windows XP.

7. In the Open text box, type **command.com**, and then click **OK**. A command prompt window opens. Examine the Application tab in Task Manager, and note that \windows\system32\command.com now appears in the Task list.

8. Click the title bar of the command prompt window. It's now the active window, but notice that Task Manager remains on top of all other open windows. This ensures that you can keep track of changes in the system while opening and closing applications.

You can customize Task Manager to suit your preferences. Among other things, you can change the setting that keeps Task Manager on top of all other open windows and change the way information is displayed. To learn more about changing Task Manager settings, make sure the command prompt window is still open, and follow these steps:

1. In Task Manager, click **Options** on the menu bar. A menu with a list of options opens. Note that the check marks indicate which options are currently applied. The Always On Top option is currently selected, which keeps the Task Manager window on top of all other open windows. List the available menu options here:

_____

_____

_____

2. Click **Always On Top** to clear the check mark, and then click the command prompt window. What happens?

_____

_____

3. Click **Options** on the Task Manager menu bar, and then click **Always On Top** to select it again.

4. On the Task Manager menu bar, click **View**. You can use the options on this menu to change how quickly the information is updated. List the available and current settings:

_____

_____

_____

Follow these steps in Task Manager to end a task and observe system use information:

1. On the Applications tab, notice that three types of information are listed in the bar at the bottom of Task Manager. What three types of information do you see, and what are their values?

_____

_____

_____

2. While observing these three values, move your mouse around the screen for several seconds and then stop. Did any of the values change?

_____

3. Next, move your mouse to drag an open window around the screen for several seconds and then stop. How did this affect the values?

_____

4. In the Task list, click **Windows Help and Support** and then click the **End Task** button.

5. Compare the number of processes, CPU usage, and commit charge (memory usage) to the information recorded in Step 1. How much memory was Windows Help and Support using?

_____

Follow these steps in Task Manager to observe process and performance information:

1. In Task Manager, click the **Processes** tab. This tab lists current processes in the Image Name column and displays information about each process, such as the percentage used by the CPU (CPU) or the memory usage (Memory).

2. Scroll down and examine each process. What process is currently using the highest CPU and Memory resources?

_____

3. Click the **View** tab and click **Select Columns**. Which column would you select to appear on the Process page if you wanted to know the process identifier for each process?

_____

4. Use the Start menu to start Windows Help and Support.

5. Drag the Help and Support window to position it so that it is visible to the left of the Task Manager window.

6. Verify that the Help window is the active window, and then observe the process information in Task Manager as you select various topics in the Help and Support window. Which process or processes begin to use more CPU resources as the mouse moves from topic to topic?

_____

7. In the Processes tab of Task Manager, click **HelpPane.exe** (**HelpSvc.exe** in Windows XP), and then click **End Process**. What message is displayed?

_____

_____

_____

8. In addition to processes for optional user applications, the Processes tab displays and allows you to end core Windows processes. *Caution*: Be careful about ending tasks; ending a potentially essential task (one that other processes depend on) could have serious consequences. Because Windows Help and Support is not critical to core Windows functions, it's safe to end this task. Click **End process** to end.

9. Click the **Performance** tab, which displays CPU usage and memory usage in bar graphs. This tab also shows a running history graph for both CPU usage and Memory usage. What other categories of information are displayed in the Performance tab?

_____

_____

10. Insert an audio CD. Configure it to begin playing, if necessary. Observe the CPU and page file or memory usage values, and record them here:

_____

_____

11. Stop the CD from playing, and again observe the CPU usage and page file or memory usage. Compare these values to the values from Step 9. Which value changed the most?

_____

12. When you're finished, close all open windows.

REVIEW QUESTIONS

1. Explain one way to launch Task Manager:

_____

2. Which Task Manager tab do you use to switch between applications and end a task?

_____

3. Why could it be dangerous to end a process with Task Manager?

_____

_____

4. How could you tell whether the processor had recently completed a period of intensive use but is now idle?

5. Did the playback of an audio CD use more system resources than moving the mouse? Explain:

LAB 5.5 EDIT THE REGISTRY WITH REGEDIT

OBJECTIVES

The goal of this lab is to learn how to save, modify, and restore the Windows registry. After completing this lab, you will be able to:

⊿ Back up and modify the registry

⊿ Observe the effects of a damaged registry

⊿ Restore the registry

MATERIALS REQUIRED

This lab requires the following:

⊿ Windows Vista/XP operating system

LAB PREPARATION

Before the lab begins, the instructor or lab assistant needs to do the following:

⊿ Verify that Windows starts with no errors.

ACTIVITY BACKGROUND

The registry is a database of configuration information stored in files called hives. Each time Windows boots, it rebuilds the registry from the configuration files and stores it in RAM. When you need to modify the behavior of Windows, you should consider editing the registry as a last resort. Errors in the registry can make your system inoperable, and there's no way for Windows to inform you that you have made a mistake. For this reason, many people are afraid to work with the registry. If you follow the rule of backing up the system before you make any change, however, you can feel confident that even if you make a mistake, you can restore the system to its original condition. In this lab, you back up, change, and restore the registry.

ESTIMATED COMPLETION TIME: 45 Minutes

Activity

Windows allows you to create a restore point so that you can restore Windows to a time before any changes were made. Follow these directions to back up the system (including the registry):

1. Open the **System Properties** dialog box by clicking **Start, Control Panel, System and Maintenance, System,** and the **System protection** task. If Windows presents a UAC dialog box, click **Continue.**

2. Click **Create** and add a name for your restore point. The current time and date will be added automatically. Click **Create** again to create the restore point.

3. When the backup is completed, click **OK** to close the System Protection dialog box and **OK** again to close the System Properties dialog box. By default, Windows stores restore points automatically.

4. Open System Properties again and click **System Restore** on the System protection tab. Select **Choose a different restore point** and click **Next**. Determine the name and description of the backup you just created by checking the date and time the file was created. Record the name, date, and time of this file:

_____

5. Click **Cancel** to close the System Restore wizard and **Cancel** again to exit from System Properties.

6. Close any open windows.

As you know, you can use Windows tools such as Control Panel to modify many features, from the color of the background to the power-saving features. Sometimes, however, the only way to make a modification is to edit the registry. These modifications are sometimes referred to as registry tweaks or hacks. In these steps, you will make a relatively small change to the registry by editing the name of the Recycle Bin. Follow these steps:

1. Click **Start**, type **regedit**, and press **Enter**. (In XP, Click **Start**, type **Run**, type **regedit**, and then click **OK**.) If Windows presents a UAC dialog box, click **Continue**. The Registry Editor opens, displaying the system's registry hierarchy in the left pane and any entries for the selected registry item in the right pane.

The registry is large, and searching through it manually (by scrolling through all the entries) can be tedious even if you have a good idea of where to look. To save time, use the Registry Editor's search feature to find the section governing the Recycle Bin:

1. To make sure you're searching the entire registry, select **Computer** and then click **Edit, Find** from the menu.

2. Make sure **Match whole string only** is checked and type **Recycle Bin** in the Find what text box. You can narrow your search by limiting which items to search. What other three ways can you further refine your search?

_____

_____

3. Click the **Find Next** button and then double-click the (**Default**) entry. The Edit String dialog box opens.

4. In the Value data text box, replace "Recycle Bin" with **Trash**, and then click **OK**.

5. Notice that "Trash" has replaced "Recycle Bin" in the right pane.

6. Close the Registry Editor, and then click **File, Exit** from the menu. You weren't prompted to save your changes to the registry because they were saved the instant you made them. This is why editing the registry is so unforgiving: There are no safeguards. You can't undo your work by choosing to exit without saving changes, as you can, for instance, in Microsoft Word.

7. Right-click the desktop, and then click **Refresh** in the shortcut menu. Note that the Recycle Bin icon is now named Trash.

Finally, you need to undo your changes to the Recycle Bin. Follow these steps to use the System Restore to restore the registry's previous version:

1. Open System Properties again and click **System Restore** on the System Protection tab. Select **Choose a different restore point** and click **Next**.

5

2. Choose the restore point you created earlier and click **Next**.

3. When you're asked to confirm your restore point, click **Finish**. Click **Yes** when the system warns you that a system restore cannot be undone.

4. After the system restore, the computer will have to reboot.

5. After the boot is completed, notice that the name of the Recycle bin has been restored.

Use Windows Help and Support or the Internet to answer the following questions about the registry:

⊿ How often does Windows save the registry automatically?

_____

⊿ Where are registry backups usually stored?

_____

⊿ What files constitute the Vista and XP registry? What type of file are they saved as during backup?

_____

_____

REVIEW QUESTIONS

1. Why does Windows automatically save the registry?

_____

_____

2. Where is the registry stored while Windows is running?

_____

3. What type of safeguards does the Registry Editor have to keep you from making mistakes?

_____

4. How many files make up the registry on your system?

_____

5. In this lab, how did you check to make sure your registry was restored?

_____

LAB 5.6 CRITICAL THINKING: USE WINDOWS UTILITIES TO SPEED UP A SYSTEM

OBJECTIVES

The goal of this lab is to help you learn how to clean up processes that might slow Windows. After completing this lab, you will be able to:

⊿ Use Windows tools to clean up startup

⊿ Investigate processes that are slowing down Windows

⊿ Configure the system to keep it clean and free of malware

MATERIALS REQUIRED

This lab requires the following:

◢ A Windows Vista/XP computer designated for this lab

◢ Internet access

LAB PREPARATION

Before the lab begins, the instructor or lab assistant needs to do the following:

◢ Make available a Windows Vista/XP computer. For the best student experience, try to use systems that are not optimized and need the benefits of this lab.

◢ Verify that Internet access is available.

ACTIVITY BACKGROUND

A troubleshooting problem you'll often face as a PC support technician is a sluggish Windows system. Customers might tell you that when their Windows computer was new, it ran smoothly and fast with no errors, but now it hangs occasionally, is slow to start up or shut down, and is slow when working. There is no one particular problem that stands out above the rest, but a customer just says, "Please make my system work faster." When solving these types of general problems, it helps to have a game plan. This activity will give you just that. You'll learn how to speed up Windows, ridding it of unneeded and unwanted processes that are slowing it down.

ESTIMATED COMPLETION TIME: 60 Minutes

 Activity

Before you make any changes to the system, first get a benchmark of how long it takes for Windows to start up. Do the following:

1. Power down the computer and turn it on. Using a watch with a second hand, note how many minutes are needed for the system to start. Startup is completed after you have logged onto Windows, the hard drive activity light has stopped, and the mouse pointer looks like an arrow. How long does startup take?

   _____

2. Describe any problems you observed during startup:

   _____

   _____

   This lab assumes that Windows might be slow starting, but does start up without errors. If you see error messages on-screen or the system refuses to boot, you need to solve these problems before you continue with a general cleanup.

You're now ready to begin a general cleanup. Do the following:

1. If valuable data is on the hard drive that is not backed up, back up that data now.

2. Run antivirus (AV) software. Here are your options:

   ◢ If AV software is not installed and you have the AV software setup CD, install it. If it fails to install (some viruses block software installations), boot into Safe Mode and install and run it from there.

◢ If you don't have access to the AV software setup CD, you can download software from the Internet. If your PC cannot connect to the Internet (such as when Internet access is blocked by an active virus), you can download the software on another PC and burn a CD with the downloaded file. But before you do that, first try to connect to the Internet using the Safe Mode with Networking option on the Advanced Boot Options menu. (This option might not load a virus that prevents Internet access.)

◢ If you don't have AV software installed and don't have access to an AV software setup CD, but you can connect the computer to the Internet, you can run an online virus scan from an AV Web site. For example, Trend Micro (*www.trendmicro.com*) offers a free online virus scan. (This free online scan has been known to find viruses that other scans do not.)

◢ List the steps you took to run the AV software:

_____

_____

_____

◢ List any malware the AV software found:

_____

_____

_____

3. Reboot the system. Is there a performance increase? How long does startup take?

_____

_____

4. If the system is still running so slowly you find it difficult to work, you can temporarily use MSconfig to control startup processes hogging system resources. Click **Start** and type **msconfig** in the Start Search box (in XP, enter **msconfig** in the Run dialog box) and press **Enter**. If Windows presents a UAC dialog box, click **Continue**. The System Configuration utility window opens. Click the **Startup** tab, as shown in Figure 5-3.

5. You can keep services from starting by unchecking them in this window. List all of the services that are run at startup and use the Internet to determine the purpose of each of them:

_____

_____

_____

_____

_____

_____

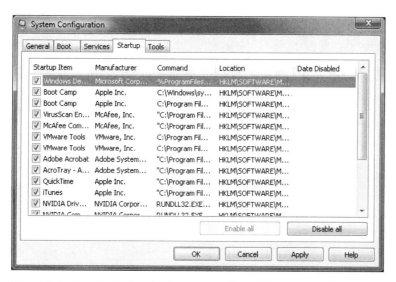

Figure 5-3 Use the System Configuration utility window to control startup processes until you can further clean up a slow Windows system
Courtesy: Course Technology/Cengage Learning

6. Uncheck all the services except the ones associated with your antivirus program. Reboot the system to cause these changes to take effect.

7. Is there a performance increase? How long does startup take?

8. Clean up the hard drive. Delete temporary files, defrag the hard drive, and check for errors. If the system is slow while doing these tasks, do them from Safe Mode. Note that you need about 15 percent free hard drive space to defragment the drive. If you don't have that much free space, find some folders and files you can move to a different media. Windows requires this much free space to run well.

9. Reboot the system. Is there a performance increase? How long does startup take?

10. Check Device Manager for hardware devices that are installed but not working or devices that are no longer needed and should be uninstalled. Did you find any devices that need fixing or uninstalling? How did you handle the situation?

CHALLENGE ACTIVITY (ADDITIONAL 15 MINUTES)

MSconfig doesn't necessarily show all the processes that run at startup. So, to get a more thorough list, you need to use a more powerful startup manager such as Autoruns from Sysinternals.

1. Go to http://technet.microsoft.com/en-us/sysinternals/default.aspx and download and install the latest version of Autoruns.

2. Run Autoruns and select the Logon tab, as shown in Figure 5-4.

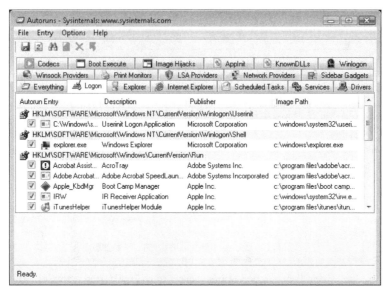

Figure 5-4   Autoruns startup manager by Sysinternals
Courtesy: Course Technology/Cengage Learning

3. How does the list of startup processes differ from the list generated by Msconfig? List any additional processes identified:

_____

_____

_____

_____

REVIEW QUESTIONS

1. If AV software is not installed and you don't have access to the Internet, how can you install it?

_____

2. Which window is used to defrag a hard drive and check it for errors?

_____

3. What two folders can contain programs to be launched when a specific user logs onto the system?

_____

4. When cleaning up startup, why should you not delete a program file you find in a startup folder?

_____

5. What utility lists all currently running processes?

_____

CHAPTER 6

Tools for Solving Windows Problems

Labs included in this chapter:

- **Lab 6.1:** Use Windows Help and Troubleshooters

- **Lab 6.2:** Restore the System State

- **Lab 6.3:** Update Drivers with Device Manager

- **Lab 6.4:** Install the XP Recovery Console as an Option on the Startup Menu

- **Lab 6.5:** Use the XP Recovery Console to Copy Files

- **Lab 6.6:** Use the Vista Recovery Environment (Windows RE) to Repair Windows

LAB 6.1 USE WINDOWS HELP AND TROUBLESHOOTERS

OBJECTIVES

The goal of this lab is to demonstrate how to use Windows Help tools to find information and how to use Windows Troubleshooters to correct common problems. After completing this lab, you will be able to:

◢ Find information on various topics in Windows Help

◢ Use a Windows Troubleshooter

MATERIALS REQUIRED

This lab requires the following:

◢ Windows Vista/XP Professional operating system

LAB PREPARATION

Before the lab begins, the instructor or lab assistant needs to do the following:

◢ Verify that Windows starts with no errors.

ACTIVITY BACKGROUND

You can use Windows Help to look up information on topics related to the operating system. To access Windows Help, use the Start menu or, with the desktop active, press F1. Windows Help is useful when you just need information. If you want help actually solving a problem, however, you should use the Windows Troubleshooters, which are interactive utilities that walk you through the problem of repairing a misconfigured system. Windows Troubleshooters are often launched automatically when Windows detects a problem. You can also start them manually from Windows Help.

ESTIMATED COMPLETION TIME: 30 Minutes

 Activity

In the following steps, you learn to use the main features of Windows Help. Note that pressing F1 starts Help for whatever application happens to be active at that time. To start Windows Help, you need to close or minimize any open applications, thereby making the desktop active, and then you can press F1 to start Windows Help. To learn more, follow the procedure for your operating system.

In Windows Vista/XP, follow these steps:

1. Log on to your computer as an administrator.

2. Close or minimize any applications that start automatically so that the desktop is active.

3. Press **F1**. (Instead of activating the desktop and pressing F1, you could simply click **Start, Help and Support**.) Windows Help opens. As you can see, the Windows Help interface is similar to a Web browser. Answer the following questions:

◢ What general categories are available in Windows Help?

◢ What steps would you follow to find information on how to locate lost files?

_____

_____

4. Move the pointer over **What's new?** (in XP, move the pointer over the **What's new in Windows XP** topic in the left pane), and note that the pointer becomes a hand, as it does in a Web browser when you move it over a link. When you point to a topic, it becomes underlined, like a hyperlink.

In Windows XP:

1. Click **What's new in Windows XP** in the left pane. This topic expands in the left pane, displaying subtopics. Click **What's new**. Subtopics are displayed in the right pane.

2. Scroll the right pane to get a sense of what information is available, and then click **What's new with files and folders** in the right pane. The topic expands to show a description of the contents as well as links to more information.

3. Click **New ways of viewing files and pictures**. The topic expands to add a brief overview and additional subcategories. Click **Viewing files and folders overview**. The right pane displays a list of ways to arrange and identify your files. Record the possible view options here:

_____

_____

_____

4. The Windows Help toolbar has buttons similar to those in a Web browser, including a Back button (a left-facing arrow) you can use to display a previous topic. Click the **Back** button in Windows Help. The What's new with files and folders screen is displayed again in the right pane.

In Windows Vista:

1. Click the **What's new?** icon and a list of subtopics appears on the left. Click **Tips for finding files** in the **Searching and organizing** section.

2. What three search methods are recommended for finding files?

_____

_____

_____

You can also look for topics in Windows Help by using the Search Help box, where you type keywords to locate the information you need. This feature is useful when you're familiar with Windows Help but don't know where to look for a specific topic in the Table of Contents. Follow these steps to use the Search feature:

1. Type **automatic updates** in the Search Help box and press **Enter**. The list of topics should now include one on how to turn on automatic updates in Windows. Follow the link to learn how to turn on automatic updates. How does Windows suggest you turn on automatic updates?

_____

_____

_____

_____

With the Add to Favorites button in XP, you can record a list of topics you want to refer to again without having to search for them. Follow these steps:

1. Click the **Add to Favorites** button and click **OK**.

2. A pop-up window is displayed, stating that the page has been added to your favorites list.

Windows Help enables you to search for information on topics related to using Windows. Windows Troubleshooters provide information on how to fix problems with Windows and its applications. You can access Troubleshooters from Windows Help. In the following steps, you use a Troubleshooter to repair a nonfunctioning sound card:

1. Search for **sound troubleshooter** in the Search Help box and click **Troubleshoot sound problems** (click **Sound Troubleshooter** in XP).

2. The Windows Troubleshooter for sound asks you for details about the problem you're troubleshooting so that it can provide a solution tailored to that problem. For this portion of the lab, assume the following:

   ◢ A sound appears to play, but you don't hear anything.

   ◢ Your speakers can't play system sounds.

   ◢ Your volume is not set too low, and audio is not muted.

3. To troubleshoot the problem, select the option for the specified scenario. In XP, click **Next** to advance through the Troubleshooter windows. What Windows utility is suggested for making sure your computer has an enabled sound card?

   _____

4. Now go back and troubleshoot a slightly different problem. This time, assume the following:

   ◢ The sound is distorted or scratchy.

   ◢ You aren't using an excessively high volume level.

   ◢ You don't have a hardware device conflict.

5. Answer the following questions:

   ◢ What options are offered to correct the problem?

   _____

   _____

   ◢ Where does Windows suggest you look for further information?

   _____

   _____

REVIEW QUESTIONS

1. Windows Help is similar in appearance to what type of program?

   _____

2. What can you do if you're not sure where to look for a specific topic?

   _____

3. What are two ways to launch Windows Help?

   _____

4. What tool accessible from Windows Help takes you step-by-step through the process of diagnosing and perhaps repairing common problems?

_____

5. Are Troubleshooters ever launched automatically? Explain:

_____

_____

LAB 6.2 RESTORE THE SYSTEM STATE

OBJECTIVES

The goal of this lab is to help you restore the system state on a Windows Vista/XP computer. After completing this lab, you will be able to:

◢ Create a restore point by using System Restore

◢ Change system settings

◢ Restore the system state with the restore point you created

MATERIALS REQUIRED

This lab requires the following:

◢ Windows Vista/XP Professional operating system

LAB PREPARATION

Before the lab begins, the instructor or lab assistant needs to do the following:

◢ Verify that Windows starts with no errors.

ACTIVITY BACKGROUND

The System Restore tool in Windows Vista/XP enables you to restore the system to the state it was in when a snapshot, called a "restore point," was taken of the system state. The settings recorded in a restore point include system settings and configurations and files needed for a successful boot. When the system state is restored to a restore point, user data on the hard drive isn't affected, but software and hardware might be. Restore points are useful if, for example, something goes wrong with a software or hardware installation. In this lab, you create a restore point, make changes to system settings, and then use the restore point to restore the system state.

ESTIMATED COMPLETION TIME: 30 Minutes

 Activity

To use the System Restore tool to create a restore point, follow these steps:

1. Click **Start**, click **All Programs**, click **Accessories**, click **System Tools**, and then click **System Restore**. If Windows opens a UAC box, click **Continue**.

In Windows XP:

1. The System Restore window opens with two choices: **Restore my computer to an earlier time** and **Create a restore point**. The first option restores your computer to an existing restore point. Read the information at the left and answer these questions:

   ◢ Can changes made by System Restore be undone? What type of data does System Restore leave unaffected?

   _____

   ◢ What is the term for the restore points the system creates automatically?

   _____

   ◢ As you've read, it's helpful to create a restore point before you install software or hardware. In what other situations might you want to create a restore point?

   _____

   _____

2. Click the **Create a restore point** option button, and then click **Next**.

3. In the next window, type a description of the restore point. The description should make it easy to identify the restore point later, such as "Restore *today's date*."

4. Click the **Create** button.

5. A message is displayed stating that the restore point was created and showing the date, time, and name of the restore point. Click the **Close** button.

In Windows Vista:

1. If there are already several restore points on your system, the System Restore window opens with two choices: **Recommended restore** and **Choose a different restore point**. Click **How does System Restore work?** and read through this section. Then click **System Restore: frequently asked questions** and answer these questions:

   ◢ Can changes made by System Restore be undone? What type of data does System Restore leave unaffected?

   _____

   ◢ What feature regularly creates and saves restore points on your computer?

   _____

2. Close Windows Help and Support and click **open System Protection** to create a restore point.

3. Click the **Create . . .** button and assign your restore point a name.

4. Click the **Create** button and a restore point is created.

5. Click **OK** and then close any open windows.

Next, you make a change to the system by changing the display settings:

1. In Control Panel, click **Appearance and Personalization** (**Appearance and Themes** in XP), and then click **Personalization** (**Display** in XP).

2. Click **Desktop Background** (or the **Desktop** tab in XP), select a different background, and then click **OK**.

3. Close the Control Panel window. Notice that the desktop background has changed to the one you selected.

Follow these steps to use the restore point you created to restore the system state:

1. Open the System Restore tool as explained earlier in this lab.

2. Click **Choose a different restore point** (**Restore my computer to an earlier time** in XP) option button, and then click **Next**.

3. A window opens showing all dates on which restore points were made.

   ◢ How many restore points were created in the current month?

   _____

   ◢ List the reasons the restore points were made:

   _____

   _____

   _____

4. Click the name of the restore point you created earlier in the lab, and then click **Next**. (In Windows XP, first select the current date.)

5. When a confirmation window is displayed, click **Finish** to continue (click **Next** in XP). If necessary, click **Yes** to proceed.

   Describe what happens when you proceed with a restore:

   _____

   _____

   _____

6. After the system restarts, logon to the Windows desktop. In Windows XP, a message is displayed stating that the restoration is complete. Click **OK**.

   ◢ Did the display settings change back to their original settings?

   _____

REVIEW QUESTIONS

1. List three situations in which you might want to create a restore point:

   _____

   _____

   _____

   _____

2. What types of restore points are created by the system, and what types are created by users?

   _____

   _____

   _____

3. How often does the system create restore points automatically?

   _____

4. Can more than one restore point be made on a specific date?

   _____

5. Does Windows track more than one restore point? Why?

_____

_____

_____

LAB 6.3 UPDATE DRIVERS WITH DEVICE MANAGER

OBJECTIVES

The goal of this lab is to explore the functions of Device Manager. After completing this lab, you will be able to:

◢ Select your display adapter in Device Manager

◢ Update the driver for your display adapter from Device Manager

MATERIALS REQUIRED

This lab requires the following:

◢ Windows Vista/XP Professional operating system

◢ Updated driver files for the display adapter

LAB PREPARATION

Before the lab begins, the instructor or lab assistant needs to do the following:

◢ Verify that Windows starts with no errors.

◢ Locate or download updated driver files for the display adapter (video card).

ACTIVITY BACKGROUND

With Device Manager, you can update device drivers as well as monitor resource use. If you find a new driver for a device, you can use Device Manager to select the device and update the driver. In this lab, you use Device Manager to update the driver for your display adapter.

ESTIMATED COMPLETION TIME: 30 Minutes

 Activity

1. Open Control Panel and click **System and Maintenance**. Select **Device Manager**, and click **Continue** if Windows needs your permission to continue. In XP, click **Performance and Maintenance**, click **System**, select the **Hardware** Tab, and click **Device Manager**.

2. Click the + sign next to **Display adapters** to expand this category, and click your display adapter to select it.

3. Open the Properties dialog box for your display adapter by right-clicking the adapter and selecting **Properties**. Then click the **Driver** tab.

4. Click the **Driver Details** button. Which folders contain the drivers used by your display adapter?

   _____

   _____

5. Return to the Driver tab in the display adapter's Properties dialog box by clicking **OK**, and then click **Update Driver**.

6. Click **Browse my computer for driver software**.

7. In Windows XP, click **No, not at this time** to keep from connecting to Windows Update and then click **Next**. Click **Install from a list or specific location (Advanced)** and then click **Next**. Click the **Include this location in the search** check box.

8. Type the location of the driver installation file, or click the **Browse** button to select a location your instructor has designated. After you have specified a location, click **Next**. Windows searches the location and reports its findings.

9. If the wizard indicates it has found a file for the device you selected in Step 2 (the display adapter), click **Next** to continue. If the wizard reports that it can't find the file, verify that you have entered the installation file's location correctly.

10. After Windows locates the drivers, it copies the driver files. If a file being copied is older than the file the system is currently using, you're prompted to confirm that you want to use the older file. Usually, newer drivers are better than older drivers. However, you might want to use an older one if you've had problems after updating drivers recently. In this case, you might want to reinstall the old driver that wasn't causing problems.

11. When the files have been copied, click **Finish** to complete the installation.

12. Close all open windows and restart the computer if prompted to do so.

CRITICAL THINKING (ADDITIONAL 30 MINUTES)

Use Device Manager to identify the installed display adapter. Next, search the device manufacturer's Web sites for new video, network card, sound card, and motherboard drivers. If you find drivers newer than the one in use, install the updated drivers.

REVIEW QUESTIONS

1. Describe the steps to access Device Manager:

   _____

   _____

2. How can you access a device's properties in Device Manager?

   _____

   _____

3. What tab in the Properties dialog box do you use to update a driver?

   _____

4. Besides typing the path, what other option do you have to specify a driver's location?

   _____

   _____

5. Why might you want to use an older driver?

_____

_____

LAB 6.4 INSTALL THE XP RECOVERY CONSOLE AS AN OPTION ON THE STARTUP MENU

OBJECTIVES

The goal of this lab is to help you install the Recovery Console as a startup option. After completing this lab, you will be able to:

⊿ Install the Recovery Console

⊿ Open the Recovery Console from the Startup menu

MATERIALS REQUIRED

This lab requires the following:

⊿ Windows XP operating system

⊿ Windows XP installation CD or installation files

LAB PREPARATION

Before the lab begins, the instructor or lab assistant needs to do the following:

⊿ Verify that Windows starts with no errors.

⊿ Provide each student with access to the Windows XP installation files, if needed.

ACTIVITY BACKGROUND

The Recovery Console tool in Windows XP allows you to start the computer when other startup and recovery options, such as System Restore, Safe Mode, and the Automated System Recovery (ASR) process, don't work. In the Recovery Console, you can use a limited group of DOS-like commands to format a hard drive, copy files from a floppy disk or CD to the hard drive, start and stop certain system processes, and perform other administrative tasks and troubleshooting tasks. If the Recovery Console isn't installed on your computer, you have to run it from the Windows XP installation CD. This lab shows you how to install the Recovery Console on your Windows XP computer so that it appears as an option when the computer starts.

ESTIMATED COMPLETION TIME: 30 Minutes

 Activity

Follow these steps to install the Recovery Console as a startup option:

1. Insert the Windows XP installation CD into your CD-ROM drive. If the Autorun feature launches, close it. If your instructor has given you another location for the installation files, what drive letter do you use to access them?

_____

2. Click **Start, Run**. The Run dialog box opens. Type **cmd** and then click **OK**. A command prompt window opens.

3. To switch to your CD-ROM drive (or other drive with the installation files), type the drive letter followed by a colon, and then press **Enter**.

4. Next, you run the Windows XP setup program stored on this drive. The path to the program might vary, depending on the release of Windows XP you're using. Try the following possibilities until you locate the command that runs the program:

   ◢ Type **\i386\winnt32.exe /cmdcons** and press **Enter**.

   ◢ Type **\english\winxp\pro\i386\winnt32.exe /cmdcons** and press **Enter**.

   ◢ Type **\english\winxp\home\i386\winnt32.exe /cmdcons** and press **Enter**.

   ◢ Which command launched the setup program?

   _____

> **Notes** If you've upgraded XP to a later service pack than the one bundled with the installation CD, you might need to boot from the CD to start setup.

5. A message box is displayed, asking if you want to install the Recovery Console. Click **Yes** to continue.

6. The Windows Setup window opens and shows that Setup is checking for updates. When the update check is finished, a progress indicator appears. When the installation is finished, a message box is displayed stating that the Recovery Console was installed successfully. Click **OK** to continue.

7. Restart your computer.

8. When the Startup menu is displayed, select **Microsoft Windows Recovery Console** and press **Enter**. What do you see when the Recovery Console opens?

   _____

   _____

   _____

   _____

9. Type **1** (to log on to your Windows installation) and press **Enter**.

10. When prompted, type the administrator password for your computer and press **Enter**.

11. Type **help** and press **Enter** to see a list of commands available in the Recovery Console. You may have to continue pressing **Enter** to scroll through the list. Answer the following questions:

    ◢ What command deletes a directory?

    _____

    ◢ What command can you use to list services that are running?

    _____

    ◢ Name at least two tasks you might not be able to perform in the Recovery Console:

    _____

    _____

12. Type **exit** and press **Enter** to close the Recovery Console and restart the computer to Windows.

REVIEW QUESTIONS

1. What is the advantage of being able to access the Recovery Console from your hard drive instead of the CD-ROM drive?

2. Describe a situation where Recovery Console would not be the best tool for solving a Windows problem:

3. Why is an administrator password needed for access to the Recovery Console?

4. Why do you think Recovery Console only supports command-line utilities?

LAB 6.5 USE THE XP RECOVERY CONSOLE TO COPY FILES

OBJECTIVES

The goal of this lab is to help you learn how to copy files using the Recovery Console. After completing this lab, you will be able to:

◢ Copy files from a storage medium to your hard drive using the Recovery Console

MATERIALS REQUIRED

This lab requires the following:

◢ Windows XP operating system

◢ A floppy disk or other storage medium such as a USB flash drive

◢ Completion of Lab 6.4

LAB PREPARATION

Before the lab begins, the instructor or lab assistant needs to do the following:

◢ Verify that Windows starts with no errors.

ACTIVITY BACKGROUND

The Windows XP Recovery Console is useful when you need to restore system files after they have been corrupted (perhaps by a virus) or accidentally deleted from the hard drive.

In this lab, you use the Recovery Console (which you installed in Lab 6.4) to restore a system file, System.ini, from a floppy disk or other storage medium such as a USB flash drive. (Windows XP doesn't need this file to boot; it's included in Windows XP for backward compatibility with older Windows software.)

ESTIMATED COMPLETION TIME: 30 Minutes

 Activity

Follow these steps to copy the file System.ini to a floppy disk and then copy it from the floppy to the hard drive using the Recovery Console:

1. Insert the floppy disk in the floppy drive.

2. Open Windows Explorer, and then locate and click the **System.ini** file (which is usually in the C:\Windows folder).

> **Notes** In these steps, a floppy disk is used as the storage medium, but you can adapt the steps to whatever storage medium you're using.

3. Copy the **System.ini** file to the floppy disk, and then eject the floppy disk from the drive.

4. Locate System.ini on your hard drive again and rename it as **System.old**. When prompted, click **Yes** to confirm that you want to rename the file.

5. Restart the computer and select the **Microsoft Windows Recovery Console** option and press **Enter**.

6. Insert the floppy disk in the floppy disk drive. In the Recovery Console, log on with the administrator password. Type **copy a:\ system.ini c:\windows\system.ini** and press **Enter**. This command copies System.ini from the floppy disk to its original location (C:\Windows). What message does Recovery Console display?

_____

7. If C:\Windows is not the active directory, change to that directory and then use the **dir** command to view its contents. Verify that System.ini was copied to this directory. You might have to use the Spacebar to scroll down.

8. Exit the Recovery Console and restart the computer.

REVIEW QUESTIONS

1. You could have used the Recovery Console to rename the System.old file instead of copying the original version from the floppy disk. What command do you use to perform this task?

_____

2. Assume you moved the System.ini file to the My Documents folder. What command do you use in the Recovery Console to move it back to the C:\Windows folder?

_____

3. When might it be useful to be able to copy files from a CD to the hard drive by using the Recovery Console?

_____

4. Why does Windows XP include the System.ini file?

_____

5. When might you want to use the Recovery Console to copy files from the hard drive to a floppy disk?

LAB 6.6 USE THE VISTA RECOVERY ENVIRONMENT (WINDOWS RE) TO REPAIR WINDOWS

OBJECTIVES

The goal of this lab is to help you learn how to use the Windows Vista Recovery Environment (Windows RE). After completing this lab, you will be able to:

- Boot to Windows RE
- Repair a Windows installation using Windows RE

MATERIALS REQUIRED

This lab requires the following:

- Windows Vista operating system
- Vista installation DVD

LAB PREPARATION

Before the lab begins, the instructor or lab assistant needs to do the following:

- Verify that Windows starts with no errors.

ACTIVITY BACKGROUND

The Windows Vista Recovery Environment (RecEnv.exe), also known as Windows RE, is an operating system launched from the Vista DVD that provides a graphical and command-line interface. In this lab, you will become familiar with Windows RE and use it to solve some simple startup problems.

ESTIMATED COMPLETION TIME: 30 Minutes

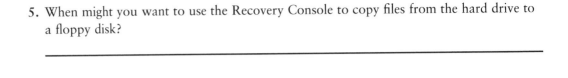 **Activity**

Follow these steps to start up and explore Windows RE:

1. Using a computer that has Windows Vista installed, boot from the Vista setup DVD. (To boot from a DVD, you might have to change the boot sequence in CMOS setup to put the optical drive first above the hard drive.) The screen in Figure 6-1 appears. Select your language preference and click **Next**.

2. The Install Windows screen appears, as shown in Figure 6-2. Click **Repair your computer**. The recovery environment (RecEnv.exe) launches and displays the System Recovery Options dialog box (see Figure 6-3).

3. Select the Vista installation to repair and click **Next**.

Figure 6-1 Select your language preference
Courtesy: Course Technology/Cengage Learning

Figure 6-2 Launch Windows RE after booting from the Vista DVD
Courtesy: Course Technology/Cengage Learning

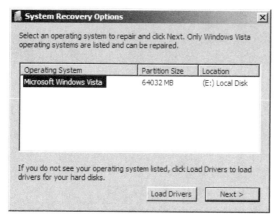

Figure 6-3 Select an installation of Vista to repair
Courtesy: Course Technology/Cengage Learning

6

4. The System Recovery Options window in Figure 6-4 appears, listing recovery options.

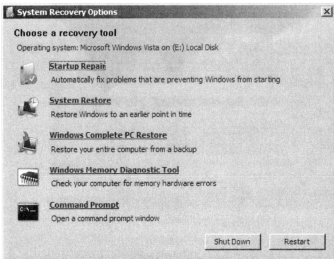

Figure 6-4   Recovery tools in Windows RE
Courtesy: Course Technology/Cengage Learning

5. The first tool, Startup Repair, can automatically fix many Windows problems, including those caused by a corrupted BCD file and missing system files. You can't cause any additional problems by using it and it's easy to use. Therefore, it should be your first recovery option when Vista refuses to load. Click **Startup Repair** and the tool will examine the system for errors (see Figure 6-5).

Based on what Startup Repair finds, it will suggest various solutions. For example, it might suggest you use System Restore or suggest you immediately reboot the system to see if the problem has been fixed (see Figure 6-6). Did Startup Repair find any errors on your system?

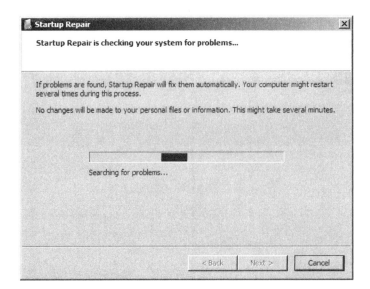

Figure 6-5   Startup Repair searches the system for problems it can fix
Courtesy: Course Technology/Cengage Learning

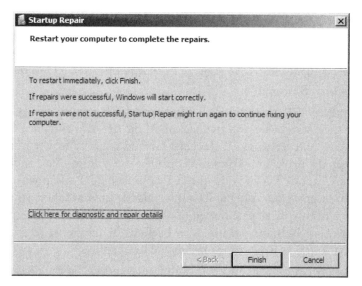

Figure 6-6 Startup Repair has attempted to fix the problem
Courtesy: Course Technology/Cengage Learning

6. To see a list of items examined and actions taken by Startup Repair, click **Click here for diagnostic and repair details**. If no problems were detected on your system, you can click **View diagnostic and repair details**. The dialog box showing the list of repairs appears, as shown in Figure 6-7. A log file can also be found at C:\Windows\System32\ LogFiles\SRT\SRTTrail.txt.

What steps would you take to print this log file?

_____

_____

7. Click **Close** to close the dialog box and then click **Finish** in the Startup Repair window to get back to the System Recovery Options window.

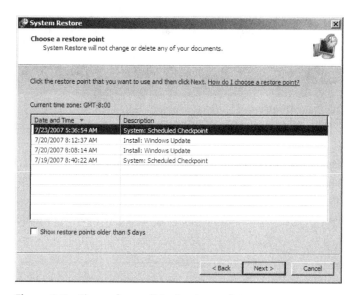

Figure 6-7 Choose from a list of restore points
Courtesy: Course Technology/Cengage Learning

8. System Restore in the System Recovery Options window works the same as Windows Vista System Restore from the desktop to return the system to its state when a restore point was made (see Lab 6.2). Click **System Restore** and click **Next**. A list of restore points appears (see Figure 6-7). Get back to the System Recovery Options windows by canceling the System Restore.

Windows Complete PC Restore can be used to completely restore drive C and possibly other drives to their state when the last backup of the drives was made. When you use Complete PC Restore, everything on the hard drive is lost because the restore process completely erases the drive and writes to it the OS, user information, applications, and data as they were captured at the time the last Complete PC Backup was made. Therefore, before using Complete PC Restore, consider how old the backup is. Perhaps you can use it to restore drive C and then boot into Windows, reinstall applications installed since the last backup, and use other backups of data more recent than the last Complete PC Backup was made to restore the data.

9. Use the Windows Memory Diagnostic Tool to test memory. Did the diagnostic tool find any memory errors?

_____

_____

10. After the computer reboots, get back to the Systems recovery Options window and click **Command Prompt** to open a command prompt window. You can use this window to repair a corrupted Vista system or recover data (see Figure 6-8).

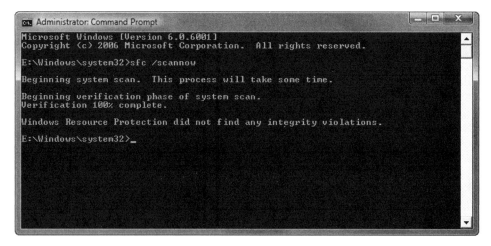

Figure 6-8   The command prompt window
Courtesy: Course Technology/Cengage Learning

11. Several of the commands in the Vista Recovery environment have been changed from the command used in the Windows XP Recovery Console. Use the help command and the Internet to answer the following questions:

◢ What Recovery Console command has been replaced with the command **BootRec /ScanOS**?

_____

◢ What Recovery Console command has been replaced with the command **BootRec /FixBoot**?

_____

◢ What Recovery Console command has been replaced with the command **BootRec /FixMbr**?

_____

12. Exit from the command prompt.

13. As you use a tool in the System Recovery Options window, be sure to reboot after each attempt to fix the problem to make sure the problem has not been resolved before you try another tool. To exit the Recovery Environment, click **Shut Down** or **Restart**.

CRITICAL THINKING (ADDITIONAL 15 MINUTES)

1. Using Windows Explorer, rename the BootMgr file in the root directory of drive C. Reboot the system. What error message do you see?

_____

_____

2. Use Windows RE to restore the BootMgr file. List the steps taken to complete the repair:

_____

_____

_____

_____

REVIEW QUESTIONS

1. If your computer would not boot, which Windows RE recovery tool would you try first? Why?

_____

_____

2. Why does Windows RE need to boot from the DVD?

_____

3. Why do you think Windows RE has still included an option for a command-line interface?

_____

4. What must be done before you can do a complete PC restore?

_____

5. Why is it important to reboot after each attempt to fix a problem with Windows RE?

_____

_____

CHAPTER 7

Fixing Windows Problems

Labs included in this chapter:

- **Lab 7.1:** Troubleshoot Failed Windows Installations
- **Lab 7.2:** Recover Data from a Computer That Will Not Boot
- **Lab 7.3:** Finding a Driver for an Unknown Device
- **Lab 7.4:** Fixing Internet Explorer
- **Lab 7.5:** Critical Thinking: Sabotage and Repair Windows XP
- **Lab 7.6:** Critical Thinking: Sabotage and Repair Windows Vista

LAB 7.1 TROUBLESHOOT FAILED WINDOWS INSTALLATIONS

OBJECTIVES

The goal of this lab is to help you learn how to troubleshoot problems with various Windows installations. After completing this lab, you will be able to:

◢ Research problems with Windows installations

◢ Transfer user data and preferences

◢ Modify an answer file

◢ Share an external drive between a PC and a MAC

MATERIALS REQUIRED

This lab requires the following:

◢ A Windows Vista/XP computer designated for this lab

◢ Internet access

LAB PREPARATION

Before the lab begins, the instructor or lab assistant needs to do the following:

◢ Verify that Internet access is available.

ACTIVITY BACKGROUND

PC support technicians are often called on to upgrade Windows or install Windows on a new hard drive. Installations don't always go smoothly, so you need to know what to do when problems arise. When researching a problem, the Microsoft support site (support.microsoft.com) is an excellent resource. You also need to know about transferring user settings and data from one computer to another. These skills are covered in this lab.

ESTIMATED COMPLETION TIME: 45 Minutes

Activity

Imagine the following scenario. As a PC support technician in a large organization, you work with a team of technicians supporting the users and equipment on a large enterprise network including personal computers, laptops, printers, and scanners. Corporations are sometimes slow to upgrade operating systems and equipment, and several users in the organization use Mac computers, so you find yourself researching many problems as they arise. Use the Internet to research the following problems:

A group of PCs are being converted from Windows 2000 to Windows XP, and your coworker, Larry, has already set up these unattended installations of Windows XP using the System Preparation (Sysprep) utility (see Lab 3.6). Larry is not available and your boss has asked you to make a change to a particular desktop computer being upgraded. He gives you the change he wants you to make but assumes you know how to implement it. Answer the following questions:

1. Can an answer file be edited after it has been created? If so, how?

2. What is the name of the answer file for the unattended Windows installation?

_____

3. You know that Windows will be installed in the C:\Windows folder. What is the path to the answer file?

_____

You are asked to enable disk quotas on a Windows XP computer that serves double duty as a user's PC and a file server running IIS. When you begin to make the change, you notice that the Properties window for the drive used as the file server (drive D) does not have the Quota tab. Answer the following questions:

1. What would cause the Quota tab to be missing?

_____

2. What command can you use from a command prompt window to convert the FAT32 drive D to a NTFS drive?

_____

3. Is there a risk any data will be lost during the conversion? What can you do to guard against this risk?

_____

_____

Linda has just received a new desktop computer on which Windows Vista has been newly installed. Her old Windows XP computer and her new computer are both connected to the network. After you finish moving her data and user preferences to the new computer, you intend to reformat the old computer's hard drive, reinstall Windows XP and applications, and assign the computer to another user. Answer the following questions:

1. What utility can be used to transfer Linda's documents and user preferences from her old Windows XP computer to this new Windows Vista computer?

_____

2. Can her applications also be transferred or do they have to be reinstalled?

_____

3. Your company policy is to keep the old computer in your storage room for one month before reformatting the hard drive. Why do you think this policy is needed?

_____

_____

Jennifer is a graphics artist who works a lot with Adobe Illustrator on her desktop PC, but occasionally works at a customer's location where she uses the same application on a Mac. She wants to use a FireWire external hard drive with her desktop PC at work that she can take with her to the off-site location and have the Mac read her large files on the external drive. Answer these questions:

1. If she uses the NTFS file system on the external drive, can files be read by the Mac using OS X?

_____

2. Can files be written to the drive by the Mac?

_____

3. Can the Mac execute software that has been installed by the PC on the external drive?

REVIEW QUESTIONS

1. Besides the Microsoft support site, were there any Web sites that you found particularly useful in researching Windows problems? What were they?

2. What file system is required if you are using disk quotas in XP?

3. What is the default file system for Mac OS X, and can it be read by a PC?

4. Why is it a good idea to reformat and reinstall the operating system before reassigning a computer?

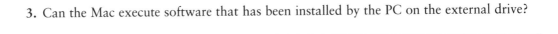

LAB 7.2 RECOVER DATA FROM A COMPUTER THAT WILL NOT BOOT

OBJECTIVES

The goal of this lab is to help you learn how to recover data from a computer that will not boot. After completing this lab, you will be able to:

◢ Copy data from a nonbooting computer

◢ Use data-recovery software

MATERIALS REQUIRED

This lab requires the following:

◢ Two Windows Vista/XP computers designated for this lab

◢ Internet access

LAB PREPARATION

Before the lab begins, the instructor or lab assistant needs to do the following:

◢ Verify that Internet access is available.

ACTIVITY BACKGROUND

If Windows is corrupted and the system will not boot, recovering your data might be your first priority. One way to get to the data is to remove your hard drive from your computer and install it as a second nonbooting hard drive in another working system. After you boot up the system, you should be able to use Windows Explorer to copy the data to another medium such as a USB flash drive. If the data is corrupted, you can try to use data-recovery software. In this lab, you will remove the hard drive from a computer and attempt to recover information.

ESTIMATED COMPLETION TIME: 45 Minutes

 Activity

First you need to create some data on the first computer that will need to be rescued:

1. Boot the first computer and log in as **Administrator**.

2. Create a new user called **User1** (see Lab 4.4).

3. Log on as **User1**.

4. You will now create some files to represent important information that might be saved in various locations on this computer. Use Notepad to create three text files named file1.txt, file2.txt, and file3.txt, and save one in each of the following locations:

    ◢ User1's Document's folder (My Documents in XP)

    ◢ The Public Documents folder (Shared Documents in XP)

    ◢ The root (probably C:\)

5. Open Internet Explorer and bookmark at least three locations on the Internet.

6. Log out and shut down this computer.

Now pretend that this computer is no longer able to boot. Since a backup or restore point has not been created recently, you have decided to remove the hard drive and attempt to recover some important files before attempting to determine why the computer won't boot.

1. Remove the main hard drive and install it as a second hard drive in another Windows machine.

> **Notes** You can save time by purchasing an external IDE/SATA-to-USB converter kit for about $30 and use the kit to temporarily connect a hard drive to a USB port on a working computer.

2. Boot this computer and log on as **Administrator**.

3. Use Windows Explorer to locate the three text files on the hard drive you just installed.

4. List the path where each of these files can be found:

    ◢ file1.txt

    _____

    ◢ file2.txt

    _____

    ◢ file3.txt

    _____

5. Determine the name and location of the file containing your IE favorites:

    _____

6. Can you think of any other locations that could contain information a user might want to recover?

_____

_____

_____

_____

In some cases, the files might be corrupt or you may not be able to access the drive at all. In these cases, you can attempt to use file-recovery software.

1. Open **Computer** (**My Computer** in XP) and right-click the drive that contains the files you would like to recover.

2. Click **Properties** and select the **Tools** tab, as shown in Figure 7-1.

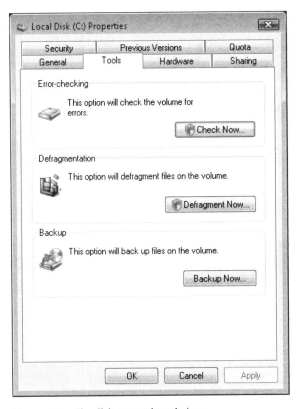

Figure 7-1 The disk properties window
Courtesy: Course Technology/Cengage Learning

3. Click **Check Now** . . . in the Error-checking section. If a UAC dialog box opens, click **Continue**.

4. Check **Scan for and attempt recovery of bad sectors** and click **Start**.

5. Did Error-checking find any errors?

6. If Error-checking did find errors but was unable to recover them, you can try using a utility designed for the brand of hard drive you're using.

7. Shut down the system you're using and return the other hard drive to its computer.

8. Boot both computers back up and ensure that everything is working before shutting them both down.

REVIEW QUESTIONS

1. Why might you want to recover lost data before attempting to resolve a boot problem?

_____

_____

2. How could scheduled backups have saved you a lot of time?

_____

_____

3. What might have caused the first computer not to boot? List three possible causes:

_____

_____

_____

4. If you suspect the first computer is not booting because it is infected with a virus, what should you ensure before installing its hard drive in your system?

_____

_____

7

LAB 7.3 FINDING A DRIVER FOR AN UNKNOWN DEVICE

OBJECTIVES

The goal of this lab is to help you learn how to find the drivers for an unknown device. After completing this lab, you will be able to:

◢ Use third-party software to determine brand and model information of an unknown device

◢ Use the Internet to find and download a driver

MATERIALS REQUIRED

This lab requires the following:

◢ A Windows Vista/XP computer designated for this lab

◢ Internet access

◢ A burnable CD and a marker for labeling

LAB PREPARATION

Before the lab begins, the instructor or lab assistant needs to do the following:

⊿ Verify that Internet access is available.

ACTIVITY BACKGROUND

Someone has come to you for help with her computer. She is unable to connect to the Internet and is not sure why. After some investigation, you realize that she has just replaced the network adapter, but has lost the driver CD for the adapter and its documentation. Windows does not recognize the device type and there is no model information on the device itself. To find the correct drivers on the Internet, you need to know the exact brand and model of the device.

ESTIMATED COMPLETION TIME: 30 Minutes

 Activity

Use the following steps to retrieve this information. By following these steps, you'll learn to use the Ultimate Boot CD, which can be a valuable utility to add to your PC repair kit.

1. Go to the Ultimate Boot CD download page at *www.ultimatebootcd.com/download. html* and read the directions about creating the Ultimate Boot CD. The CD is created using an ISO image. An ISO image is a file that contains all the files that were burned to an original CD or DVD. This ISO image is then used to create copies of the original CD or DVD. The process has three steps: (1) Download the ISO image as a compressed, self-extracting .exe file; (2) decompress the compressed file to extract the ISO file having an .iso file extension; (3) use CD-burning software to burn the CD from the ISO image.

2. Follow the directions to download to your hard drive a self-extracting executable (.exe) file containing the ISO image. What is the most recent nonbeta version of the software?

   _____

3. Read through the section called Frequently Asked Questions and answer the following questions:

   ⊿ What utilities are included for partitioning hard drives?

   _____

   _____

   ⊿ How could you load the Ultimate Boot Disk on a USB flash drive?

   _____

   _____

   ⊿ Name several programs that you can use to burn an ISO image under Windows:

   _____

   _____

4. Double-click the downloaded file to execute it and extract the ISO image. (For Version 4.1.1, the new file will be named ubcd411.iso.)

5. You'll need software to burn the ISO image to the CD. (Do not just burn the .iso file to the CD. The software extracts the files inside the ISO image and burns these files to the CD to create a bootable CD holding many files.) The Ultimate Boot CD Web site suggests some free CD-burning software that supports ISO images. Download and execute one of these products to burn the ISO image to the CD. Using a permanent marker, label the CD "Ultimate Boot CD," and include the version number that you downloaded.

6. Boot the computer from the CD and find a tool that will retrieve the brand and model number of the NIC (network adapter). What software on the CD did you decide to use?

7. Use the program to find the make and model number of the NIC installed in your system and write down this information:

8. Using the acquired information, search the Internet for the correct driver. What is the name of this driver and where did you find it on the Internet?

9. Does this driver match the driver currently installed on your system?

10. When you're finished, remove the CD and reboot your system.

REVIEW QUESTIONS

1. Name some advantages to using a boot CD over just running diagnostic programs in Windows:

2. What are ISO images and can Windows use them without additional software?

3. Describe two other situations where the Ultimate Boot CD would be useful:

4. How much does the Ultimate Boot CD cost?

LAB 7.4 FIXING INTERNET EXPLORER

OBJECTIVES

The goal of this lab is to help you fix problems that can occur with Internet Explorer. After completing this lab, you will be able to:

◢ Repair Internet Explorer

◢ Disable IE add-ons

◢ Clean the browser history

◢ Reset Internet Explorer settings

◢ Repair a Corrupted Cache Index

MATERIALS REQUIRED

This lab requires the following:

◢ A Windows Vista/XP computer designated for this lab

◢ Internet access

LAB PREPARATION

Before the lab begins, the instructor or lab assistant needs to do the following:

◢ Verify that Internet access is available.

ACTIVITY BACKGROUND

When application problems occur, our first instinct is to restart the system. However, before you do the restart, make sure you understand the problem that is currently displayed on the screen so that you know how to reproduce it after the restart. If you are concerned that the source of the problem might be a failing OS or hard drive, save any important data to another media before you begin. The system might not boot after you restart and saving the data then will be more complicated. After you restart the system, log on as an administrator and verify whether the problem still exists.

This lab supposes that you have problems with Internet Explorer 8.0. The steps may vary slightly if you are using a different version of the program.

ESTIMATED COMPLETION TIME: 90 Minutes

 Activity

Begin troubleshooting by following these steps:

1. Log on as an administrator.

2. *Verify that you have Internet access.* Before you assume the problem is with Internet Explorer, verify that the local network is working and you have Internet access. Don't just assume you have Internet access if your home page opens. It might be a cache file stored locally on your computer. Try opening a new Web page such as *www.microsoft.com*. Can you access the Internet?

If the Web page won't open, try to use an application other than IE that requires Internet access. Open a command prompt window and try to ping the Web site by typing **ping www.microsoft.com**. If the ping command does not work, then treat the problem as a network problem.

3. *Verify that all Vista updates are current.* Windows Vista considers Internet Explorer and Windows Mail (formerly Outlook Express) program files to be part of the full set of Windows system files. Therefore, updates to Windows Vista include updates to these apps, and these updates might solve the problem. Does Windows have the latest updates?

4. *Using updated antivirus software, scan the system for viruses.* If your AV software finds malware, scan again to make sure the system is infection free. Is your system virus free?

5. *Use the Error Reporting feature of Vista to search for solutions.* Click **Start**, click **All Programs**, click **Maintenance**, and click **Problem Reports and Solutions** to open the Problem Reports and Solution window, as shown in Figure 7-2. Do you see any problems that pertain to Internet Explorer?

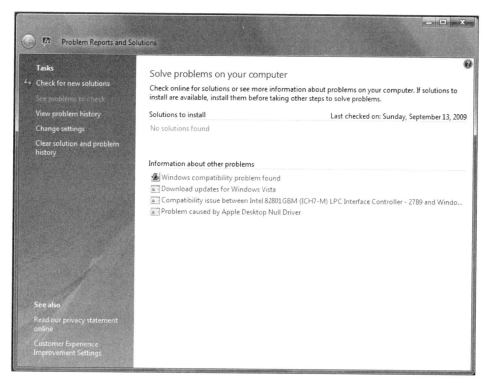

Figure 7-2 Use the Problem Reports and Solutions tool to view a history of past problems
Courtesy: Course Technology/Cengage Learning

6. *Verify that other applications are not causing the problem.* Other applications might be in conflict with IE. Close all other open applications and check Task Manager to make sure all are closed.

7. If the problem still persists, then follow the instructions given next where you'll learn to eliminate add-ons, IE history, IE settings, the cache index, and corrupted OS files as sources of the problem.

Most Internet Explorer problems are caused by add-ons. You can temporarily disable all add-ons so they can be eliminated as the source of a problem. Follow these steps:

1. Click **Start, All Programs, Accessories, System Tools,** and **Internet Explorer (No Add-ons).** (Alternately, you can enter **iexplore.exe –extoff** in the Start Search box.) Internet Explorer opens, showing the Information bar message in Figure 7-3.

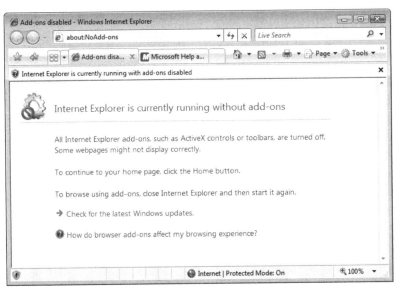

Figure 7-3   Internet Explorer is running with no add-ons
Courtesy: Course Technology/Cengage Learning

2. If the problem has disappeared, then you can assume the source of the problem is an add-on. Click the yellow information bar and click **Manage Add-ons.** What types of add-ons are listed?

_____

_____

3. To return Internet Explorer to run with add-ons, close the IE window and then open IE as usual.

The IE problem might be caused by a corrupted browser history, which might prevent access to particular Web sites. Also, deleting the browser history is a good best practice to protect your privacy when you are finished using Internet Explorer on a public computer. To clean the history, follow these steps:

1. In Internet Explorer, click **Tools** and **Internet Options.** The Internet Options dialog box appears, as shown on the left in Figure 7-4.

2. Under Browsing history, click **Delete.** The Delete Browsing History dialog box appears, as shown in the right of Figure 7-4. You can select particular items to delete or select all to clean out the entire browsing history. When using a public computer, definitely click all of the check boxes to completely delete history files. List the types of data that can be deleted:

_____

_____

_____

_____

3. When you're finished, click **OK** to close the Internet Options window.

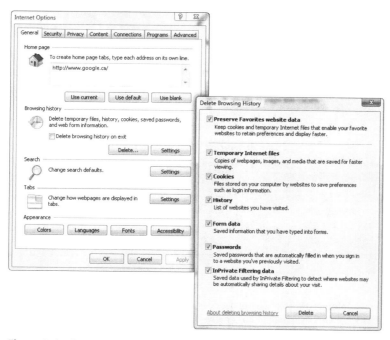

Figure 7-4 Internet Options dialog box
Courtesy: Course Technology/Cengage Learning

After you have eliminated add-ons and the browser history as the source of the problem, the next step is to eliminate IE settings. There are two approaches to doing that: resetting IE to default settings (all customized settings are lost and all add-ons are deleted), or the less drastic approach of manually changing one setting at a time, searching for the one that might be causing the problem.

If Internet Explorer does not use many customized settings, resetting IE is the quickest way to eliminate settings as the problem. Follow these steps to reset Internet Explorer:

1. If necessary, open Internet Explorer and click **Tools**. From the Tools menu, select **Internet Options**. The Internet Options box appears, as shown earlier in Figure 7-4. (Alternately, you can enter **inetcpl.cpl** in the Start Search box.)

2. Click the **Advanced** tab and then click **Reset** (see Figure 7-5). Note in the box on the right that Vista warns that all cookies, passwords, toolbars, and add-ons will be deleted. Therefore, use this method with caution and consider exporting cookies before you reset. Click **Reset** to complete the task. What personal settings are not affected by the default resetting Internet Explorer?

_____

_____

Sometimes IE problems are caused by a corrupted index file in the cache folder. To solve the problem, you need to delete the hidden file index.dat. The easiest way to delete the file is to delete the entire IE cache folder for the user account that has the problem. The next time the user logs on, the folder will be rebuilt. To delete the folder, follow these steps:

1. Log onto the system using a different account that has administrative privileges.

2. Use Windows explorer to delete C:\Users*username*\AppData\Local\Microsoft\ Windows\Temporary Internet Files. You will not be able to delete the folder if this user is logged on.

3. Log out and log back in as your original user and open Internet Explorer. Did Internet Explorer rebuild the folder?

_____

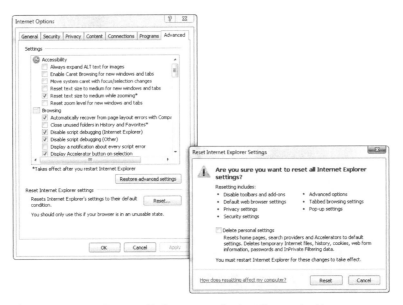

Figure 7-5   Reset Internet Explorer customized settings and add-ons
Courtesy: Course Technology/Cengage Learning

If you still have a problem with IE and you are certain the problem is not with the network or with Internet access, follow the steps listed below to repair Internet Explorer. However, know that each step is progressively more drastic than the next and you might find that, in using the method described, you change other Windows configuration settings and components. Therefore, after you try a step, check to see if your problem is fixed. Don't move on to the next step unless your problem is still present.

1. Use the Windows Vista System File Checker (sfc.exe) to check Windows system files and replace corrupted ones. Close all open applications and open a command prompt. Type **sfc /scannow**, as shown in Figure 7-6. Did your system find any corrupted files?

2. *Upgrade Internet Explorer.* At the time of this writing, Internet Explorer 8 was the most recent version. However, by the time you are reading this, a new version of Internet Explorer may be available. What is the most recent version of Internet Explorer available?

```
Administrator: Command Prompt

Microsoft Windows [Version 6.0.6001]
Copyright (c) 2006 Microsoft Corporation.  All rights reserved.

E:\Windows\system32>sfc /scannow

Beginning system scan.  This process will take some time.

Beginning verification phase of system scan.
Verification 100% complete.

Windows Resource Protection did not find any integrity violations.

E:\Windows\system32>_
```

Figure 7-6   Use System File Checker to verify Vista system files
Courtesy: Course Technology/Cengage Learning

3. *Run Internet Explorer in Safe Mode with Networking.* Press **F8** at startup to display the Advanced Boot Options menu and select Safe Mode with Networking from the menu. If Internet Explorer works in Safe Mode, then you can assume the problem is not with IE but with the operating system, device drivers, or other applications that load at startup which are conflicting with IE. In this situation, approach the problem as a Windows problem rather than an Internet Explorer problem.

4. *Repair a corrupted Windows Vista installation.* If Internet Explorer refuses to work, even in Safe Mode with Networking, you can assume that the Vista installation is corrupted.

REVIEW QUESTIONS

1. What troubleshooting techniques from this lab might work to fix any Windows application?

_____

_____

_____

_____

2. Why can't you assume Internet Explorer is working if you can open your home page?

_____

_____

3. Why is deleting the browser history a good idea?

_____

_____

4. What should you do before restarting the system if an application is not working properly?

_____

_____

LAB 7.5 CRITICAL THINKING: SABOTAGE AND REPAIR WINDOWS XP

OBJECTIVES

The goal of this lab is to learn to troubleshoot Windows XP by repairing a sabotaged system. After completing this lab, you will be able to:

◢ Troubleshoot and repair a system that isn't working correctly

MATERIALS REQUIRED

This lab requires the following:

◢ Windows XP Professional installed on a PC designated for sabotage

◢ Windows XP Professional installation CD or installation files

◢ A workgroup of 2 to 4 students

LAB PREPARATION

Before the lab begins, the instructor or lab assistant needs to do the following:

⊿ Verify that Windows starts with no errors.

⊿ Provide each workgroup with access to the Windows XP installation files, if needed.

ACTIVITY BACKGROUND

You have learned about several tools and methods you can use to recover Windows XP when it fails. This lab gives you the opportunity to use these skills in a troubleshooting situation. Your group will sabotage another group's system while that group sabotages your system. Then your group will repair its own system.

ESTIMATED COMPLETION TIME: 45 Minutes

 Activity

1. If your system's hard drive contains important data, back it up to another medium. Is there anything else you would like to back up before another group sabotages the system? Record the name of that item here, and then back it up:

   _____

2. Trade systems with another group, and sabotage the other group's system while they sabotage your system. Do one thing that will cause the system to fail to boot, display errors after the boot, or prevent a device or application from working. The following list offers some sabotage suggestions. Do something in the following list, or think of another option. Be inventive and have fun, but do *not* alter the hardware.

   Notes Windows XP has several features designed to prevent sabotage, so you might find it a little challenging to actually prevent the system from booting by deleting or renaming system files.

   ⊿ Find a system file in the root directory that's required to boot the computer, and rename it or move it to a different directory. (Don't delete the file.)

   ⊿ Using the Registry Editor (Regedit.exe), delete several important keys or values in the Registry.

   ⊿ Locate important system files in the \Windows directory, and rename them or move them to another directory.

   ⊿ Put a corrupted program file in the folder that will cause the program to launch automatically at startup. Record the name of that program file and folder here:

   _____

   ⊿ Use display settings that aren't readable, such as black text on a black background.

   ⊿ Disable a critical device driver.

3. Reboot the system and verify that a problem exists.

4. How did you sabotage the other team's system?

_____

_____

_____

5. Return to your system and troubleshoot it.

6. Describe the problem as a user would describe it to you if you were working at a help desk:

_____

_____

7. What is your first guess as to the source of the problem?

_____

8. List the steps you took in the troubleshooting process:

_____

_____

_____

9. How did you finally solve the problem and return the system to good working order?

_____

_____

_____

REVIEW QUESTIONS

1. What would you do differently the next time you encountered the same symptoms?

_____

_____

2. What Windows utilities did you use or could you have used to solve the problem?

_____

_____

3. In a real-life situation, what might cause this problem to happen? List three possible causes:

_____

_____

_____

4. If you were the PC support technician responsible for this computer in an office environment, what could you do to prevent this problem from happening in the future or limit its impact on users if it did happen?

_____

_____

LAB 7.6 CRITICAL THINKING: SABOTAGE AND REPAIR WINDOWS VISTA

OBJECTIVES

The goal of this lab is to learn to troubleshoot Windows Vista by repairing a sabotaged system. After completing this lab, you will be able to:

◢ Troubleshoot and repair a system that isn't working correctly

MATERIALS REQUIRED

This lab requires the following:

◢ Windows Vista installed on a PC designated for sabotage

◢ Windows Vista Professional installation DVD or installation files

◢ A workgroup of 2 to 4 students

LAB PREPARATION

Before the lab begins, the instructor or lab assistant needs to do the following:

◢ Verify that Windows starts with no errors.

◢ Provide each workgroup with access to the Windows Vista installation files, if needed.

ACTIVITY BACKGROUND

You have learned about several tools and methods you can use to recover Windows Vista when it fails. This lab gives you the opportunity to use these skills in a troubleshooting situation. Your group sabotages another group's system while that group sabotages your system. Then your group repairs its own system.

ESTIMATED COMPLETION TIME: 45 Minutes

 Activity

1. If your system's hard drive contains important data, back it up to another medium. Is there anything else you would like to back up before another group sabotages the system? Record the name of that item here, and then back it up:

_____

2. Trade systems with another group, and sabotage the other group's system while it sabotages your system. Do one thing that will cause the system to fail to boot, display errors after the boot, or prevent a device or application from working. The following list offers

some sabotage suggestions. Do something in the following list, or think of another option. (Do *not* alter the hardware.)

◿ Find a system file in the root directory that's required to boot the computer, and rename it or move it to a different directory. (Don't delete the file.)

◿ Using the Registry Editor (Regedit.exe), delete several important keys or values in the Registry.

◿ Locate important system files in the \Windows directory, and rename them or move them to another directory.

◿ Put a corrupted program file in the folder that will cause the program to launch automatically at startup. Record the name of that program file and folder here:

_____

◿ Use display settings that aren't readable, such as black text on a black background.

◿ Disable a critical device driver.

3. Reboot the system and verify that a problem exists.

4. How did you sabotage the other team's system?

_____

_____

_____

5. Return to your system and troubleshoot it.

6. Describe the problem as a user would describe it to you if you were working at a help desk:

_____

_____

7. What is your first guess as to the source of the problem?

_____

8. List the steps you took in the troubleshooting process:

_____

_____

_____

9. How did you finally solve the problem and return the system to good working order?

_____

_____

_____

7

REVIEW QUESTIONS

1. What would you do differently the next time you encountered the same symptoms?

   _____

   _____

2. What Windows utilities did you use or could you have used to solve the problem?

   _____

   _____

3. In a real-life situation, what might cause this problem to happen? List three possible causes:

   _____

   _____

   _____

4. If you were the PC support technician responsible for this computer in an office environment, what could you do to prevent this problem from happening in the future or limit its impact on users if it did happen?

   _____

   _____

Networking Essentials

Labs included in this chapter:

LAB 8.1 CONNECT TWO COMPUTERS

OBJECTIVES

The goal of this lab is to install and configure an Ethernet network interface card (NIC). After completing this lab, you will be able to:

- Remove a NIC (and network protocols, if necessary)
- Install a NIC (and network protocols, if necessary)
- Perform a loopback test

MATERIALS REQUIRED

This lab requires the following:

- Windows Vista/XP operating system
- A NIC and drivers
- Windows installation CD/DVD or installation files
- A PC toolkit with antistatic ground strap
- A crossover cable or two patch cables and a small repeater (hub)
- A workgroup partner

LAB PREPARATION

Before the lab begins, the instructor or lab assistant needs to do the following:

- Verify that Windows starts with no errors.
- Provide each student with access to the Windows installation files, if needed.

ACTIVITY BACKGROUND

A computer connects to a wired network through a network interface card (NIC). In this lab, you install a NIC, configure necessary network settings, and verify that the NIC is functioning correctly. Working with a partner, you create a simple network of two PCs. By default, Windows Vista/XP has the protocols already installed for two computers to communicate.

ESTIMATED COMPLETION TIME: 30 Minutes

 Activity

Follow these steps to install and configure your NIC:

1. Physically install your NIC as you would other expansion cards.

2. Boot the system. The Found New Hardware Wizard detects the NIC and begins the driver installation process. In some cases, Windows doesn't allow using non-Microsoft drivers. If this option is available, however, click **Locate and install driver software (recommended)** (**Have Disk** in XP) and provide the manufacturer's drivers for the NIC. Reboot if prompted to do so. If you need help in installing the driver, see Lab 6.3.

Next, you give the computer an IP address, a computer name, and a workgroup name, as shown in the following chart. Write your name and your partner's name in the chart, and then follow these steps to assign an IP address to the computer:

> **Notes** If you want to force Windows to use manufacturers' drivers, run the setup program on the CD or floppy disk that comes bundled with the NIC *before* you physically install the NIC. After you boot with the new card installed, Windows then finds the already installed manufacturers' drivers and uses them.

To configure the IP address in Windows Vista:

1. Click **Start**, right-click **Network**, and click **Properties**. The Network and Sharing Center window appears.

2. Click **Manage network connections**, right-click **Local Area Connection**, and click **Properties** in the shortcut menu. If Windows needs your permission to continue, click **Continue**. The Local Area Connection Properties dialog box opens, as shown in Figure 8-1.

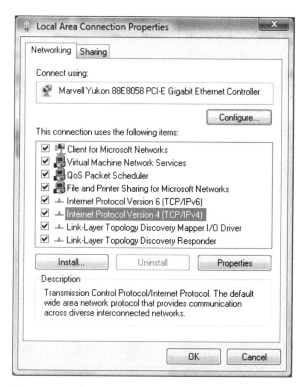

Figure 8-1 The Local Area Connection Properties dialog box
Courtesy: Course Technology/Cengage Learning

3. In the list of connection items, click **Internet Protocol Version 4 (TCP/IPv4)**, and then click the **Properties** button. The Internet Protocol (TCP/IP) Properties dialog box opens. Click **Use the following IP address** and enter your IP address (192.168.1.1 or 192.168.1.2) and subnet mask (255.255.255.0). Click **OK** and **Close** and then close all open windows.

Your names:		
IP address:	192.168.1.1	192.168.1.2
Computer name:	Lab1	Lab2
Workgroup name:	NIC LAB	NIC LAB

To configure the IP address in Windows XP:

1. Click **Start,** right-click **My Network Places,** and click **Properties** in the shortcut menu. The Network Connections window appears.

2. Right-click **Local Area Connection** and click **Properties** in the shortcut menu. The Local Area Connection Properties dialog box opens.

3. In the list of connection items, click **Internet Protocol (TCP/IP),** and then click the **Properties** button. The Internet Protocol (TCP/IP) Properties dialog box opens. Click **Use the following IP address** and enter your IP address (192.168.1.1 or 192.168.1.2) and subnet mask (255.255.255.0). Click **OK** in the Internet Protocol (TCP/IP) Properties dialog box, and then close all open windows.

Next, you assign a computer name and workgroup name to your computer.

In Windows Vista, follow these steps:

1. Click **Start,** right-click **Computer,** and click **Properties.** The System window opens.

2. Click **Change settings** and click **Continue** if Windows needs your permission to continue. Click the **Change. . .** button and the Computer Name/Domain Changes dialog box opens (see Figure 8-2).

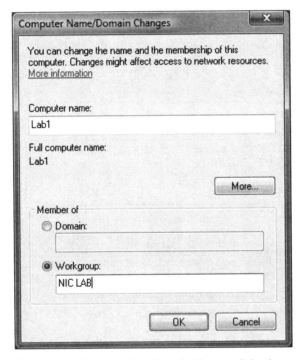

Figure 8-2 Computer Name/Domain Changes dialog box
Courtesy: Course Technology/Cengage Learning

3. Enter the computer name (**Lab1** in the example shown in Figure 8-2). Each computer name must be unique within a workgroup or domain.

4. Click **Workgroup** and enter the name of the workgroup (**NIC LAB** in this example).

5. Click **OK** and close any open windows. Restart your computer when prompted for changes to take effect.

In Windows XP, follow these steps:

1. Click **Start,** right-click **My Computer,** and click **Properties** in the shortcut menu. The System Properties dialog box opens.

2. In Windows XP, click the **Computer Name** tab, and then click the **Change** button. The Computer Name Changes dialog box opens.

3. Enter the computer name (**Lab1** or **Lab2**). Each computer name must be unique within a workgroup or domain.

4. Click **Workgroup** and enter the name of the workgroup (**NIC LAB** in this example).

5. Click **OK** and close any open windows. Restart your computer when prompted for changes to take effect.

Now follow these steps to test your NIC:

1. Open a command prompt window.

2. Type **ping 127.0.0.1** and press **Enter**. Ping is a TCP/IP utility used to test whether an address can be reached and is able to respond. Any 127.*x.x.x* address is a loopback address, which is essentially a stand-in for your computer's own address. When you use a loopback address in a ping test, the Ping utility sends packets to your local computer's NIC, thereby allowing you to verify that your computer's NIC has a functioning TCP/IP connection.

3. Examine the results of the loopback test and answer these questions:

   ◢ How many bytes were sent in each packet?

   _____

   ◢ How many packets were sent with one Ping command?

   _____

   ◢ How many responses were received from one Ping command?

   _____

   ◢ Were any packets lost?

   _____

Next, use the Ipconfig utility to verify your IP configuration. Do the following to check your NIC's configuration:

1. At the command prompt, type **ipconfig /all |more** and press **Enter**. An IP configuration report is displayed one screen at a time. If necessary, press **Enter** to see each new line. Answer the following questions:

   ◢ Is the configuration the same information you configured originally?

   _____

   ◢ What is the physical address (MAC address) of your NIC?

   _____

In Windows, another way to test a NIC is to use its assigned IP address in a ping test, as follows:

1. Use the ping command with the IP address you assigned to your computer. The results should be similar or identical to the loopback test results, except for the address listed in the Ping results. Was the ping successful?

   _____

8

2. Now, before attaching any network cables, ping your partner's IP address. Describe what happened to the request:

_____

_____

_____

Now you will create a small network and then test it:

1. Close the command prompt window, and shut down both computers.

2. Connect the two PCs with the crossover cable or attach both PCs to the hub with a patch cable.

3. Reboot the computers, and open a command prompt window.

4. Ping your partner's IP address. How do these results differ from your earlier attempt to ping your partner's IP address?

_____

_____

CHALLENGE ACTIVITY (ADDITIONAL 15 MINUTES)

For an additional challenge, try connecting two computers with different operating systems, one with Windows Vista and one with Windows XP.

REVIEW QUESTIONS

1. Where do you configure network adapters and protocols?

_____

2. What two text boxes are used to identify a computer on a workgroup?

_____

_____

3. Other than the IP address, what information is required for TCP/IP communication?

_____

4. What are two ways to use the Ping utility to test a local computer's NIC?

_____

_____

5. What conclusion should you draw from a loopback test that reports dropped packets or an unreachable host?

_____

_____

LAB 8.2 INSPECT CABLES

OBJECTIVES

The goal of this lab is to help you visually inspect a set of cables and use a multimeter to test them. After completing this lab, you will be able to:

◢ Identify two Cat 5e wiring systems

◢ Test cables with a multimeter

◢ Draw pin-outs for cable connectors

◢ Determine whether a cable is a patch cable (also known as a straight-through cable) or a crossover cable

◢ Visually inspect cables and connectors

MATERIALS REQUIRED

This lab requires the following:

◢ A variety of cables, including a patch cable and a crossover cable

◢ A multimeter

◢ Internet access

LAB PREPARATION

Before the lab begins, the instructor or lab assistant needs to do the following:

◢ Verify that Internet access is available.

ACTIVITY BACKGROUND

For a network connection to function properly, the cables must be connected correctly and be without any defects. In this lab, you physically inspect cables and the connector, and then test the cable for continuity and pin-outs using a multimeter.

ESTIMATED COMPLETION TIME: 45 Minutes

8

 Activity

1. Open your browser, and go to **http://www.lanshack.com/**. You can also search the Internet for information about a patch cable diagram, a crossover cable diagram, and a Cat 5e wiring diagram. List the two standards for unshielded twisted pair (UTP) wiring schemes. What Web site did you use?

2. For both wiring schemes, print a wiring diagram for a patch cable and a crossover cable.

Follow these steps to visually inspect cables:

1. Examine the length of the cable for obvious damage, such as a cut or abrasion in the outer sleeve with further damage to the twisted pairs inside. A completely cut strand is an obvious problem, but the conductor inside the cable might be broken even if the insulator is intact. Any visible copper is an indication you need a new cable.

2. Inspect the RJ-45 connectors. In particular, look for exposed twisted pairs between the clear plastic connector and the cable sleeve. This indicates that the cable was assembled

improperly or excessive force was used when pulling on the cable. The cable sleeve should be crimped inside the RJ-45 connector. Sometimes you can identify a nonconforming wiring scheme by noting the color of the insulation through the clear connector, but you should check the cable with a multimeter to verify its condition.

3. Next, verify that the retaining clip on the connector is present. When an assembled cable is pulled, this clip often snags on carpet or other cables and breaks off. This results in a connector that's likely to become loose or fall out of the jack. Worse still, this connection might be intermittent. Some cables have hooded guards to prevent the clip from snagging when pulled, but these guards can cause problems when seating the connector in the jack if the guard has slid too far toward the end of the cable.

4. Test your cables with a multimeter, and fill in Table 8-1.

	End A		End B		Questions About the Cable
Pin #	**Insulator color**	**Pin tied to pin at End B**	**Insulator color**	**Pin tied to pin at End A**	**Is the cable good or bad?**
1					
2					**Wired with what scheme?**
3					
4					
5					**Is the cable a crossover or patch cable?**
6					
7					
8					
Pin #	**Insulator color**	**Pin tied to pin at End B**	**Insulator color**	**Pin tied to pin at End A**	**Is the cable good or bad?**
1					
2					**Wired with what scheme?**
3					
4					
5					**Is the cable a crossover or patch cable?**
6					
7					
8					
Pin #	**Insulator color**	**Pin tied to pin at End B**	**Insulator color**	**Pin tied to pin at End A**	**Is the cable good or bad?**
1					
2					**Wired with what scheme?**
3					
4					
5					**Is the cable a crossover or patch cable?**
6					
7					
8					

(Cable 1, Cable 2, Cable 3 label the three row-groups)

Table 8-1 Pin connections for selected cables

REVIEW QUESTIONS

1. If you can see a copper conductor in a cable, what should you do with the cable?

2. What type of connector is used with Cat 5e cable?

3. Based on your research, which cabling scheme is more common, straight-through or crossover?

4. On a patch cable, pin 3 on one end connects to pin _____ on the opposite end of the cable.

5. On a crossover cable, pin 2 on one end connects to pin _____ on the other end of the cable.

LAB 8.3 COMPARE OPTIONS FOR A HOME LAN

OBJECTIVES

The goal of this lab is to help you research the costs and capabilities of wired and wireless home LANs. After completing this lab, you will be able to:

◢ Research wired and wireless Ethernet

◢ Research 802.11 standards

◢ Identify the strengths and weaknesses of each option

MATERIALS REQUIRED

This lab requires the following:

◢ Internet access

LAB PREPARATION

Before the lab begins, the instructor or lab assistant needs to do the following:

◢ Verify that Internet access is available.

8

ACTIVITY BACKGROUND

As the price of equipment and computers falls, installing a home LAN has become increasingly popular. In this lab, you research wired and wireless Ethernet and determine which option is best in certain situations.

ESTIMATED COMPLETION TIME: 30 Minutes

 Activity

Use your favorite search site to investigate and answer the following questions about wireless LAN standards:

1. List the 802.*x* standards for specifying wireless networks:

2. What industry name is associated with 802.11g?

_____

3. What is the simplest form of a wireless network? What devices are needed to create this type of network, and what mode does this type of network use?

_____

_____

_____

4. What device connects wireless users to a wired network?

_____

5. What standard speeds are supported by 802.11x?

_____

_____

_____

6. What kind of encryption is used with 802.11n?

_____

7. Give four examples of devices (besides PCs) that will probably eventually run on wireless LANs:

_____

_____

_____

_____

8. What does the acronym Wi-Fi stand for?

_____

9. What is the approximate maximum range for 802.11b, 802.11g, and 802.11n technologies?

_____

_____

_____

10. What inherent feature of 802.11b, seen as a major problem by businesses, might affect your decision to use Wi-Fi at home?

_____

_____

11. In the context of how they physically interface with a computer, what are the three basic types of wireless adapters?

_____

_____

_____

12. What mode requires a wireless access point?

_____

13. How many 802.11x devices can be used at one time with a single access point?

_____

14. What radio band and speed does 802.11a use?

_____

15. Which standard offers a faster transfer rate: 802.11a, 802.11b, 802.11g, or 802.11n? List their transfer rates:

_____

_____

_____

_____

16. List the components required to connect four PCs in ad hoc mode and include their prices. List the device and extra expense needed to connect the same four PCs to a cable modem:

_____

_____

_____

_____

_____

Use the Internet to research and answer these questions on an Ethernet home LAN:

1. What is the maximum cable length for a 100BaseT Ethernet LAN?

_____

2. Must you use a hub to connect three PCs? Two PCs? Explain:

_____

_____

_____

8

3. What type of cabling is typically used for 100BaseT?

_____

4. Are special tools required when working with Cat 5e cabling to create patch or crossover cables?

_____

5. What feature of Windows Vista or Windows XP allows more than one computer to share a connection to the Internet?

_____

6. What type of cable connector is used for fast Ethernet?

_____

7. What standard supports a speed of 100 Mbps using two sets of Cat 3 cable?

_____

8. What is the name for a cable that connects a computer to a hub?

_____

9. Suppose you have a LAN consisting of a 100BaseT hub, two computers with 10BaseT NICs, and a computer with a 10/100BaseT NIC. At what speed would this LAN operate? Why?

_____

_____

10. Given a budget of $200 to connect five computers, would you choose a wired system or wireless? Explain your choice:

_____

_____

_____

11. What is the name for a cable that connects a hub to a hub?

_____

12. In theory, if a file is transferred in 4.5 seconds on a fast Ethernet LAN, how long would the same file transfer take on a 10BaseT LAN?

_____

13. Give three examples of ways to physically interface a NIC to a computer:

_____

_____

_____

14. What device can you use to connect two or more PCs to a single cable modem?

_____

15. List the components, including cables, required to connect four PCs. Include the price of each component. List the changes and additional devices required to connect all four PCs to a cable modem and provide a hardware firewall:

_____

_____

_____

_____

_____

REVIEW QUESTIONS

1. Based on your research, does wireless or 100BaseT offer the best performance for the money?

_____

_____

2. Is wireless or 100BaseT easier to configure in a home? Why?

_____

_____

3. What factors dictate the transmission range of 802.11x?

_____

_____

4. What determines the speed of a LAN that consists of both 10 Mbps and 100 Mbps devices?

_____

_____

5. Could you combine a wireless and wired LAN in the same home? Why would you?

_____

_____

_____

8

LAB 8.4 UNDERSTAND THE OSI MODEL

OBJECTIVES

The goal of this lab is to help you understand some of the concepts and principles of networking technology. After completing this lab, you will be able to:

▲ Describe the OSI layers

▲ Apply the OSI layer principles to networking

MATERIALS REQUIRED

This lab requires the following:

▲ Windows Vista/XP operating system

▲ A DHCP server

▲ Internet access

LAB PREPARATION

Before the lab begins, the instructor or lab assistant needs to do the following:

▲ Verify that Windows starts with no errors.

▲ Verify that Internet access is available.

ACTIVITY BACKGROUND

Network architects use a variety of principles and concepts for communication when designing and implementing networks. Collectively, this architectural model is called the OSI (Open Systems Interconnection) model. The OSI model consists of seven layers. As a PC support technician, you do not need to understand network architecture. However, you might find it interesting to know a little about these fundamental concepts, which can help you better understand how the TCP/IP protocols work.

ESTIMATED COMPLETION TIME: 30 Minutes

 Activity

Using the Internet for your research, answer the following questions:

1. What are the seven OSI layers? Enter their names in the empty boxes on the left side of Table 8-2.

2. TCP/IP is a suite of protocols that follow the concepts of the OSI model. The four TCP/IP layers are shown on the right side of Table 8-2. E-mail is one example of a TCP/IP application that works in the Application layer. What are two more examples of applications that work in this layer?

OSI Layer		TCP/IP Protocol Stack Layer
7		Application Layer (E-mail using SMTP and IMAP protocols)
6		
5		
4		Transport Layer (TCP protocol)
3		Internet Layer (IP protocol)
2		Network Interface Layer (Network card using Ethernet protocol)
1		

Table 8-2   Describing the OSI model

3. The TCP protocol works at the Transport layer of TCP/IP. Briefly describe the function of the TCP protocol as used in Internet communications:

_____

_____

4. The IP protocol, working at the Internet layer, is responsible for locating the network and host for a data packet being transmitted by TCP. What is the name of each address on the Internet that identifies a unique network and host?

_____

5. Other than a network card (NIC), what is one more example of a device that works at the Network layer of the TCP/IP stack?

_____

6. Other than IP, what is another example of a protocol that works at the Internet layer of TCP/IP?

_____

7. At what TCP/IP layer does a MAC address function?

_____

8. At what TCP/IP layer does the TLS protocol work?

_____

9. At what TCP/IP layer does the HTTPS protocol work?

_____

8

10. Why do you think TCP/IP is often called a protocol stack rather than a protocol suite?

_____

_____

REVIEW QUESTIONS

1. List the four layers of the protocol stack used when an e-mail client requests e-mail over the Internet:

   _____

   _____

2. What protocol does a Web browser normally use?

   _____

3. At what TCP/IP layer does a Web browser work?

   _____

4. When more than one application is running on a server, how does IP know which service should be presented a data packet?

   _____

5. When configuring a network connection to the Internet, you might need to enter the IP address of the computer, the DNS server, the subnet mask, and the default gateway. Of these four items, which is used to determine whether a remote computer is on the same network or a remote network?

   _____

6. Of the four items in Question 5, which is used to relate a domain name to an IP address?

   _____

LAB 8.5 SHARE RESOURCES ON A NETWORK

OBJECTIVES

The goal of this lab is to understand the process of sharing resources and using these shared resources on a remote computer on the network. After completing this lab, you will be able to:

◿ Share resources

◿ Control access to shared resources

◿ Connect to shared resources

MATERIALS REQUIRED

This lab requires the following:

◿ Two or more Windows Vista/XP computers on a network

◿ Windows installation CD/DVD or installation files

⊿ Local printer attached to computer (optional)

⊿ A workgroup of 2 to 4 students

LAB PREPARATION

Before the lab begins, the instructor or lab assistant needs to do the following:

⊿ Verify that Windows starts with no errors.

⊿ Provide each student with access to the Windows installation files, if needed.

ACTIVITY BACKGROUND

The primary reason to network computers is to make it possible to share files, printers, Internet connections, and other resources. To share resources in a Windows workgroup, you need to make sure each computer has two Windows components installed: Client for Microsoft Networks and File and Print Sharing. Those components are installed by default in Windows XP/Vista. In this lab, you will share resources and connect to these shared resources on another computer.

ESTIMATED COMPLETION TIME: 30 Minutes

 Activity

To share resources on a Windows peer-to-peer network, computers must belong to the same workgroup. Do the following to verify that all computers in your group belong to the same Windows workgroup:

1. Determine the workgroup name (see Lab 8.1). What is the workgroup name for this computer?

   _____

2. Change the workgroup name, if necessary, so that all computers in your group belong to the same workgroup. If you're asked to reboot the PC, wait to do that until after you have installed the components in the next set of steps.

For each computer, follow these steps to see whether Client for Microsoft Networks and File and Print Sharing are installed, and, if necessary, install those components:

In Windows Vista:

1. Click **Start**, right-click the **Network**, and click **Properties** in the shortcut menu. The Network and Sharing Center window opens.

2. Under Sharing and Discovery, ensure that File sharing and Printer sharing are both set to on and that Password protected sharing is set to off.

3. Close all open Windows and reboot.

In Windows XP:

1. Click **Start**, right-click **My Network Places**, and click **Properties** in the shortcut menu. The Network Connections dialog box opens. Click your active connection and click **Change settings of this connection**.

2. If Client for Microsoft Networks is not listed as an installed component, you need to install it. To do that, click **Install**. The Select Network Component Type dialog box opens.

3. Click **Client**, and then click **Add**. The Select Network Client dialog box opens.

4. In the Select Network Client dialog box, click **Microsoft**, and then click **Client for Microsoft Networks** in the right pane. Click **OK** to continue. You return to the Local Area Connection Properties dialog box.

8

5. If File and Print Sharing for Microsoft Networks isn't listed as an installed component in the Network Properties dialog box, you need to install it. To do that, click **Install**. The Select Network Component Type dialog box opens again.

6. Click **Service**, and then click **Add**. The Select Network Service dialog box opens.

7. Click **File and Printer Sharing for Microsoft Networks**, and then click **OK**. If necessary, insert the Windows installation CD or point to the location of the installation files, as instructed in the dialog box that opens. When the service is installed, you return to the Local Area Connection Properties dialog box.

8. Click **OK** to close the Local Area Connection Properties dialog box and save your new settings. The Systems Settings Change message box opens and notifies you that before the settings take effect, the system must be restarted. Click **Yes** to reboot.

Now that you have installed file and printer sharing, you're ready to set up folders or printers on your PC to be shared by others on the network. Follow these steps to share folders and control access to their contents:

In Windows Vista:

1. Open Windows Explorer, and create three folders at the root of drive C named **Reader, Contributor**, and **Co-owner**. Create a text file called **readtest.txt** in the Reader folder, a text file called **contest.txt** in the Contributor folder, and a text file called **cotest.txt** in the Co-owner folder. Type a short sentence in each text file, save your changes, and close the files.

2. In the right pane of Windows Explorer, right-click the **Reader** folder and click **Share. . .** in the shortcut menu. From the drop-down menu, select **Everyone** and click **Add**.

3. Make sure the permission level is set to **Reader** and click **Share**. If Windows opens a UAC, click **Next**. This setting gives users read-only access to all files in the Read folder.

4. Click **Done** to close the Window.

5. Repeat Steps 2 through 4 for the other two folders you just created, selecting the access types associated with their names.

In Windows XP:

1. Open Windows Explorer, and create three folders at the root of drive C named **Read, Full**, and **Change**. Create a text file called **readtest.txt** in the Read folder, a text file called **fulltest.txt** in the Full folder, and a text file called **changetest.txt** in the Change folder. Type a short sentence in each text file, save your changes, and close the files.

2. In the right pane of Windows Explorer, right-click the **Read** folder and click **Sharing and Security** in the shortcut menu. The Read Properties dialog box opens, with the Sharing tab selected.

3. Select **Share this folder** and click the **Permissions** button.

4. When the Permissions for Read window opens, select read in the allow column and click **OK**. This gives everyone permission to read the contents of this folder.

5. Repeat Steps 2 through 4 for the other two folders you just created, selecting the permissions associated with their names. For the Full folder, allow Full Control. For the Change folder, allow Change.

So far, you have verified that all computers sharing resources are in the same workgroup, have installed Windows components to share resources, and have set up the folders to be shared. Now you're ready to use shared resources over the network. Follow these steps to access shared folders:

1. Click **Start** and then click **Network**. The Network window displays a list of computers on the network.

2. Double-click your partner's computer icon to display the shared resources available on that computer.

3. Double-click the **Reader** (**Read** in XP) folder.

4. The contents of the Reader (Read in XP) folder are displayed in Windows Explorer.

5. Double-click **readtest.txt**. The file opens in Notepad. Attempt to save the file, and record your results:

_____

_____

6. Now attempt to save the file in the Documents folder (My Documents in XP) on your computer. Record the results on the following lines. Why did your results in Step 5 differ from your results here?

_____

_____

_____

7. Close Notepad, click the **Network** icon (**My Network Places** in XP) in the left pane of Windows Explorer, and double-click the icon for your partner's computer in the right pane.

8. Open the other two files and attempt to save them in the Documents folder (My Documents in XP) on your computer, and record the results on the following lines. Did you note any difference between the results of Step 5 and 6? If so, explain the difference:

_____

_____

_____

9. Close Notepad, return to the desktop, and open your **Documents** (**My Documents** in XP) folder.

10. Rename the cotest.txt (fulltest.txt in XP) file with a new name of your choice. Attempt to copy, or drag and drop, this file into the Co-owner folder (Full folder in XP) on your partner's PC. Were you successful? Why or why not?

_____

_____

You have just seen how you can use Network to access shared folders on the network. You can make these shared folders appear to be a local drive on your PC, thereby making it more convenient to access these folders. When a shared folder on the network appears to be a local drive on your PC, the folder is called a network drive. Follow these steps to map a network drive and configure it to connect at logon:

1. Click **Start** and click **Network**. A list of computers on your network is listed in the right pane.

2. Double-click the icon for your partner's computer. A list of shared resources is displayed.

3. Right-click the **Co-owner** folder and click **Map Network Drive. . .** in the shortcut menu. In XP, click the **Full** folder and click **Map Network Drive** off the Tools menu. The Map Network Drive dialog box opens.

4. In the Drive drop-down list box, click the drive letter you want to assign to this folder.

5. Click the **Reconnect at logon** check box, and then click **Finish**.

6. The drive is connected, and a window opens displaying the contents of the Full folder. The title bar includes the drive letter you assigned.

7. Check Windows Explorer and verify that the drive letter is now listed under Computer (My Computer in XP).

8. Log off and then log back on to test that the drive reconnects. What did you have to do to reconnect when you logged back on?

_____

_____

REVIEW QUESTIONS

1. What is the main advantage of connecting computers into networks?

_____

_____

2. What term refers to the process of allowing others to use resources on your computer?

_____

3. What two Windows network components must be installed before you can grant others access to resources on your computer and use their resources?

_____

4. How can you provide full access to some of your files while giving read-only access to other files shared on the network?

_____

_____

5. Explain how to allow some people to make changes to files in shared folders while allowing others to just view and read the contents of the same folder:

_____

_____

_____

_____

LAB 8.6 SIMULATE MODEM PROBLEMS

OBJECTIVES

The goal of this lab is to help you simulate, diagnose, and remedy common modem problems. After completing this lab, you will be able to:

◢ Diagnose problems with a modem

◢ Remedy problems with a modem

MATERIALS REQUIRED

This lab requires the following:

⊿ Windows XP operating system

⊿ A modem installed in a PC and connected to a phone line

⊿ A PC toolkit with antistatic ground strap

⊿ Modem installation drivers

⊿ Windows installation CD/DVD or installation files

⊿ A standard phone

⊿ A lab partner with whom you can swap PCs

LAB PREPARATION

Before the lab begins, the instructor or lab assistant needs to do the following:

⊿ Verify that Windows starts with no errors.

⊿ Provide each student with access to the Windows installation files, if needed.

ACTIVITY BACKGROUND

Although high-speed connections are quickly growing in popularity, dial-up are still common in many rural areas where high-speed Internet is not available. Dial-up connections are notoriously unreliable. One of the challenges of troubleshooting these connections is determining whether a dial-up failure is related to a problem with the modem or the phone line. In this lab, you diagnose and remedy common modem problems. Mastering these skills makes it easier for you to determine when the modem is the source of trouble in a dial-up connection.

ESTIMATED COMPLETION TIME: 90 Minutes

 Activity

1. To verify that your modem is working, start HyperTerminal, dial any reliable phone number, and listen for the sound of the modem dialing and attempting to connect. (The actual connection isn't necessary at this point.) Disconnect the call and close HyperTerminal.

2. Sabotage your modem by introducing one of these problems:

   ⊿ If your modem has jumpers or DIP switches, record the original settings on the following lines, and then change the settings:

   _____

   _____

   ⊿ In BIOS or Device Manager, disable the modem's COM port.

   ⊿ Loosen the modem card in the expansion slot so that it doesn't make good contact.

   ⊿ Unplug the phone cord from the wall.

   ⊿ Change the port to which the phone line connects on the back of the modem.

   ⊿ Uninstall the modem in Device Manager.

   ⊿ Change or disable the IRQ for the modem.

   ⊿ Using Device Manager, disable the modem in the current hardware configuration.

8

3. Swap PCs with your partner, and then troubleshoot and repair your partner's PC.

4. Answer these questions:

◢ What is the initial symptom of a problem as a user would describe it?

_____

_____

◢ How did you discover the source of the problem?

_____

_____

_____

_____

◢ What did you do to solve the problem?

_____

_____

_____

_____

5. Introduce another problem from the list in Step 2, and swap again. Continue this process until you have introduced and remedied all the problems listed in Step 2.

6. Suppose a user says, "I can't dial out using my modem." List the first three things you would check, in the order you would check them:

_____

_____

_____

REVIEW QUESTIONS

1. What was the easiest problem to diagnose and why?

_____

_____

2. Which problems aren't apparent in Device Manager but would result in no dial tone when dialing?

_____

_____

3. Did all the problems listed in Step 2 actually prevent the modem from working? Which (if any) did not?

_____

_____

4. What was the simplest way to determine whether there was definitely a dial tone?

_____

_____

5. Why are modems much less common in computers today?

_____

_____

LAB 8.7 CRITICAL THINKING: USE NETBEUI INSTEAD OF TCP/IP

OBJECTIVES

Most networks use the TCP/IP network protocol suite. The goal of this lab is to demonstrate how to replace TCP/IP with NetBEUI. After completing this lab, you will be able to:

◢ Install NetBEUI

◢ Remove TCP/IP

◢ Observe the results of using NetBEUI

MATERIALS REQUIRED

This lab requires the following:

◢ Windows XP operating system

◢ A NIC configured to use only TCP/IP

◢ IP address information or a DHCP server on the network

◢ Internet access

◢ Windows XP Professional installation CD or installation files

◢ A network workgroup consisting of two computers

◢ A workgroup of 2 to 4 students

LAB PREPARATION

Before the lab begins, the instructor or lab assistant needs to do the following:

◢ Verify that Windows starts with no errors.

◢ Provide each student with access to the Windows installation files, if needed.

◢ Verify that Internet access is available.

8

ACTIVITY BACKGROUND

TCP/IP is probably the network protocol you're most familiar with, but it's not the only network protocol, nor is it the best for all situations. IBM originally developed NetBIOS Enhanced User Interface (NetBEUI) to make it possible to use NetBIOS names as official network addresses. NetBEUI is faster than TCP/IP and much easier to configure. Its main disadvantage is that it's nonroutable (meaning it can communicate only with computers on its network). In this lab, you configure one computer in your workgroup to use NetBEUI, and then observe the effect of this change on both computers in the workgroup. Then you use NetBEUI as the only network protocol in your workgroup.

ESTIMATED COMPLETION TIME: 30 Minutes

 Activity

First, you need to determine what the network looks like before you install NetBEUI and remove TCP/IP. Follow these steps:

1. On one of the two computers in the workgroup, open My Network Places via Windows Explorer. Click **View workgroup computers**. A list of computers on your network is displayed. Take and print a screen shot of this list.

> **Notes** To take a screen shot, press **Alt+Print Screen**, which copies the window into the Clipboard. Open Windows Paint, and click **Edit, Paste** from the menu. To print the screen shot, click **File, Print** from the menu. Close Windows Paint without saving your work.

2. Repeat Step 1 for the other computer on your network.

Now follow these steps to install NetBEUI as the network protocol on one of the computers in your workgroup:

1. Insert the Windows XP installation CD and locate the Valueadd\MSFT\Net\NetBEUI folder.
2. Copy the Nbf.sys file to the C:\System32\Drivers folder and copy the Netnbf.inf file to the C:\Windows\Inf folder. (*Note:* The Inf folder is hidden by default.)
3. In Windows Explorer, right-click **My Network Places** and click **Properties** in the shortcut menu. The Network Connections window opens.
4. Right-click the **Local Area Connection** icon and click **Properties** in the shortcut menu. The Local Area Connection Properties dialog box opens.
5. Click **Install**. The Select Network Component Type dialog box opens.
6. Click **Protocol**, and then click **Add**. The Select Network Protocol dialog box opens.
7. Click **NetBEUI Protocol**, and then click **OK**. The Select Network Protocol and Select Network Component Type dialog boxes close.

Your next job is to uninstall TCP/IP on the computer where you installed NetBEUI. You begin by recording the TCP/IP configuration information for that computer, and then uninstall TCP/IP. (You need this configuration information when you reinstall TCP/IP at the end of this lab.) Follow these steps:

1. Right-click **My Network Places** and click **Properties** in the shortcut menu. The Network Connections or Network and Dial-Up Connections window opens.
2. Right-click the **Local Area Connection** icon and click **Properties** in the shortcut menu. The Local Area Connection Properties dialog box opens.

3. Click **Internet Protocol (TCP/IP)** in the list of components, and then click **Properties**. The TCP/IP Properties dialog box opens.

4. Record the configuration information available in this window:

_____

_____

_____

_____

5. Click **Cancel** to close the TCP/IP Properties dialog box.

6. In the Local Area Connection Properties dialog box, click **Internet Protocol (TCP/IP)**, and then click **Uninstall**. A message appears informing you that you're about to remove the protocol from all connections.

7. Click **Yes** to continue. Internet Protocol (TCP/IP) is removed from the Local Area Connection Properties dialog box.

8. The Local Network dialog box opens and informs you that you must restart the computer before the changes can take effect.

9. Click **Yes** to restart the computer.

Follow these steps to observe the effects of using NetBEUI:

1. Go to the computer that you didn't alter (the computer still running TCP/IP).

2. If it's not already open, open the **My Network Places** window. Click **View workgroup computers** and answer these questions:

   ◢ What computers are displayed?

   _____

   _____

   _____

   _____

   ◢ Compare the current screen to the screen shot you created earlier. What computers are missing?

   _____

   _____

   ◢ Why are they missing?

   _____

   _____

3. Go to the computer where you installed NetBEUI.

8

4. Open My Network Places, and then click **View workgroup computers** (Windows XP). Answer the following questions:

◢ What computers are displayed?

_____

_____

_____

_____

◢ Compare the current screen to the screen shot you created earlier. What computers are missing?

_____

_____

◢ Why are they missing?

_____

_____

5. Press **F5** to refresh the list of computers on the network. Did any new ones appear? Why or why not?

_____

_____

_____

_____

6. On the computer where you installed NetBEUI, attempt to connect to the Internet, and then answer these questions:

◢ What message did you receive?

_____

_____

_____

_____

◢ Why do you think you were unable to connect to the Internet?

_____

_____

Next, you use some network utilities to test your network connections. You start by running a loopback ping test, as you did in Lab 8.1. Follow these steps:

1. On the computer running TCP/IP (the one you didn't change), open a command prompt window, type **ping 127.0.0.1**, and press **Enter**. Record the results of the loopback test:

_____

_____

_____

2. Next, you use the Ipconfig utility to test network configuration and connectivity. Type **ipconfig /all** and press **Enter**. Record the results of the command:

_____

_____

_____

3. On the computer where you installed NetBEUI, open a command prompt window, and then repeat Steps 1 and 2. Record the results. Why did you get these results?

_____

_____

_____

_____

Follow these steps to reinstall TCP/IP:

1. On the computer where you installed NetBEUI, right-click **My Network Places** and click **Properties** in the shortcut menu. The Network Connections or Network and Dial-up Connections window opens.

2. Right-click the **Local Area Connection** icon and click **Properties** in the shortcut menu. The Local Area Connection Properties dialog box opens.

3. Click **Install**. The Select Network Component Type dialog box opens.

4. Click **Protocol**, and then click **Add**. The Select Network Protocol dialog box opens.

5. Click **TCP/IP Protocol**, and then click **OK**. The Select Network Protocol and Select Network Component Type dialog boxes close.

6. The Local Network dialog box opens and informs you that you must restart the computer before the changes can take effect. Click **Yes** to restart the computer.

You've finished reinstalling TCP/IP. Now you need to reconfigure the necessary TCP/IP settings. Follow these steps:

1. Right-click **My Network Places** and click **Properties** in the shortcut menu. The Network Connections or Network and Dial-Up Connections window opens.

2. Right-click the **Local Area Connection** icon and click **Properties** in the shortcut menu. The Local Area Connection Properties dialog box opens.

3. Click **Internet Protocol (TCP/IP)**, and then click **Properties**. The Internet Protocol (TCP/IP) Properties dialog box opens.

4. Reconfigure the settings to match the ones you recorded earlier in this lab.

5. Click **OK** twice to close the Internet Protocol (TCP/IP) Properties and Local Area Connection Properties dialog boxes and save your settings.

6. Test your settings by connecting to another computer or the Internet.

CHALLENGE ACTIVITY (ADDITIONAL 20 MINUTES)

1. Install NetBEUI and remove TCP/IP on one more computer in your workgroup so that NetBEUI is the only network protocol installed on two computers.

2. Using NetBEUI, transfer files from one computer to the other.

3. Install TCP/IP and configure it, and then remove NetBEUI as an installed networking protocol.

REVIEW QUESTIONS

1. Is it possible to have more than one network protocol installed on the same network? Explain how you arrived at your answer:

   _____

   _____

   _____

2. If you had to access the Internet from your computer, which protocol would you use?

   _____

3. What features of NetBEUI make it appealing for a small network that doesn't need Internet access?

   _____

   _____

4. Of the two network protocols covered in this lab, which is better suited for trouble-shooting problems? Why?

   _____

   _____

5. What type of computer name is used on a NetBEUI network?

   _____

Networking Practices

Labs included in this chapter:

- **Lab 9.1:** Install Software to Delete Cookies
- **Lab 9.2:** Use FTP to Download a Browser
- **Lab 9.3:** Configure and Use Remote Access Service
- **Lab 9.4:** Use Remote Desktop
- **Lab 9.5:** Share an Internet Connection
- **Lab 9.6:** Set Up a Wireless Router
- **Lab 9.7:** Troubleshoot with TCP/IP Utilities
- **Lab 9.8:** Solve Network Connectivity Problems

LAB 9.1 INSTALL SOFTWARE TO DELETE COOKIES

OBJECTIVES

The goal of this lab is to help you install software that deletes cookies each time you boot your computer. After completing this lab, you will be able to:

◢ Locate, download, and install the software

◢ Delete cookies using the software you downloaded

MATERIALS REQUIRED

This lab requires the following:

◢ Internet access

◢ Windows Vista/XP operating system

LAB PREPARATION

Before the lab begins, the instructor or lab assistant needs to do the following:

◢ Verify that Windows starts with no errors.

◢ Verify that Internet access is available.

ACTIVITY BACKGROUND

When you visit certain Web sites, cookies are placed on your system to collect information about you, including what Web sites you visit. Although cookies can be useful by storing your preferences for when you revisit sites, they can also be a security risk, passing on information you don't want to make accessible to others. For example, this information could be passed on to companies that then sell it to a mailing list or use it for advertising purposes. Several utilities on the market can clean cookies from your computer. One is Webroot's Window Washer, which is available for trial download. In this lab, you install Window Washer and use it to delete cookies.

> **ESTIMATED COMPLETION TIME: 45 Minutes**

 Activity

Follow these steps to download Webroot's Window Washer software. As you know, Web sites change often, so your steps might differ slightly from the following:

1. Open your browser, and go to **www.webroot.com**.
2. Find the Free Downloads section.
3. Scroll down and click the link to download a free trial of Window Washer.
4. The File Download – Security Warning dialog box opens, indicating that you have chosen to download the installation file for Window Washer. Click the **Run** button.

5. A dialog box opens indicating the progress of the installation. Depending on your connection speed, it could take a few minutes. While you're waiting, look on the Webroot site for information about Window Washer and record a short description of what it does:

_____

_____

_____

_____

6. When the download is finished, an Internet Explorer - Security Warning dialog box opens. Click **Run** to verify that you want to install and run the trial version of Window Washer.

7. If a UAC dialog box opens, click **Continue**.

8. The Window Washer installation program launches. In the first window, click **I Agree** to accept the license agreement.

9. Select the **Typical Installation** option, if necessary, and then click **Next**. The Installation Status window shows the progress of the installation. When a completion message is displayed, click **Next**.

10. In the Custom Wash Item Detection window, leave the defaults selected, and then click **Next**. Leave the e-mail check box and text box blank, and then click **Next**.

11. In the Successful Installation window, click to clear **Run Window Washer**, and then click **Finished**.

Follow these steps to use Window Washer to delete cookies:

1. Open Internet Explorer, if necessary, and browse the Web for a couple of minutes, visiting a variety of sites, such as news sites and commercial sites. Click a few links and ads on those sites. Close Internet Explorer.

2. Open Windows Explorer, and then open the **Cookies** folder, which is usually located under C:\Users*username*\AppData\Roaming\Microsoft\Windows\Cookies (C:\Documents and Settings*username* in Windows XP). If the Cookies folder is hidden, open the Folder Options dialog box, select the **View** tab, and clear the **Hide protected operating system files** check box. Cookies are stored as text files.

   ◢ How many cookies are listed?

   _____

   ◢ What sites appear to have stored cookies on your computer?

   _____

   _____

   _____

3. Click **Start**, point to **All Programs**, and then click **Webroot**. If the Webroot folder does not open automatically, click **Window Washer**.

4. On the right side of the window, notice that no data is listed under Wash Statistics for the Last wash item. Click the **Wash My Computer Now** button.

5. If a Ready to Wash window opens, click **Start**.

6. The Wash screen opens. When the Washing completed screen appears, click **Finished**.

9

7. In Windows Explorer, open the **Cookies** folder again to verify that the cookies are gone.

8. When you're finished, close any open windows.

If you still see cookies in the Cookies folder after you run Window Washer, you might need to verify that you selected all the options indicating which files you want to delete before running Window Washer again.

REVIEW QUESTIONS

1. What other items can Window Washer clean besides cookies?

   _____

   _____

2. List some reasons you might not want cookies on your system:

   _____

   _____

   _____

3. What information did the Webroot site provide about how Window Washer works?

   _____

   _____

4. Can you specify your own wash items—that is, items that aren't already listed in Window Washer? Explain:

   _____

   _____

5. How might cookies be useful?

   _____

   _____

LAB 9.2 USE FTP TO DOWNLOAD A BROWSER

OBJECTIVES

The goal of this lab is to help you use FTP from the command prompt to download a browser. After completing this lab, you will be able to:

⊿ Use common FTP commands from a command prompt

⊿ Download a browser via FTP

MATERIALS REQUIRED

This lab requires the following:

⊿ Windows Vista/XP operating system

⊿ Internet access

LAB PREPARATION

Before the lab begins, the instructor or lab assistant needs to do the following:

◢ Verify that Windows starts with no errors.

◢ Verify that Internet access is available.

ACTIVITY BACKGROUND

File Transfer Protocol (FTP) is a quick and easy way to transfer files over the Internet without converting them to ASCII text first. You might use FTP when transmitting files too large to be sent as e-mail attachments, for example. For this lab, imagine that your Web browser has been rendered inoperable by a virus or because you accidentally deleted some vital files, but you can still connect to the Internet. How can you get your browser back? If you're using a network, it might be possible for you to go to another computer on the network, use that computer's browser to download a new browser, and then transfer the downloaded browser file to your computer. Another option is to reinstall Windows on your computer, a process that installs Internet Explorer. However, if these options aren't available or practical, you can use FTP to download a browser. If you have no user-friendly GUI FTP software installed on your computer, you can use FTP from the command prompt. In this lab, you use FTP commands from the command prompt to locate and download the latest version of Netscape.

ESTIMATED COMPLETION TIME: 45 Minutes

 Activity

Follow these steps to connect to the Netscape FTP site from a command prompt and download the latest version of the Netscape browser:

1. When you download the browser, you should store the file in a location on your hard drive that's easy to find. In Windows Explorer, create a folder on your C drive called **Downloads**.

2. Leave Windows Explorer open, and open a command prompt window.

3. When the command prompt window opens, the C:\Users*username* directory (C:\Documents and Settings*username* in Windows XP) is probably the active directory. When you use FTP, the files you download are stored in whatever directory was active when you began the session. To change to the Downloads directory, type **cd c:\downloads** and press **Enter**.

4. When the Downloads directory is active, type **ftp** and press **Enter**. How did the command prompt change?

5. To enter the Netscape FTP site, type **open ftp.netscape.com** and press **Enter**.

6. A message is displayed, stating that you're connected to the Netscape site and the server is ready, followed by a user prompt. Many sites, including this one, allow limited access to the site via an anonymous logon. Type **anonymous** at the user prompt and press **Enter**.

7. A message asks you to specify your password. Type **anonymous** and press **Enter**. What message do you see?

8. You now have access to certain files on the Netscape FTP site. Browse to the location of the latest version of the Netscape browser. Note which options such as operating systems, versions, and languages are available. Use the **dir** command to list the contents of various directories and the **cd** command to change directories as necessary. If necessary, unblock the Windows Firewall and respond to the UAC to continue. At the time of this writing, Netscape 9.0 was located in the path *ftp.netscape.com/pub/netscape9/ en-US/9.0/windows/win32/netscape-navigator-9.0.exe*. The names and locations of downloadable files can change as versions and site structure change, so you might find the file stored in a different directory. The exact filename might be different as well, depending on what the most current browser version is. If the location or name of the latest version of the browser setup file differs from the one mentioned earlier in this step, record the correct information here:

---

9. After you have located the file, type **bin** and press **Enter**. This command sets the download mode to specify that you want the file downloaded as a binary (not ASCII) file.

10. To download the file, type **get netscape-navigator-9.0.exe** (substituting the correct filename if you noted a different one in Step 8). Remember that FTP commands are case sensitive.

11. Press **Enter**. What messages are displayed?

---

12. Return to Windows Explorer (in XP, click **View, Refresh** from the menu), open the **Downloads** folder, and verify that the file was downloaded successfully.

13. To verify that the browser setup program you downloaded works, double-click the file you downloaded. The setup program opens.

14. At this point, you can follow the instructions to install the browser or simply close the setup program.

15. Return to the command prompt window. Type **bye** and press **Enter** to close the FTP session and close any open windows.

REVIEW QUESTIONS

1. List all the FTP commands you used in this lab, with a short description of each:

---

2. In what mode did you download the browser setup file? Why is using this mode necessary?

_____

_____

_____

_____

3. For what other operating systems and languages is Netscape available for download?

_____

_____

4. If you were using FTP to upload a text file created in Notepad, which mode (ASCII or binary) should you choose to upload it and why?

_____

_____

5. You're downloading FileABC.txt from the FTP site of CompanyXYZ.com. The file is located in the /pub/documentation/ folder of that site and uses *guest* as both the username and password. Your FTP client defaults to binary mode for download. List in order all the commands you would use to open the FTP connection, download the file, and close the connection:

_____

_____

_____

_____

_____

_____

LAB 9.3 CONFIGURE AND USE REMOTE ACCESS SERVICE

OBJECTIVES

The goal of this lab is to give you practice using Remote Access Service to allow dial-up access to a computer. After completing this lab, you will be able to:

◢ Set up Remote Access Service

◢ Configure Remote Access Service

◢ Connect to a network through a dial-up connection

MATERIALS REQUIRED

This lab requires the following:

◢ Two Windows XP computers

◢ A modem and telephone line for each computer

◢ A workgroup of 2 to 4 students

9

LAB PREPARATION

Before the lab begins, the instructor or lab assistant needs to do the following:

⊿ Verify that Windows starts with no errors.

⊿ Provide students with the phone numbers of both machines.

ACTIVITY BACKGROUND

You can set up your Windows computer to receive dial-up connections from other comput-ers. You might want to do this if you travel and want to be able to transfer files to and from your home computer while away. You can allow incoming calls by default by using Remote Access Service (RAS). In this lab, you connect two Windows XP machines through a dial-up connection.

ESTIMATED COMPLETION TIME: 45 Minutes

 Activity

Follow these steps to configure one machine to accept a remote connection:

1. Click **Start**, right-click **My Network Places,** and click **Properties.** The Network Connections window opens.

2. Click **Create a new connection,** and then click **Next.**

3. Click **Set up an advanced connection,** and then click **Next.**

4. Click **Accept incoming connections,** and then click **Next** again.

5. Click to select the modem installed in your machine, and then click **Next.**

6. Click **Do not allow virtual private connections,** and then click **Next.**

7. Select the user that you want to use this connection and click **Add.** Enter the informa-tion and record it here:

_____

8. Click **Next** to advance to the next screen.

9. Click **Next** in the Networking Software screen to accept the default settings.

10. Finally, click **Finish.**

Follow these steps to connect remotely to your first machine:

1. Click **Start**, right-click **My Network Places,** and click **Properties.** The Network Connections window opens.

2. Click **Create a new connection,** and then click **Next.**

3. Click **Connect to the network at my workplace,** and then click **Next.**

4. Click **Dial-up connection,** and then click **Next.**

5. Enter a name for this connection, and then click **Next.**

6. Next, enter the phone number of the machine accepting the remote connection.

7. If prompted, click **Anyone's use** to specify how this connection can be used, and then click **Next.**

8. Click **Finish** to complete the wizard. A window for the new connection should open automatically.

9. Enter the name and password of the new user account you created while configuring the first machine.

10. Finally, click **Dial** to connect to the remote machine. How long did it take to connect?

_____

11. When you're finished, disconnect from the remote machine and close any open windows.

CRITICAL THINKING (ADDITIONAL 15 MINUTES)

Change the workgroup identity on one of the computers so that the two computers no longer belong to the same workgroup. Attempt to connect and transfer files. At what point did the process fail?

_____

_____

REVIEW QUESTIONS

1. Which Windows XP component handles dial-up connections?

_____

2. Why doesn't remote access work if both computers aren't on the same workgroup?

_____

3. Why might you need to have more than one object in the Dial-up section of the Network Connections window?

_____

_____

4. How does each computer disconnect from a Dial-Up Server session?

_____

_____

5. Can you think of any disadvantages of connecting through RAS?

_____

_____

LAB 9.4 USE REMOTE DESKTOP

9

OBJECTIVES

The goal of this lab is to learn how to log on to another computer remotely by using Windows Remote Desktop. After completing this lab, you will be able to:

▲ Configure Remote Desktop

▲ Use Remote Desktop to log on to another computer remotely

MATERIALS REQUIRED

This lab requires the following:

▲ Windows Vista/XP Professional operating system

▲ A network workgroup consisting of two computers

▲ A workgroup of 2 to 4 students

LAB PREPARATION

Before the lab begins, the instructor or lab assistant needs to do the following:

▲ Verify that Windows starts with no errors.

▲ Verify that a network connection is available.

ACTIVITY BACKGROUND

Windows allows users to connect remotely from other Windows machines. With a remote connection, you can control a computer from another location, such as work or home. This feature might be useful if you need to access files or programs from another location, for example. In this lab, you configure one computer to accept a remote connection, and then connect to it from another machine.

ESTIMATED COMPLETION TIME: 30 Minutes

 Activity

To configure a computer to accept a remote connection, follow these steps:

1. Log on to an account with administrative privileges. Write down the account name and password:

   _____

2. To determine the computer name, open Control Panel, click **System and Maintenance** (**Performance and Maintenance** in XP), and click **System**. In XP, click the **Computer Name** tab. Write down the computer name:

   _____

3. In Vista, click **Remote settings** in the System window and click **Continue** if a UAC dialog box opens. If necessary, click the **Remote** tab, and then click **Allow connections from computers running any version of Remote Desktop (less secure)**. Note that you would click **Allow users to connect remotely to this computer** in XP. See Figure 9-1.

   > **Notes** The administrator already has access. You could grant access to other users with the Select Users (Select Remote Users in XP) button.

4. Click **OK** in the System Properties dialog box and log off the system. You must be logged off before you can remotely log on.

To establish a remote connection, follow these steps:

1. Move to another computer on the same network, and log on.

2. Click **Start**, click **All Programs**, click **Accessories** (in XP SP1 or earlier, click **Communications**), and click **Remote Desktop Connection**.

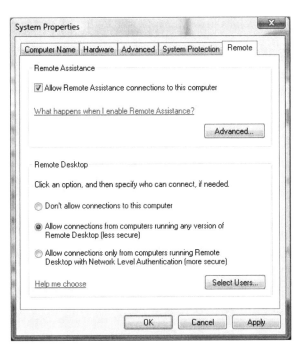

Figure 9-1 Allowing users to connect remotely to a computer
Courtesy: Course Technology/Cengage Learning

> **Notes** Windows Firewall in XP SP2 or later blocks the port used by remote access if the Don't allow exceptions check box is selected when configuring firewall settings.

3. Enter the computer name (of the remote computer) or its IP address (which you learned how to determine in Lab 8.1), and then click **Connect**.

4. Log on to the other computer remotely with the account information you wrote down earlier.

5. When you're finished, log off to close the connection.

REVIEW QUESTIONS

1. Describe two situations when you might want to use Remote Desktop Connection:

_____

_____

_____

_____

2. How can you tell if you are connected remotely to another computer?

_____

3. How can you determine the name of the remote computer before connecting?

_____

_____

4. How might other programs, such as firewalls, interfere with a remote connection?

_____

_____

_____

LAB 9.5 SHARE AN INTERNET CONNECTION

OBJECTIVES

The goal of this lab is to share an Internet connection between two computers using Windows ICS. After completing this lab, you will be able to:

◢ Configure two computers to use ICS

MATERIALS REQUIRED

This lab requires the following:

◢ Two computers running the Windows Vista operating system

◢ Internet access

LAB PREPARATION

Before the lab begins, the instructor or lab assistant needs to do the following:

◢ Verify that Windows starts with no errors.

◢ Verify that Internet access is available.

ACTIVITY BACKGROUND

In Lab 8.1, you learned how to connect two computers with a single crossover cable or a pair of patch cables and a hub. Now let's look at how to connect two or more computers in a small network so they can share this one Internet connection. The computer with the direct connection to the Internet will act as the host and share its connection.

Windows Internet Connection Sharing (ICS) is designed to manage these types of connections. Using ICS, the host computer stands as a gateway between the network and the Internet and ICS manages the gateway. These types of connections, which don't use a router as a gateway, were popular when routers were quite expensive. Now that routers are relatively inexpensive, one computer serving as a gateway to the Internet for other computers is not as popular as it once was.

ESTIMATED COMPLETION TIME: 20 Minutes

 Activity

Follow these steps to configure Windows on two computers so that they can share the Internet connection:

1. Depending how you connect to the Internet, your gateway computer (the one connected directly to the Internet) will probably require two network cards: one to connect to the Internet and the other to the other computer. If necessary, add a second network card to this computer.

2. Log on as Administrator on your gateway computer, open the Network and Sharing Center, and click **Manage network connections**. The Network Connections window opens.

3. Right-click the connection that you want to share, select **Properties** from the shortcut menu, and respond to the UAC box. In the Properties box, click the **Sharing** tab (see the left side of Figure 9-2).

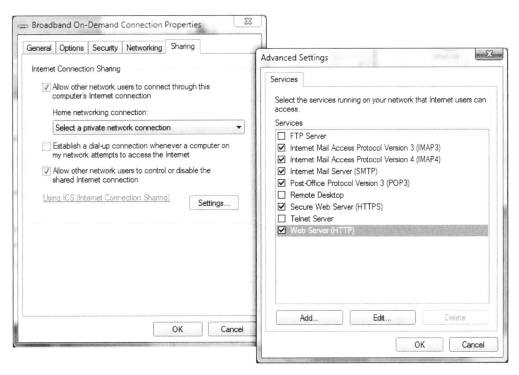

Figure 9-2   Allow others on your network to use this Internet connection
Courtesy: Course Technology/Cengage Learning

4. Check **Allow other network users to connect through this computer's Internet connection.** You can check the second box if you want to allow users on the network to be able to control the shared connection.

5. Click **Settings** to open the Advanced Settings window shown on the right side of Figure 9-2. Select the services that you want to allow Internet users to access on your network. A dialog box appears; click **OK** to close the box. Do this for each service you want to share.

6. Click **OK** twice to close both boxes.

The disadvantage of this type of shared connection is that the host computer must always be running for another computer on the network to reach the Internet. Another disadvantage is this network is not as secure as it would be if we had a hardware firewall installed. Both these problems can be solved by using a router in our network. How to set up a router on a network is covered in Lab 9.6.

1. Log on to the other computer and test the Internet connection by opening your browser and going on the Internet.

2. Can both computers access the Internet at the same time?

_____

3. What happens to the Internet connection when no one is logged on the gateway computer?

_____

9

4. What happens to the Internet connection when the gateway computer is shut down altogether?

_____

5. When you're finished, shut down both systems and remove the second network card from the gateway computer.

REVIEW QUESTIONS

1. What are two disadvantages of using ICS?

_____

_____

2. What device has mostly eliminated the need for ICS?

_____

3. If you had two computers, a desktop and a laptop, which would be the better choice to act as the gateway? Why?

_____

_____

4. Why are two network cards required on the gateway computer?

_____

_____

LAB 9.6 SET UP A WIRELESS ROUTER

OBJECTIVES

The goal of this lab is to install and configure a wireless router. After completing this lab, you will be able to:

◢ Install and configure a wireless router

◢ Configure PCs to connect to a wireless router

MATERIALS REQUIRED

This lab requires the following:

◢ Windows Vista/XP computer designated for this lab

◢ A wireless router with setup CD or user's manual

◢ A wireless NIC

LAB PREPARATION

Before the lab begins, the instructor or lab assistant needs to do the following:

◢ Verify that Windows starts with no errors.

◢ Verify that a network connection is available.

ACTIVITY BACKGROUND

In Lab 9.5, you learned how to share an Internet connection using ICS. A more popular way to share a connection is to use a router. Routers offer several advantages over ICS, including:

⏶ A gateway computer will not be a bottleneck to slow down performance for other computers using the Internet.

⏶ Access to the Internet does not depend on a gateway computer being turned on.

⏶ The router can add additional security by providing a hardware firewall and limiting access to the Internet.

⏶ The router can provide additional features such as functioning as a DHCP server.

In this lab, you will set up and configure a wireless router and then connect to it from a remote system.

ESTIMATED COMPLETION TIME: 30 Minutes

Activity

Follow these steps to set up your router:

1. If your router comes with a setup CD (see Figure 9-3), run the setup program on one of your computers on the network (it doesn't matter which one). Follow the instructions on the setup screen or in the accompanying user's manual to disconnect the Internet connection from your host computer and connect it to the router.

Figure 9-3 A typical wireless router with setup CD and instruction manual
Courtesy: Course Technology/Cengage Learning

2. Connect the computers on your network to the router. A computer can connect directly to a network port on the router (see Figure 9-4), or you can connect through a switch or hub to the router. Plug in the router and turn it on.

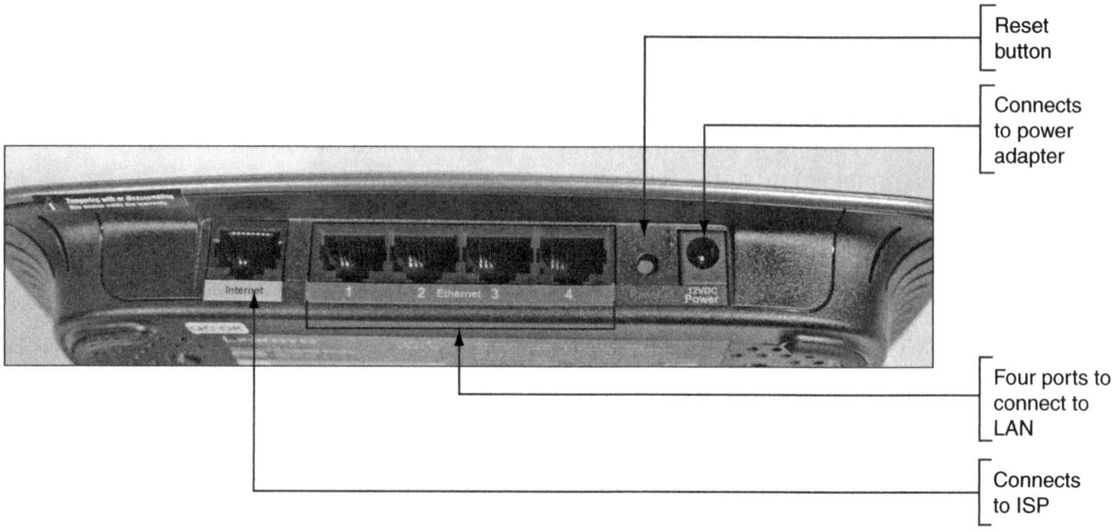

Reset
button

Connects
to power
adapter

Four ports to
connect to
LAN

Connects
to ISP

Figure 9-4 Connectors and ports on the back of a Linksys router
Courtesy: Course Technology/Cengage Learning

3. Firmware on the router (which can be flashed for updates) contains a configuration program that you access using a Web browser from anywhere on the network. In your browser address box, enter the IP address of the router (for our router, it's 192.168.1.1) and press **Enter**. What is the name and IP address for your router?

_____

4. You'll probably be required to sign in to the utility using a default password. The first thing you want to do is reset this password so that others cannot change your router setup. What is your new router password?

_____

5. The main Setup window appears, as shown in Figure 9-5. For most situations, the default settings on this and other screens should work without any changes. The setup program will take you through the process of configuring the router. After you've configured the router, you might have to turn your cable or DSL modem off and back on so that it correctly syncs up with the router. What basic steps did the setup program have you follow to configure the router?

_____

_____

_____

_____

6. Spend some time examining the various features of your router. What security features does it appear to have?

_____

_____

_____

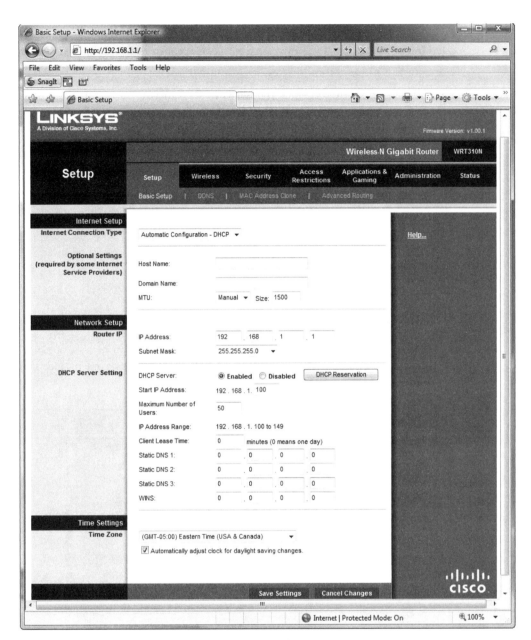

Figure 9-5 Basic Setup screen used to configure a Linksys router
Courtesy: Course Technology/Cengage Learning

7. What is the IP address of the router on the ISP network?

_____

_____

8. Why is it necessary for the router to have two IP addresses?

_____

_____

_____

Follow these steps to connect to your wireless router from another PC.

1. On your computer, attach your wireless NIC and install the necessary drivers.

2. Boot the computer and log on as Administrator.

3. Mouse over or double-click the network icon in your notification area. Vista reports when wireless networks are available (see Figure 9-6).

Figure 9-6   Windows reports when wireless networks are available
Courtesy: Course Technology/Cengage Learning

4. Click **Connect to a network**. A list of available networks appears (see Figure 9-7). List all the networks that are available:

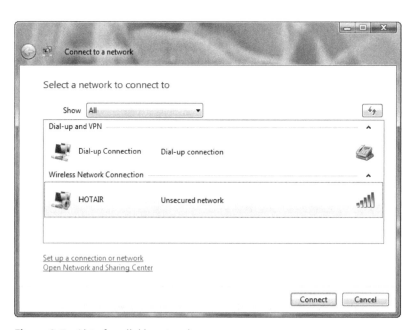

Figure 9-7   List of available networks
Courtesy: Course Technology/Cengage Learning

5. If you select an unsecured network, Vista warns you about sending information over it. Click **Connect Anyway**.

6. Vista reports the connection is made using the window in Figure 9-8. If you are comfortable with Vista automatically connecting to this network in the future, check **Save this network**. Close the window. If you mouse over the network icon in the notification area or double-click it, you can see the network to which you are connected.

Figure 9-8   Decide if you want to save this network connection
Courtesy: Course Technology/Cengage Learning

7. To verify firewall settings and check for errors, open the Network and Sharing Center
window (see Figure 9-9). Verify that Vista has configured the network as a public network
and that Sharing and Discovery settings are all turned off. In the figure, you can see there is
a problem with the Internet connection from the HOTAIR network to the Internet.

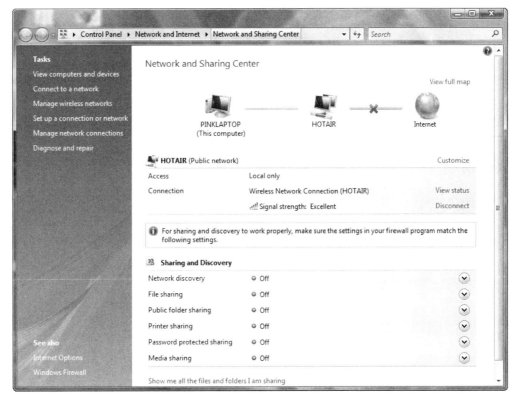

Figure 9-9   Verify that your connection is secure
Courtesy: Course Technology/Cengage Learning

9

8. Open your browser to test the connection.

9. What speed is your Wireless connection? How does this compare with your wired network?

_____

_____

10. When you're finished, reset and uninstall the wireless router and NIC.

REVIEW QUESTIONS

1. What are some of the additional features available on your router?

_____

_____

2. Name two ways your router can limit Internet access:

_____

_____

3. Name one advantage and one disadvantage of a wireless connection compared to a wired network:

_____

_____

4. Most wireless routers have a reset switch. Give an example of when this might be useful:

_____

_____

LAB 9.7 TROUBLESHOOT WITH TCP/IP UTILITIES

OBJECTIVES

The goal of this lab is to help you use Windows Vista/XP TCP/IP utilities to troubleshoot connectivity problems. After completing this lab, you will be able to:

◢ Use the Ipconfig utility

◢ Use the Ping utility

◢ Use the Tracert utility

◢ Identify the point at which your packets will no longer travel

MATERIALS REQUIRED

This lab requires the following:

◢ Windows Vista/XP operating system

◢ A DHCP server

◢ Internet access

LAB PREPARATION

Before the lab begins, the instructor or lab assistant needs to do the following:

◢ Verify that Windows starts with no errors.

◢ Verify that Internet access is available.

ACTIVITY BACKGROUND

Perhaps nothing frustrates users more than a suddenly unavailable network connection. As a PC technician, you might be asked to restore these connections, and sometimes you even have to deal with several failed connections at one time. When troubleshooting network connections, it helps to know whether many users in one area of a network are having the same connection problem. That information can help you narrow down the source of the problem. After you have an idea of what machine is causing the problem, you can use a few TCP/IP utilities to test your theory without physically checking the system. In this lab, you learn to use TCP/IP utilities to isolate connection problems.

ESTIMATED COMPLETION TIME: 30 Minutes

 Activity

Follow these steps to display IP settings in Windows:

1. Click **Start,** right-click **Network (My Network Places** in XP) and click **Properties** in the shortcut menu. In Windows Vista, the Network and Sharing Center opens; in Windows XP, the Network Connections window opens.

2. In Vista, click **Manage network connections**. Right-click **Local Area Connection** and click **Properties** in the shortcut menu. If Windows opens a UAC, click **Continue**. The Local Area Connection Properties dialog box opens.

3. Click **Internet Protocol Version 4 (TCP/IPv4), (Internet Protocol (TCP/IP)** in XP) and then click the **Properties** button. When the Internet Protocol Version 4 (TCP/IPv4) dialog box opens, notice the different options. What two ways can you set up the IP configuration?

\
\

4. Verify that **Obtain an IP address automatically** is selected.

5. Click **OK** to close the Internet Protocol Version 4 (TCP/IPv4) dialog box, and then close the Local Area Connection Properties dialog box. Close any open Windows.

Follow these steps to adjust the command prompt so that you can view more information at a time:

1. Open a command prompt window.

2. Right-click the title bar of the command prompt window and click **Properties** in the shortcut menu. The Command Prompt Properties dialog box opens.

3. Click the **Layout** tab, if necessary. In the Screen Buffer Size section, type **150** for width and **300** for height. These settings enable you to scroll in the command prompt window and view the last 300 lines of 150 characters. If you want, you can adjust settings in the Window Size section, but generally, it's best to adjust a command prompt window after it opens so that you don't make the window too large for your monitor's display settings. Click **OK** to save the settings.

9

4. The Apply Properties dialog box opens. To specify that you want to apply the properties every time you open a command prompt window, click **Save properties for future windows with same title**, and then click **OK**.

Follow these steps to learn how to display IP information from the command line:

1. At the command prompt, type **ipconfig** and press **Enter**. What is the IP address and subnet mask?

_____

_____

_____

2. To get more information about your IP settings, type **ipconfig /all** and press **Enter**. Answer these questions:

◢ What is the purpose of DHCP?

_____

_____

◢ What is the address of the DHCP server?

_____

◢ What is the address of the DNS server?

_____

◢ What is the address of the Default Gateway?

_____

◢ What is the physical address (MAC)?

_____

◢ What is the address of the DHCP server?

_____

3. Because your system is using DHCP to obtain an IP address, type **ipconfig /renew** and press **Enter**. The command prompt window again displays IP information.

4. Again, type **ipconfig /all** and press **Enter**. Compare the current IP address lease information to the information in the screen shot. What information changed?

_____

_____

5. Next, type **ipconfig /release** and press **Enter**. What message is displayed? What implications do you predict this command will have on connectivity?

_____

_____

6. Using your screen shot as a reference, attempt to ping the DHCP server and the DNS server. What are the results?

_____

_____

7. Type **ipconfig** and press **Enter**. Note that your adapter has no IP address and no subnet mask. These two parameters are necessary to communicate with TCP/IP.

8. To get an IP address lease again, type **ipconfig /renew** and press **Enter**. New IP information, which might be the same address as before, is assigned.

9. Find your new IP address lease information. List the command you used to find this information and the lease information:

_____

_____

_____

In Windows, you can use the Network and Sharing Center (Network Connections in XP) window to release and renew the IP address.

1. Click **Start** and right-click **Network** (**My Network Places** in XP) and click **Properties** in the shortcut menu. In Vista, click **Diagnose and repair**.

2. In XP, the Network Connections window opens. Click the network connection you want to repair, and then click **Repair this connection**. You can also right-click the network connection you want to repair and click **Repair** in the shortcut menu.

If you're connected to the Internet, follow these steps to determine what route your packets take to reach an Internet address:

1. If necessary, open a command prompt window.

2. Type **tracert** followed by a single space and then a domain name on the Internet (for example, **tracert www.yahoo.com**). Press **Enter**.

3. The DNS server resolves the domain name to an IP address, and that address is listed, indicating you can reach at least one DNS server. This information tells you that your packets are traveling at least that far. Next, each hop (or router your packet passed through) is listed with the time in milliseconds the packet took to reach its destination. How many hops did the packet take to reach the domain you specified?

_____

4. Now use the Tracert command with an illegal name, such as **www.mydomain.c**. What are the results of this command?

_____

5. When you're finished, close any open windows.

When troubleshooting connectivity problems, always consider the number of users experiencing the problem. If many users have similar difficulties, it's unlikely the problem lies with any one user's computer. Therefore, you can probably eliminate the need to run extensive local tests on each computer. Instead, you can examine a device that all computers commonly use.

9

As a general rule, when troubleshooting, you should start by examining devices close to the computer exhibiting problems and then move farther away. The following steps show you how to apply this principle by examining the local computer first, and then moving outward to other devices on the network.

1. Verify that the computer is physically connected (that both ends of the cable are connected).

2. Verify that the NIC is installed and TCP/IP is bound to the NIC.

3. Perform a loopback test to verify that the NIC is functioning correctly.

4. Check the IP settings with the **ipconfig /all** command. Verify that an IP address is assigned.

5. Ping other computers on the local network. If you get no response, begin by examining a hub or punchdown panel (a panel where cables convene before connecting to a hub).

6. If you can ping other computers on the local network, ping the default gateway, which is the first stop for transmissions being sent to addresses that aren't on the local network.

7. Continue troubleshooting connections, beginning with nearby devices and working outward until you discover an IP address that returns no response. That device will be the source of the trouble.

8. If the device is under your supervision, take the necessary steps to repair it. If the device is out of your control, contact the appropriate administrator.

REVIEW QUESTIONS

1. Name four additional pieces of information that the Ipconfig command with the /all switch provides that the Ipconfig command alone does not:

   _____

   _____

   _____

   _____

2. What type of server resolves a domain name to an IP address?

   _____

3. In Windows Vista/XP, what command discards the IP address?

   _____

4. What command do you use to determine whether you can reach another computer on the local network? Would this command work if the default gateway were down?

   _____

   _____

5. If many users suddenly encountered connection problems, would you suspect problems with their local computers or problems with other devices on the network? Explain:

   _____

   _____

   _____

LAB 9.8 SOLVE NETWORK CONNECTIVITY PROBLEMS

OBJECTIVES

The goal of this lab is to troubleshoot and remedy common network connectivity problems. After completing this lab, you will be able to:

⊿ Diagnose and solve connectivity problems

⊿ Document the process

MATERIALS REQUIRED

This lab requires the following:

⊿ Windows Vista/XP operating system

⊿ A PC connected to a network and to the Internet

⊿ Windows installation CD/DVD or installation files

⊿ A PC toolkit with antistatic wrist strap

⊿ A workgroup partner

LAB PREPARATION

Before the lab begins, the instructor or lab assistant needs to do the following:

⊿ Verify that Windows starts with no errors.

⊿ Provide each student with access to the Windows installation files, if needed.

ACTIVITY BACKGROUND

To a casual user, Internet and network connections can be confusing. When users have a connectivity problem, they usually have no idea how to remedy the situation. In this lab, you introduce and solve common connectivity problems.

ESTIMATED COMPLETION TIME: 60 Minutes

 Activity

1. Verify that your network is working correctly by browsing the network and connecting to a Web site.

2. Do one of the following:

   ⊿ Change your PC's IP address.

   ⊿ Change your PC's subnet mask.

   ⊿ Remove your PC's network cable.

   ⊿ Remove TCP/IP from your PC.

   ⊿ Remove your PC's adapter in the Local Area Connection Properties dialog box.

   ⊿ Unseat or remove your PC's NIC, but leave it installed in the Local Area Connection Properties dialog box.

   ⊿ Disable your PC's NIC in Device Manager.

   ⊿ Release your PC's IP address (if DHCP is enabled).

9

3. Swap PCs with your partner and troubleshoot your partner's PC.

4. On a separate sheet of paper, answer these questions about the problem you solved:

◢ What is the initial symptom of the problem as a user might describe it?

_____

_____

◢ What steps did you take to discover the source of the problem?

_____

_____

_____

_____

◢ What steps did you take to solve the problem?

_____

_____

_____

_____

5. Repeat Steps 1 through 4 until you and your partner have used all the options listed in Step 2. Be sure to answer the questions in Step 4 for each troubleshooting situation.

REVIEW QUESTIONS

1. What problem could you solve by issuing only one command? What was the command you used?

_____

_____

2. Which problem (or problems) forced you to reboot the computer after repairing it?

_____

_____

_____

_____

3. What two pieces of information are necessary for TCP/IP communication on the local network?

_____

4. What TCP/IP utility was the most useful, in your opinion, for troubleshooting these problems? Why?

_____

_____

5. Why should you always check for physical problems like unplugged network cables before considering logical problems like missing drivers?

_____

_____

9

Security Essentials

Labs included in this chapter:

- **Lab 10.1:** Audit Computer and Network Activity in XP
- **Lab 10.2:** Monitor Security Events in Vista
- **Lab 10.3:** Research PC Security
- **Lab 10.4:** Secure a Private Folder
- **Lab 10.5:** Work with Offline Files
- **Lab 10.6:** Challenge Activity: Set Up a VPN

LAB 10.1 AUDIT COMPUTER AND NETWORK ACTIVITY IN WINDOWS XP

OBJECTIVES

The goal of this lab is to help you learn how to use event logging in Windows XP and CMOS setup so that you can audit events as needed to help secure a computer or network. After completing this lab, you will be able to:

◢ Use Windows tools for event logging

◢ Use CMOS setup for event logging

MATERIALS REQUIRED

This lab requires the following:

◢ Two Windows XP computers connected to a network

LAB PREPARATION

Before the lab begins, the instructor or lab assistant needs to do the following:

◢ Make a networked Windows XP computer available for each student or workgroup.

◢ The computer should not belong to a Windows domain.

ACTIVITY BACKGROUND

It is often necessary to monitor or audit computer or network events, such as logon events, failed hardware events, data access events, and other event activity. Auditing is necessary when you are looking for security breaches or troubleshooting hardware or software problems. This lab covers event logging for both of these situations.

ESTIMATED COMPLETION TIME: 90 Minutes

🕾 Activity

Samuel works as a PC support technician in a patent attorney's office. The attorneys are especially interested in a high level of security because their clients often trust them with information they are expected to protect. The attorneys know that, in the past, hackers have tried to steal inventions by penetrating the office's computers and networks. Therefore, Samuel wants to implement all available techniques to audit the Windows XP computers that contain client records on the local wired and wireless network.

Samuel has decided he wants to audit events in four areas: network activity, Windows logon, access to private folders, and errors that occur when a computer is booted. All four areas are covered in this lab. Follow these steps to configure your computer for the lab:

1. Log on as Administrator and create a user account named **Attorney Miller**.

2. In Miller's My Documents folder, create a folder named Miller_Client_Inventions.

   If you are using the NTFS file system, any folder that is part of your user profile in the Documents and Settings folder can be made private using the folder Properties window. For example, to make the folder shown in Figure 10-1 private, check **Make this folder private**.

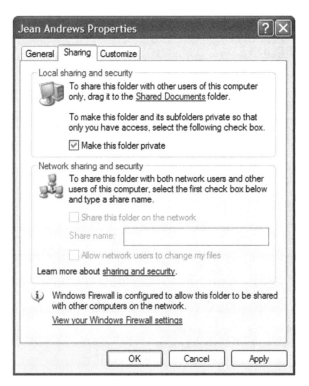

Figure 10-1 A folder that belongs to a user profile can be made private
Courtesy: Course Technology/Cengage Learning

3. Make Attorney Miller's My Documents folder private so that other users who are logged on to the computer or the network cannot see this folder. (See Lab 8.5.) Is the Miller_Client_Inventions folder also private? How do you know?

_____

_____

4. Create a folder named **C:\Client_Inventions**. Share the folder so that all users have full access to it.

5. Create two document files in the folder. Name the files Smith_Invention and Williams_Invention. Encrypt the contents of the Client_Inventions folder. To encrypt a folder, click the **Advanced** button on the **General** tab of the folder Properties window (see Figure 10-2), check the **Encrypt contents to secure data** check box, and click **OK**.

6. From another computer on the network, verify that you can see the two files in the Client_Inventions folder. Can you open either file from the remote computer? Why or why not?

_____

Follow these steps to audit network activity:

1. Using Windows Firewall, enable security logging. In the Windows Firewall window, under Security Logging, click the **Settings** button on the **Advanced** tab. Under Logging options, configure the Log Settings dialog box, as shown in Figure 10-3.

2. From another computer on the network, try to access the Client_Inventions folder. Examine the log file that shows this event. What is the name and path to the log file?

_____

10

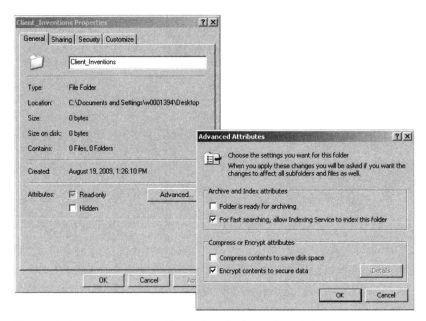

Figure 10-2   Encrypt a file or folder using the Properties window
Courtesy: Course Technology/Cengage Learning

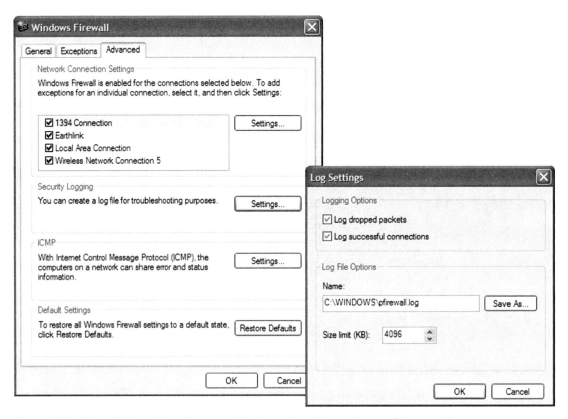

Figure 10-3   Using Windows Firewall, you can log dropped packets and successful connections
Courtesy: Course Technology/Cengage Learning

3. In the log file, how is a user or computer identified?

4. What is one good reason to use static IP addressing in this office rather than dynamic IP addressing?

Using Windows XP Professional, you can use Group Policy and Event Viewer to monitor Windows logon events. (Windows XP Home Edition does not support this feature.) Do the following:

1. Log on to the system as an administrator.

2. Click **Start, Control Panel,** double-click **Administrative Tools,** and double-click **Local Security Policy.** Select **Audit Policy** in the **Local Policy** folder and double-click **Audit account logon events,** as shown in Figure 10-4.

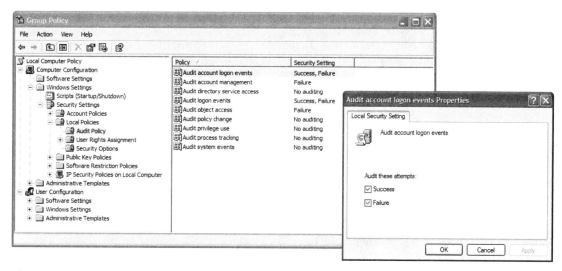

Figure 10-4 Set Windows XP Professional to monitor logging on to the system
Courtesy: Course Technology/Cengage Learning

3. Configure Windows to log all logon events, regardless of whether they are successes or failures. Do the same for the policy named **Audit logon events.**

4. Log off your computer and then log back on.

5. From another computer on the network, attempt to view the contents of the Client_Inventions folder.

6. Click **Start, Control Panel,** double-click **Administrative Tools,** and open **Event Viewer.** Look at the Security events log. How many logged events have occurred since you started this lab?

7. How are remote computers identified in the event log?

8. Double-click an event to see detailed information about the event, as shown in Figure 10-5.

10

Figure 10-5 Details about a logged event are displayed in the Event Properties
dialog box for that event
Courtesy: Course Technology/Cengage Learning

9. In Event Viewer, right-click **Security** to open the Security Properties window. Set the
Security events log so that events will not be overwritten. (See Figure 10-6.) Close Event
Viewer.

10. Using the Registry Editor, export the HKLM\SYSTEM\CurrentControlSet\Control\Lsa
key. Then change the DWORD value of the key to 1, which causes the system to halt if
the Security event log fills up. Answer these questions:

◢ What command did you use to launch the Registry Editor?

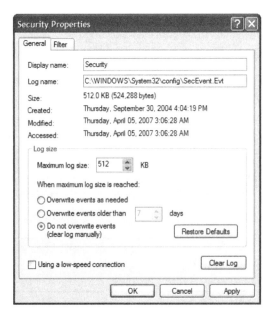

Figure 10-6 Control the Security log file settings
Courtesy: Course Technology/Cengage Learning

◢ What menu in the editor did you use to export the Registry key?

_____

◢ What did you name the exported key?

_____

11. How often do you think you need to clear the Security events log?

_____

12. Describe what you must do if you forget to clear the log, which will cause the system to halt:

_____

_____

_____

Do the following to monitor access to private folders:

1. Click **Start, My Computer,** and **Folder Options** from the **Tools** menu. Click the **View** tab and turn off simple file sharing by unchecking **Use simple file sharing (recommended)**.

2. Click **Start, Control Panel,** double-click **Administrative Tools,** and double-click **Local Security Policy.** Use the Local Security Policy to set the Audit object access policy so that both successes and failures are monitored.

3. Right-click the **Client_Inventions** folder, click **Properties,** and click **Advanced.** Using the **Auditing** tab of the Advanced Security Settings window for the Client_Inventions folder, configure Windows to monitor the folder for all successful and failed accesses by all users (Everyone).

4. Using Windows Explorer, open the Client_Inventions folder and then open a file inside the folder.

5. Open Event Viewer. How many logged events are recorded for this folder?

_____

6. When you're finished, close any open windows.

In Windows, failed hardware events are recorded in Event Viewer in the System log. However, some computer BIOSs can log failed hardware events during or after startup. Do the following to find out if your BIOS has this ability:

1. Reboot your system and enter CMOS setup.

2. Look on all menus for the ability to record errors during or after startup. Did you find this option? If so, describe exactly what type of error is recorded and how to enable the option:

_____

_____

10

Notes To refresh a window in Windows Explorer or Event Viewer, press the **F5** key. To lock a workstation without waiting for the screen saver to activate, press Win+L.

To return event logging to the way it was before you started this lab, do the following:

1. Turn off network monitoring.
2. Restore the Group Policy settings so that logon events and object access events are not logged.
3. Restore the Registry key you changed by double-clicking the exported key file. Then delete the exported file.
4. Remove all auditing from the Client_Inventions folder.
5. Turn on simple file sharing.

Answer the following questions. You might find it interesting to discuss your answers with others in this lab.

1. Sometimes, too much information keeps you from effectively monitoring a system. In this lab, you have monitored many types of failed and successful events, which all generate a lot of data to plow through. How do you think Samuel could improve the monitoring methods and options used in this lab?

_____

_____

_____

2. The current network is configured as a Windows workgroup. Give two reasons Samuel should recommend that the attorneys convert the network to a Windows domain:

_____

_____

_____

_____

REVIEW QUESTIONS

1. What is the name of the Windows XP Firewall log file that monitors network activity?

_____

2. What happens when the allowable size of the log file that monitors network activity has been exceeded?

_____

3. Which applet in Control Panel is used to turn simple file sharing on and off?

_____

4. What is the name of the Group Policy console program file?

_____

5. What are the two main categories of policies in the Group Policy console?

_____

LAB 10.2 MONITOR SECURITY EVENTS IN VISTA

OBJECTIVES

The goal of this lab is to use Event Viewer to monitor security events such as failed attempts to log into the system or changes to files and folders. After completing this lab, you will be able to:

⊿ Set Event Viewer to track failed login attempts

⊿ Set Event Viewer to monitor changes to files and folders

MATERIALS REQUIRED

This lab requires the following:

⊿ Windows Vista operating system installed on an NTFS partition

LAB PREPARATION

Before the lab begins, the instructor or lab assistant needs to do the following:

⊿ Verify that Windows starts with no errors.

ACTIVITY BACKGROUND

As part of managing the security of a computer or network, your organization might ask you to report incidents of suspicious events such as attempts to log on or change certain files. You can track either of these events with the Windows Event Viewer. In this lab, you will configure Windows to monitor these events.

ESTIMATED COMPLETION TIME: 30 Minutes

Activity

Follow these steps to set Event Viewer to track failures when people are attempting to log on to the system:

1. Log on as an administrator and create a new standard user account called **Newuser**.
2. Click **Start, Control Panel, System and Maintenance,** and **Administrative Tools.**
3. Double-click **Local Security Policy.** If a UAC box opens, click **Continue.** The Local Security Policy window opens. (Windows Vista Home Editions do not support this feature.)
4. Double-click **Local Policies** and select **Audit Policy,** as shown in Figure 10-7.
5. Double-click **Audit account logon events.** The Audit logon events Properties dialog box opens. Check **Failure** and click **OK.** Do the same for **Audit logon events** and then close the Local Security Policy window.
6. Examine the other local security policies and determine which would be used to monitor when a password is changed:

   _____

7. To see the events that are logged, open **Event Viewer** and select **Security** in Windows Logs in the left pane (see Figure 10-8). Does Event Viewer currently list any logon failures?
8. Log out and attempt to log back in to an account with the wrong password.
9. Now successfully log back in as Administrator.

10

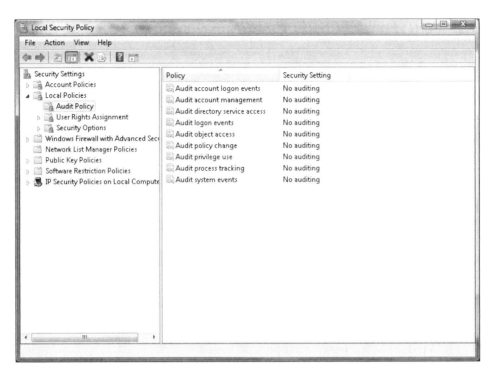

Figure 10-7   Event tracking can be enabled using the Local Security Policy window
Courtesy: Course Technology/Cengage Learning

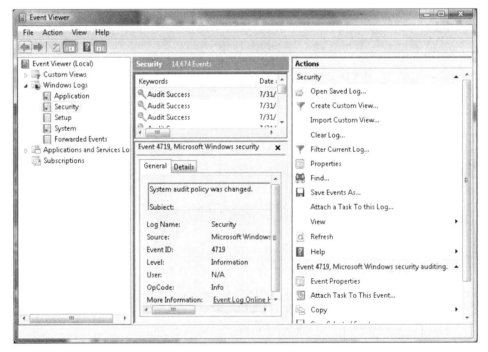

Figure 10-8   Event Viewer can be used to examine logs of past events
Courtesy: Course Technology/Cengage Learning

10. Open Event Viewer and select Security again. What information did Event Viewer record about the failed login attempt?

11. When you're finished, close any open windows.

Follow these steps to monitor changes to files and folders:

1. Open the Local Security Policy window as you did previously in Steps 2-4 and double-click **Audit object access**. Check **Failure** and click **OK**.

2. Close the Local Security Policy Window.

3. Open the **Properties** window of the C:\Users\Public folder and click the **Security** tab, as shown in Figure 10-9.

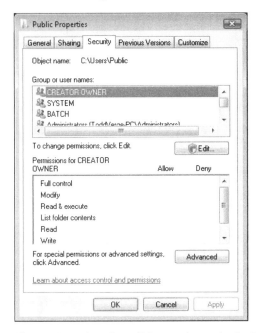

Figure 10-9   Security policies can be set in the Properties window
Courtesy: Course Technology/Cengage Learning

4. Click **Advanced**, select the **Auditing** tab, and click **Continue**. If a UAC box opens, click **Continue**.

5. The Advanced Security Settings window opens, as shown in Figure 10-10. You can now add users or groups that you want to monitor.

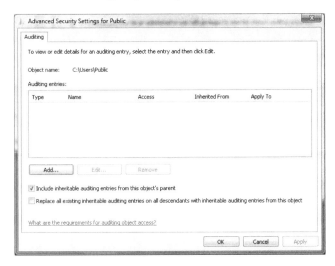

Figure 10-10   In the Advanced Security Settings window, you can add groups or users you want to monitor
Courtesy: Course Technology/Cengage Learning

10

6. Click **Add**, click **Advanced**, click **Find Now**, select **Newuser**, and click **OK**.

7. Click **OK** to close the Select User or Group window.

8. Check the **Full control** boxes for **Successful** and **Failed** attempts, as shown in Figure 10-11, and click **OK** to close the Auditing Entry window.

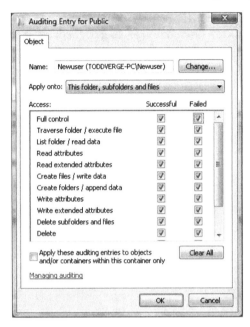

Figure 10-11 The Auditing Entry window allows you to select which events will be tracked
Courtesy: Course Technology/Cengage Learning

9. Close all windows to exit and log out as Administrator.

10. Log in as Newuser and open the C:\Users\Public folder. While you're there, use Notepad to create a short text file. What did you name your text file?

_____

11. Log out as Newuser and log back in as Administrator.

12. Open **Event Viewer**, select **Event Viewer (local)**, and double-click **Audit Success** in the Summary of Administrative Events section.

13. Explore the recent events in this section until you find the ones that are associated with Newuser's attempt to access the C:\Users\Public folder. How many separate events were created?

_____

14. Which one of the events recorded the creation of the new text file?

_____

REVIEW QUESTIONS

1. How could you use the Local Security Policy to determine if someone was trying to hack into a user account?

_____

_____

2. Why is it important to also record failed attempts to access files?

_____

3. Besides failed logon attempts, name two other events that would seem suspicious:

_____

_____

4. What would be a more efficient way to monitor the activities of a collection of users?

_____

_____

5. Why would accessing one file create several separate events?

_____

_____

LAB 10.3 RESEARCH PC SECURITY

OBJECTIVES

The goal of this lab is to research various ways to secure a computer. During this lab, you will research how to:

◢ Enable and manage Windows Firewall

◢ Enable Windows Defender

◢ Unhide file extensions

MATERIALS REQUIRED

This lab requires the following:

◢ Windows Vista/XP Professional operating system

◢ Internet access

LAB PREPARATION

Before the lab begins, the instructor or lab assistant needs to do the following:

◢ Verify that Windows starts with no errors.

◢ Verify that Internet access is available.

ACTIVITY BACKGROUND

There is no single solution for protecting your PC from the wide variety of security threats that you face every day. Running a personal firewall as well as a selection of third-party software and monitoring tools can provide some protection from malware. You can also avoid a lot of problems by following a handful of basic rules like not opening unknown e-mail attachments and always limiting the use of administrative accounts. It's important to keep in mind, however, that no defense will ever substitute for keeping

10

good backups. Data loss isn't a matter of *if* but *when*. In this lab, you will use the Internet as well as any built-in Windows Help files to research several popular methods of protecting your computer.

ESTIMATED COMPLETION TIME: 30 Minutes

Activity

A firewall is hardware or software that keeps worms or hackers from getting into your system. It works by examining the information coming in and out of the PC and blocking any unwanted data. Windows already has a built-in software firewall. Answer the following questions about the Windows Firewall:

1. Vista automatically configures Windows Firewall based on the type of network it believes you are connected to. What are the three types of network profiles, and which one offers the most protection through the firewall?

   _____

   _____

   _____

2. List the steps required to open the Network and Sharing Center in Vista:

   _____

   _____

   _____

   _____

3. What are the main differences between the Public and Private network settings?

   _____

   _____

4. Why might you need to grant a firewall exception for File and Print Sharing on a public network?

   _____

   _____

5. List the steps necessary to make this change:

   _____

   _____

   _____

   _____

Windows Defender is an antiadware and antispyware program integrated into Windows Vista. By default it downloads updates and scans your system every day at 2:00 AM. It also monitors your system and reports suspicious activity using a bubble that appears in the lower-right corner of the screen. Use Windows Help and the Internet to answer these questions:

1. How would you determine if Windows Defender had been turned off?

_____

2. What steps would you follow to turn on Windows Defender?

_____

_____

3. How would you use Windows Defender to perform a quick scan of the system right away?

_____

_____

4. Is Windows Defender also available for Windows XP?

_____

5. A Trojan is malware such as a virus that disguises itself as a harmless file like a picture and when you double-click to open it, it installs itself on your system. The key to avoiding a Trojan is to always examine the extension to make sure it is consistent with the file type you are expecting. However, sometimes Windows hides file extensions, making this more difficult. How would you change your folder options to show hidden files and folders and not hide the extensions for known file types?

_____

_____

_____

_____

REVIEW QUESTIONS

1. How could opening an unknown e-mail attachment be a security risk?

_____

2. Why would the firewall for a public network be more restrictive?

_____

_____

3. What would you suspect if you saw a file named coolpic.exe?

_____

_____

4. Can a firewall be configured to grant an exception for one program rather than be turned off altogether?

_____

10

LAB 10.4 SECURE A PRIVATE FOLDER

OBJECTIVES

The goal of this lab is to help you learn how to apply Windows tools to secure a private folder. After completing this lab, you will be able to:

◢ Share a folder on the network.

◢ Control which users can read or modify the folder

MATERIALS REQUIRED

This lab requires the following:

◢ Two Windows Vista/XP computers connected on a network for each workgroup of two or more students

◢ Microsoft Excel or an equivalent open source spreadsheet application (optional)

◢ Access to a printer (optional)

LAB PREPARATION

Before the lab begins, the instructor or lab assistant needs to do the following:

◢ Make a networked Windows Vista/XP computer available for each student or student workgroup.

ACTIVITY BACKGROUND

In an office environment, employees often share files and folders as they work together on a common project. Sensitive information in these shared files and folders often needs to be kept private from others in the organization. A PC support technician will probably be asked to solve these types of security issues for the office. In this lab, you learn how to apply Windows security tools and features to solve these security problems.

ESTIMATED COMPLETION TIME: 60 Minutes

 Activity

Michael is team leader of the payroll department of Peaceful Arbor, Inc., a corporation that manages assisted living facilities. He and his two other team members, Sharon and Jason, share payroll files that others in the accounting department are not allowed to view. The payroll data is stored on the file server in the C:\Payroll folder, and everyone in the accounting department who is not on the payroll team knows not to open the folder. Recently, Michael suspects that others have been poking around where they don't belong, so he has turned to Linden, the PC support technician, for help.

Working with a team member, re-create the problem on your two networked lab computers by doing the following:

1. On Computer 1, which will be your file server, create a user account named Linden and assign administrative privileges to the account. Be sure to assign a password to this account. What is the password?

2. On Computer 1, create the folder C:\Payroll. Create three spreadsheet files named MasterPayroll.xls, October2009.xls, and November2009.xls. Put some sample data in each file, and store all three files in the C:\Payroll folder. If you don't have access to a spreadsheet program, substitute three text files.

3. On Computer 1, create the folder C:\Budget. Create two spreadsheet files named Budget2009.xls and Budget2010.xls. Put some sample data in each file, and store the files in the C:\Budget folder.

4. Configure Computer 2 so that passwords of at least six characters are required for all user accounts. To do this, use the policy Minimum password length, shown in Figure 10-12.

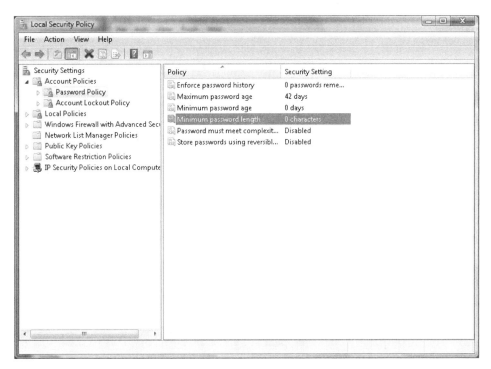

Figure 10-12 Password policy can be set in the Local Security Policy window
Courtesy: Course Technology/Cengage Learning

5. On Computer 2, create a limited user account named Michael. Michael belongs to the payroll team and needs full access to the Payroll folder. He also needs access to the Budget folder. What is the password to the Michael account?

6. On Computer 2, create a limited user account named Sharon. Sharon belongs to the payroll team and needs full access to the Payroll folder. She does not need any access to the Budget folder. What is the password to the Sharon account?

7. Create a limited user account named Jason on Computer 2. Jason belongs to the accounting department and needs full access to the Budget folder, but should not have any access to the Payroll folder. What is the password to the Jason account?

10

8. Using Windows tools, set the permissions and access controls so that Michael, Sharon, and Jason can read and write to the folder they need, but cannot view the contents of the folder they are not allowed to see. List the steps you took to do the job:

_____

_____

_____

_____

_____

_____

_____

_____

9. Test your security measures by doing the following:

◢ Log on to Computer 2 as Michael. Edit a file in the Budget folder and a file in the Payroll folder.

◢ Log on to Computer 2 as Sharon. Edit a file in the Payroll folder.

◢ Verify that Sharon cannot view the contents of the Budget folder.

◢ Log on to Computer 2 as Jason. Edit a file in the Budget folder.

◢ Verify that Jason cannot view the contents of the Payroll folder.

10. When you are convinced you have solved the problem, do the following to further test your system:

◢ Ask someone on another team to try to hack through your security measures using Computer 2. Was this person able to break through? If so, how?

_____

_____

◢ Ask the same person to attempt to hack through your security measures using Computer 1. Was this person able to break through? If so, how?

_____

_____

11. Correct any security problems that have come to light by your testing. What, if anything, did you need to do?

_____

_____

_____

12. Set up event logging so that you can view a log of unauthorized attempts to view a folder. How did you do it?

_____

_____

_____

_____

13. Test your auditing method by logging on to Computer 2 as Jason and attempting to view the Payroll folder. If possible, print the screen that shows the logged event.

14. When you're finished, remove the new accounts and undo any changes.

REVIEW QUESTIONS

1. Did your system use simple file sharing?

_____

2. Would this setup be sufficient for securing the payroll information at a large company? Why or why not?

_____

_____

3. What utility is used to require that each user account have a password?

_____

4. Why is it important for people besides your own team to test a security system that your team has put in place?

_____

5. Why is auditing an important component of file security?

_____

LAB 10.5 WORK WITH OFFLINE FILES

OBJECTIVES

The goal of this lab is to help you learn to work with offline files. After completing this lab, you will be able to:

◢ Enable offline files in Windows

◢ Make network files available offline

◢ Sync offline files with the network

10

MATERIALS REQUIRED

This lab requires the following:

◢ At least two systems running the Windows Vista operating system

◢ The ability to network both computers

◢ Internet access

LAB PREPARATION

Before the lab begins, the instructor or lab assistant needs to do the following:

◢ Verify that Windows starts with no errors.

◢ Verify that Internet access is available.

◢ Set up a simple network with two computers.

ACTIVITY BACKGROUND

Sometimes, you need access to network files when the network is not available. Maybe you're traveling and you can't find a wireless connection or maybe the server is being updated and it's temporarily unavailable. Windows allows you to work with offline files and then sync up the changes with the network files later. In this lab, you will set up some network files so they can be changed offline.

ESTIMATED COMPLETION TIME: 45 Minutes

Activity

1. Begin with two networked Windows computers and use one of the methods from Lab 9.7 to test your network connection. What method or utility did you use?

   _____

2. On Computer 1, which will be your server, create a shared folder that contains a small text file. (See Lab 8.5.) What is the name and path of your shared folder and file?

   _____

   _____

3. On Computer 2, create a drive mapping to the shared folder and open the text file to test your connection.

4. Click **Start, Control Panel, Network and Internet**, and **Offline Files** to open the Offline Files configuration window pictured in Figure 10-13. If necessary, select the **General** tab and check to see if Offline Files are enabled and then click **OK**.

You can work with offline files by following these steps:

1. On Computer 2, open Windows Explorer, right-click the drive mapping to the shared folder, and select **Always Available Offline**.

2. Windows will then make a copy of the network files on your local machine.

3. Temporarily remove Computer 2 from the network by unplugging the network cable or disabling the wireless connection. Windows will automatically enable offline files whenever the network is not available.

4. Open Windows Explorer and open the offline version of the shared text file.

Figure 10-13 Check to see if Offline Files are enabled
Courtesy: Course Technology/Cengage Learning

5. Make a small change to this file. What change did you make?

_____

6. Open the Offline Files configuration window and answer the following questions:

◢ What objects are listed when you click **View your offline files**?

_____

_____

◢ How would you change the amount of space available for storing offline files on your computer?

_____

◢ What other options or features are available for working offline?

_____

_____

7. Now reconnect Computer 2 with the network.

8. Windows updates offline files automatically but not continuously. To make sure the file is updated, open Windows Explorer, select the shared folder, and click **Sync** from the toolbar.

9. Log on to Computer 1, if necessary, and open the shared file. Did the file update with offline changes made from Computer 2?

_____

10. Will the Sync button also update the offline content with changes made on the network?

_____

10

REVIEW QUESTIONS

1. What are some reasons you might choose to set up offline files?

   _____

   _____

2. How is working with offline files different from simply making a second copy of the files you need to access?

   _____

   _____

   _____

   _____

3. Why might encrypting your offline files be necessary?

   _____

   _____

4. Why might you choose to work with offline files even if the network is available?

   _____

   _____

LAB 10.6 CHALLENGE ACTIVITY: SET UP A VPN

OBJECTIVES

The goal of this lab is to help you set up a secure VPN. After completing this lab, you will be able to:

- Set up a VPN in Windows
- Use third-party software to securely access the Internet from a public network

MATERIALS REQUIRED

This lab requires the following:

- Windows Vista operating system
- Internet access
- VPN server (optional)

LAB PREPARATION

Before the lab begins, the instructor or lab assistant needs to do the following:

- Verify that Windows starts with no errors.
- Verify that Internet access is available.

◢ Set up a VPN server and record the server's IP address (optional).

◢ Set up a user account on the VPN server and record the username and password (optional).

ACTIVITY BACKGROUND

A Virtual Private Network (VPN) offers a very secure connection between two computers. It uses a process called tunneling to form a private connection that encrypts communications independently of the type of network being used. VPNs are often used when a user has to connect to a network over a nonsecure public network such as a wireless hotspot. In this lab, you will learn how to set up a VPN connection in Windows as well as a third-party utility.

ESTIMATED COMPLETION TIME: 45 Minutes

 Activity

To connect to a VPN server in Windows, follow these steps:

1. Log on as Administrator.

2. Click **Start**, click **Connect To**, and click **Set up a connection or network**.

3. Select **Connect to a workplace**, as shown in Figure 10-14, and click **Next**.

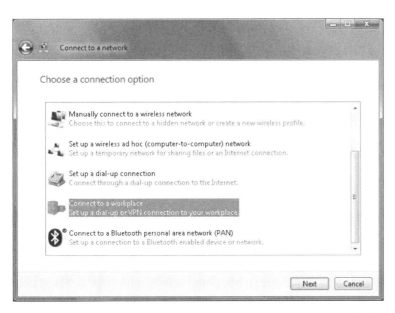

Figure 10-14 Select Connect to a workplace to set up a VPN connection in Windows
Courtesy: Course Technology/Cengage Learning

4. Click **Use my Internet connection** (VPN).

5. Enter the Internet address and Destination name provided by your instructor (optional) to connect to a real VPN, or just enter the IP address of another computer on your network. What name and address did you use?

_____

_____

10

6. To connect to an actual VPN server, enter the user name and password provided by your instructor. Otherwise, click **Cancel** to close the window. What name and password did you use?

_____

_____

Several companies offer programs to secure Internet access from public wireless connections using VPNs. One such program is Hotspot Shield from AnchorFree. To set up a secure connection, follow these steps:

1. Log on as an administrator.

2. Open your browser and go to **www.hotspotshield.com**.

3. Click the **Download** button and follow the on-screen instructions to download and install Hotspot Shield. During the installation process:

   ◢ Deselect the Include the Hotspot Shield Community Toolbar check box.

   ◢ Accept the default configuration.

   ◢ Click **Install** if any Windows Security windows open.

4. When the installation is complete, launch Hotspot Shield and wait for an automatic connection to a VPN server.

5. Look at several Web sites. How do you know that Hotspot Shield is running?

_____

6. When you're finished, uninstall Hotspot Shield and close any open windows.

REVIEW QUESTIONS

1. Will VPNs work on both wired and wireless networks?

_____

_____

2. What process do VPNs use to form a private connection between computers?

_____

3. Why would it be dangerous to do online banking transactions through a public Internet hotspot without a VPN?

_____

_____

4. How does a VPN connection differ from using Remote Desktop?

_____

_____

5. Why is a VPN more secure than other forms of wireless encryption such as WEP?

_____

_____

_____

_____

10

Security Practices

Labs included in this chapter:

- **Lab 11.1:** Protect Your Computer from Viruses and Adware

- **Lab 11.2:** Use Encryption

- **Lab 11.3:** Secure a Wireless LAN

- **Lab 11.4:** Investigate Startup Processes

- **Lab 11.5:** Deal with a Rootkit

LAB 11.1 PROTECT YOUR COMPUTER FROM VIRUSES AND ADWARE

OBJECTIVES

The goal of this lab is to help you use antivirus and antiadware software to protect your computer. After completing this lab, you will be able to:

⊿ Install antivirus software

⊿ Scan your system for viruses and adware

MATERIALS REQUIRED

This lab requires the following:

⊿ Windows Vista/XP operating system

⊿ Internet access

⊿ *Optional:* An installed antivirus program

LAB PREPARATION

Before the lab begins, the instructor or lab assistant needs to do the following:

⊿ Verify that Windows starts with no errors.

⊿ Verify that Internet access is available.

ACTIVITY BACKGROUND

One of the best ways to protect your computer against malicious software is to always run current antivirus and antispyware software. Many excellent antivirus programs, such as Norton AntiVirus or McAfee VirusScan, are available commercially. As well, many Web-based programs are available to scan and disinfect your system. In this lab, you "infect" your computer with a fake virus, and then use a Web-based antivirus program to disinfect your system.

ESTIMATED COMPLETION TIME: 60 Minutes

Activity

1. Open your browser, and go to **www.eicar.org**. Attempt to download the **eicar.com** malware test file. If you're already running an antivirus program, you'll probably be alerted that the file is infected and the download will be blocked or isolated.

2. What alert or warning does your antivirus program display when you try to download this file?

   _____

3. Next, go to **http://housecall.trendmicro.com** and click **Launch HouseCall**. On the next page, accept the terms of use and click the **Launch HouseCall** button.

4. Follow the on-screen instructions, and then click the appropriate button to do a complete scan of the computer. Depending on your system, this process might take some time.

5. When the scan is finished, you can choose to delete any infected files. How many infections did HouseCall find?

   _____

6. Exit the program and close your browser.

Occasionally, some infected files, particularly adware, manage to avoid detection by one program or another. For this reason, running several antiadware programs on your computer is often useful. Follow these steps to download and run two antiadware programs:

1. Open your Web browser, if necessary, and go to **www.lavasoft.com**. Click to download **Ad-Aware Free**, and install it on your system. Leave your Web browser open.

2. Use this program to perform a system scan of your computer, which could take several minutes. How many critical objects were recognized?

   _____

3. Next, go to **www.spybot.info**. Click **English**, click to download **Spybot Search and Destroy**, and install it on your system.

4. Use the program to check your computer for problems. Did Spybot find any adware that the first program missed?

   _____

5. Exit the program.

REVIEW QUESTIONS

1. List some ways your computer might become infected with a virus:

   _____

2. Why is it important to allow your antivirus program to update its virus-definition files automatically?

   _____

3. Why do some companies bundle adware with their programs?

   _____

4. Why does scanning your hard drive for viruses take so long?

   _____

5. What can you do if you aren't running antivirus software and suspect your computer is infected?

   _____

LAB 11.2 USE ENCRYPTION

OBJECTIVES

The goal of this lab is to help you work with encryption and observe the effects of trying to use an encrypted file without permission. After completing this lab, you will be able to:

◢ Encrypt a directory

◢ Save files to the encrypted directory

◢ Access the encrypted files as a different user

11

MATERIALS REQUIRED

This lab requires the following:

⊿ Windows Vista/XP Professional operating system installed on an NTFS partition

⊿ A blank floppy disk or USB flash drive

LAB PREPARATION

Before the lab begins, the instructor or lab assistant needs to do the following:

⊿ Verify that Windows starts with no errors.

ACTIVITY BACKGROUND

Despite your best efforts, unauthorized users might gain access to sensitive files. To protect these files from this type of security breach, you can use file encryption, which prevents unauthorized users from being able to view files, even if they do manage to gain access to them. You can encrypt individual files or entire directories. As with disk quotas, you can use file encryption only on NTFS drives. FAT file systems don't support file encryption. In this lab, you create and encrypt an entire directory, and then create a test file in that encrypted directory.

ESTIMATED COMPLETION TIME: 30 Minutes

Activity

Follow these steps to create an encrypted directory and a test file in that directory:

1. Log on as an administrator.

2. In Windows Explorer, create two new directories in the NTFS root. Name the directories **Encrypt** and **Normal**.

3. Right-click the **Encrypt** folder, and then click **Properties**. The Encrypt Properties dialog box opens.

4. Click the **Advanced** button to open the Advanced Attributes dialog box.

5. Click the **Encrypt contents to secure data** check box to encrypt the contents of the Encrypt folder.

6. Click **OK** to apply the settings and close the Advanced Attributes dialog box. You return to the Encrypt Properties dialog box.

7. Click **OK** to apply encryption.

8. In Windows Explorer, double-click the **Encrypt** folder to open it.

9. From the Windows Explorer menu, click **File**, point to **New**, and click **Text Document**. Double-click **New Text Document** and type **This file is encrypted**. Close the file, saving it as **Secure.txt**.

Follow these steps to see the effects of encrypting a file in Windows:

1. Double-click **Secure.txt** in the Encrypt folder and record what happens:

_____

2. Log off as an administrator, and log on again as a different user.

3. Double-click **Secure.txt** in the Encrypt folder and record the results:

_____

4. Copy **Secure.txt** to the Normal folder and record the results:

_____

5. Log off, and then log on again as an administrator.

6. Copy **Secure.txt** to the Normal folder and record the results:

_____

7. Copy **Secure.txt** to some form of removable media that is not formatted with NTFS, such as a USB flash drive or a blank, formatted floppy disk, and record the results:

_____

8. Log off, and then log on again as the previous user.

9. Double-click **Secure.txt** in the Normal folder and record the results:

_____

10. Double-click **Secure.txt** in the removable drive and record the results:

_____

_____

11. Right-click the **Secure.txt** file in the removable drive, and then click **Properties**. The file's Properties dialog box opens. Is there an Advanced button?

_____

12. Right-click the **Secure.txt** file in the Normal folder, and then click **Properties**. The file's Properties dialog box opens.

13. Click the **Advanced** button, click to clear the **Encrypt contents to secure data** check box, and then click **OK**. Record the results:

_____

_____

REVIEW QUESTIONS

1. Which file system must be used to enable encryption?

_____

2. How do you encrypt a single file?

_____

3. What happens when an unauthorized user tries to open an encrypted file?

_____

_____

4. What happens when an unauthorized user tries to unencrypt a file?

_____

_____

11

5. What happens to an encrypted file that's removed from an NTFS partition?

_____

_____

LAB 11.3 SECURE A WIRELESS LAN

OBJECTIVES

The goal of this lab is to learn how to set up and configure security options on your wireless router. After completing this lab, you will be able to:

◢ Download a manual for a wireless router

◢ Explain how to improve wireless security

◢ Describe some methods of securing a wireless LAN

MATERIALS REQUIRED

This lab requires the following:

◢ Windows Vista/XP Professional operating system

◢ Internet access

◢ Adobe Acrobat Reader installed for viewing .pdf files

◢ Wireless router (optional)

◢ Laptop or desktop with compatible wireless access (optional)

LAB PREPARATION

Before the lab begins, the instructor or lab assistant needs to do the following:

◢ Verify that Windows starts with no errors.

◢ Verify that Internet access is available.

ACTIVITY BACKGROUND

Wireless networks have become common in recent years and are a simple way to include a laptop in your home network. Without adequate security, however, you can open up your network to a wide range of threats. In this lab, you learn how to enable and configure some security features of your wireless router.

ESTIMATED COMPLETION TIME: 45 Minutes

🔧 Activity

1. Open your Web browser, and go to **www.linksys.com**.

2. Click **Downloads**.

3. In the drop-down list of products, click **Routers**, and then click **WRT54G2**.

> **Notes** Your instructor might choose to substitute the manual for another wireless router instead of having you download the Linksys user guide.

4. Click the **User Guide** link. The manual opens in a separate window in .pdf format. Use it to answer the following questions:

  ◢ Most wireless routers can be configured with a Web-based utility by entering the router's IP address in the browser's Address text box. What's the default IP address of this router?

  _____

  ◢ Describe how you would log in to the router for the first time:

  _____

  _____

  _____

Most routers are easily configured with a setup utility that asks a series of questions about your network and Internet service provider. The default settings, however, might not enable all your router's security features. These are the six most important steps in securing your LAN:

  ◢ Updating the router's firmware from the manufacturer's Web site so any known security flaws have been fixed

  ◢ Setting a password on the router itself so that other people can't change its configuration

  ◢ Disabling remote configuration of the router

  ◢ Changing the network's name (called a service set identifier—SSID) and turning off the SSID broadcast to anyone who's listening

  ◢ Using some kind of encryption (WEP is good, WPA is better, WPA2 is better still.)

  ◢ Enabling MAC filtering so that you can limit access to only your computers

Now continue to use the manual to answer the following additional questions:

  ◢ Which window in the router's Web-based utility do you use to change the user name and password?

  _____

  ◢ List the steps for changing the router's SSID:

  _____

  _____

  _____

  _____

  ◢ How many hexadecimal characters must be used for 64-bit Wired Equivalent Privacy (WEP) encryption?

  _____

11

◢ Describe the steps to limit access to everything but your laptop through MAC filtering:

_____

_____

_____

_____

CHALLENGE ACTIVITY (ADDITIONAL 30 MINUTES)

Set up an actual secure wireless connection by following these steps:

1. Set up a nonsecure wireless connection with the router, as covered in Lab 9.6.

2. Go to the router manufacturer's Web site and update the router's firmware (if necessary) to the latest version. Did your router require an update? What version of the firmware is it now running?

_____

3. Set a strong password for the router. What password did you use?

_____

4. Disable remote configuration for the router so the router cannot be configured wirelessly. List the steps you went through to complete this task:

_____

_____

_____

_____

5. Change the router's name (SSID). What was the router's default name and what did you change it to?

_____

6. Disable the broadcast of the new SSID.

7. Set up some kind of encryption on the router. What form of encryption did you use?

_____

8. Enable MAC filtering so that only your wireless PC or laptop can connect. How did you determine the MAC address of your wireless computer?

_____

_____

9. Connect to the network with your wireless computer, as covered in Lab 9.6, and test your wireless connection by opening your browser.

10. When you're finished, undo the changes you made on the wireless client and reset the router.

REVIEW QUESTIONS

1. How are most wireless routers automatically configured?

2. Why should you update your router's firmware before making any other security changes?

3. How could not changing your router's password compromise all of your other security changes?

4. Why wouldn't "password" or "linksys" make a good password for your router?

5. How can you configure your router once you've disabled remote configuration?

LAB 11.4 INVESTIGATE STARTUP PROCESSES

OBJECTIVES

The goal of this lab is to help you identify malicious software running on your computer by examining all running processes. After completing this lab, you will be able to:

◢ Identify all processes running on your computer at startup

◢ Use the Internet to determine the function of each process

MATERIALS REQUIRED

This lab requires the following:

◢ Windows Vista/XP Professional operating system

◢ Internet access

LAB PREPARATION

Before the lab begins, the instructor or lab assistant needs to do the following:

◢ Verify that Windows starts with no errors.

◢ Verify that Internet access is available.

ACTIVITY BACKGROUND

There's an old saying that a rose is a weed in the vegetable garden. Malicious software, for the same reason, is any software you don't want using up valuable resources on your computer.

11

The amount of malicious software on your computer tends to grow over time and eventually slows your computer down. It gets in your system by associating itself with software that you do want, such as updated drivers or applications. The first step in removing it is realizing it's there. In this lab, you learn to investigate all the startup processes on your computer and identify any you want to remove.

ESTIMATED COMPLETION TIME: 45 Minutes

Activity

1. Use Task Manager to list all the running processes on your machine. (You might want to refer to Lab 5.4 for a review of this process.)

2. On a separate piece of paper, make a list of each process running on the computer. How many processes are running?

_____

3. Now reboot the computer in Safe Mode, and use Task Manager to list the running processes again. How many processes are running now?

_____

4. Which processes didn't load when the system was running in Safe Mode?

_____

_____

_____

_____

5. Use the Internet to research each process identified in Step 4, and write a one-sentence explanation of each process on a separate piece of paper.

6. Did you find any malicious processes running? If so, list them:

_____

_____

_____

7. Suppose one of the processes running on your computer is named whAgent.exe. What program is associated with this process?

_____

8. Why isn't disabling the Lsass.exe process a good idea?

_____

9. How could you use Msconfig to temporarily disable a process?

_____

_____

10. List the steps you could take to remove this program from your computer:

_____

_____

_____

_____

REVIEW QUESTIONS

1. Why might antivirus and antispyware software not detect malicious software?

_____

_____

2. Why would you expect fewer processes to be running in Safe Mode?

_____

_____

3. How might a malicious process get onto your computer?

_____

_____

4. Why is it a good idea to temporarily disable a process before removing it altogether?

_____

_____

LAB 11.5 DEAL WITH A ROOTKIT

OBJECTIVES

The goal of this lab is to help you identify and remove a rootkit running on your system. After completing this lab, you will be able to:

◢ Download and install antirootkit software

◢ Use antirootkit software to scan your PC for rootkits

MATERIALS REQUIRED

This lab requires the following:

◢ Windows Vista/XP Professional operating system

◢ Internet access

◢ Ultimate Boot CD created in Lab 7.3 (optional)

11

LAB PREPARATION

Before the lab begins, the instructor or lab assistant needs to do the following:

◢ Verify that Windows starts with no errors.

◢ Verify that Internet access is available.

ACTIVITY BACKGROUND

A rootkit is a type of malware that uses sophisticated methods to hide itself on the system. They can prevent Windows components such as Windows Explorer, Task Manager, or the registry editor from displaying the rootkit processes. This stealthy behavior makes them difficult for your antivirus software to detect. If you have already tried other methods, such as antivirus software, to clean your system, and you still believe your system might be infected, you can try using antirootkit software. In this lab, you will use a popular antirootkit program called Rootkit Revealer by Sysinternals.

ESTIMATED COMPLETION TIME: 60 Minutes

 Activity

1. Before running antirootkit software, it's best to double-check that your problem isn't a simple virus. For best results, run the antivirus software from another PC by temporarily moving the hard drive or run the antivirus software from a bootable CD. The Ultimate Boot CD created in Lab 7.3 contains several antivirus programs. Which antivirus program did you use?

   _____

2. Log on as an administrator.

3. Open your browser and go to *http://technet.microsoft.com*. In the search box at the top, search for **Rootkit Revealer,** and follow the links to download the latest version. What is the latest version of Rootkit Revealer available?

   _____

4. Read through the information on Rootkit Revealer and answer the following questions:

   ◢ What versions of Windows support the program?

   _____

   ◢ What are the four types of rootkits listed and how do they differ?

   _____

   _____

   _____

   _____

◢ In your own words, how does Rootkit Revealer find rootkits?

_____

_____

_____

_____

5. Download and install the program on your computer.

6. When the installation is complete, close any open applications, including your antivirus software, and launch the product. Figure 11-1 shows the Rootkit Revealer running on the Vista desktop.

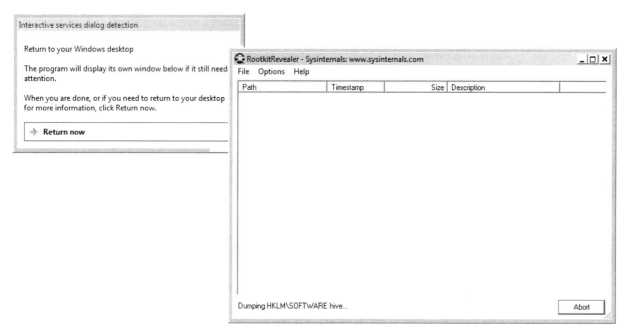

Figure 11-1 Rootkit Revealer scanning for rootkits
Courtesy: Course Technology/Cengage Learning

> **Note** While Rootkit Revealer is running, it takes control of the system so that you cannot use your computer.

7. Did you find any discrepancies that might indicate a rootkit is running? If so, list them:

_____

_____

_____

8. When you're finished, close any open programs.

11

REVIEW QUESTIONS

1. How are rootkits different from other forms of malware?

   _____

   _____

2. Why does running antivirus software from another operating system do a better job?

   _____

   _____

3. Why are kernel-mode rootkits more dangerous than user-mode ones?

   _____

   _____

   _____

4. Why should all other applications be closed before scanning for rootkits?

   _____

   _____

   _____

GLOSSARY

This glossary defines terms related to managing and maintaining a personal computer.

100BaseT An Ethernet standard that operates at 100 Mbps and uses twisted-pair cabling. *Also called* Fast Ethernet. Variations of 100BaseT are 100BaseTX and 100BaseFX.

80 conductor IDE cable An IDE cable that has 40 pins but uses 80 wires, 40 of which are ground wires designed to reduce crosstalk on the cable. The cable is used by ATA/66 and higher IDE drives.

802.11a/b/g *See* IEEE 802.11a/b/g.

A (ampere or amp) A unit of measurement for electrical current. One volt across a resistance of one ohm produces a flow of one amp.

A+ Certification A certification awarded by CompTIA (The Computer Industry Association) that measures a PC technician's knowledge and skills.

access point (AP) A device connected to a LAN that provides wireless communication so that computers, printers, and other wireless devices can communicate with devices on the LAN.

ACPI (Advanced Configuration and Power Interface) Specification developed by Intel, Compaq, Phoenix, Microsoft, and Toshiba to control power on notebooks and other devices.

active matrix A type of video display that amplifies the signal at every intersection in the grid of electrodes, which enhances the pixel quality over that of a dual-scan passive matrix display.

active partition The primary partition on the hard drive that boots the OS. Windows Vista/XP calls the active partition the "system partition."

adapter address *See* MAC (Media Access Control) address.

adapter card A small circuit board inserted in an expansion slot used to communicate between the system bus and a peripheral device. *Also called* interface card.

administrator account In Windows Vista/XP, an account that grants the administrator rights and permissions to all hardware and software resources, such as the right to add, delete, and change accounts and change hardware configurations.

Advanced Options menu A Windows Vista/XP menu that appears when you press F8 when Windows starts. The menu can be used to troubleshoot problems when loading Windows Vista/XP. In Vista, the menu is called the Advanced Boot Options Menu.

adware Software installed on a computer that produces pop-up ads using your browser; the ads are often based on your browsing habits.

Aero user interface The Vista user interface. *Also called* Aero glass.

AirPort The term Apple uses to describe the IEEE 802.11b standard.

alternating current (AC) Current that cycles back and forth rather than traveling in only one direction. In the United States, the AC voltage from a standard wall outlet is normally between 110 and 115 V. In Europe, the standard AC voltage from a wall outlet is 220 V.

ammeter A meter that measures electrical current in amps.

antistatic wrist strap *See* ground bracelet.

antivirus software Utility programs that prevent infection or scan a system to detect and remove viruses. McAfee Associates VirusScan and Norton AntiVirus are two popular antivirus packages.

APIPA (Automatic Private IP Address) An IP address in the address range 169.254.x.x, used by a computer when it can't successfully lease an IP address from a DHCP server.

ASCII (American Standard Code for Information Interchange)   A popular standard for writing letters and other characters in binary code. Originally, ASCII characters were 7 bits, so there were 127 possible values. ASCII has been expanded to an 8-bit version, allowing 128 additional values.

ASR (Automated System Recovery)   The Windows XP process that allows you to restore an entire hard drive volume or logical drive to its state at the time the backup of the volume was made.

AT   A form factor, generally no longer produced, in which the motherboard requires a full-size case. Because of their dimensions and configuration, AT systems are difficult to install, service, and upgrade. *Also called* full AT.

ATAPI (Advanced Technology Attachment Packet Interface)   An interface standard, part of the IDE/ATA standards, that allows tape drives, CD-ROM drives, and other drives to be treated like an IDE hard drive by the system.

ATX   The most common form factor for current PCs, originally introduced by Intel in 1995. ATX motherboards and cases make better use of space and resources than did the AT form factor.

autodetection   A feature on newer system BIOS and hard drives that automatically identifies and configures a new drive in CMOS setup.

autorange meter   A multimeter that senses the quantity of input and sets the range accordingly.

Baby AT   An improved and more flexible version of the AT form factor. Baby AT was the industry standard from approximately 1993 to 1997 and can fit into some ATX cases.

backup   An extra copy of a file, used if the original becomes damaged or destroyed.

bandwidth   In relation to analog communication, the range of frequencies a communications channel or cable can carry. In general use, the term refers to the volume of data that can travel on a bus or over a cable stated in bits per second (bps), kilobits per second (Kbps), or megabits per second (Mbps). *Also called* data throughput *or* line speed.

bank   An area on the motherboard that contains slots for memory modules (typically labeled bank 0, 1, 2, and 3).

baseline   The level of performance expected from a system, which can be compared to current measurements to determine what needs upgrading or tuning.

basic disk   A way to partition a hard drive, used by DOS and all versions of Windows, that stores information about the drive in a partition table at the beginning of the drive. *Compare to* dynamic disk.

binary numbering system   The numbering system used by computers; it has only two numbers, 0 and 1, called binary digits, or bits.

BIOS (basic input/output system)   Firmware that can control much of a computer's I/O functions, such as communication with the hard drive and the monitor. *Also called* ROM BIOS.

BIOS setup   The program in the system BIOS that can change the values in CMOS RAM. *Also called* CMOS setup.

bit (binary digit)   A 0 or 1 used by the binary numbering system.

blue screen   A Windows Vista/XP error displayed on a blue screen that causes the system to halt. *Also called* stop error.

Bluetooth   A standard for wireless communication and data synchronization between devices, developed by a group of electronics manufacturers and overseen by the Bluetooth Special Interest Group. Bluetooth uses the same frequency range as IEEE 802.11b but doesn't have as wide a range.

Blu-ray Disc (BD)   An optical disc technology that uses the UDF version 2.5 file system and a blue laser beam, which has a shorter wavelength than the beam used by DVD or CD discs. A Blu-ray disc can store more data than a DVD.

Boot.ini A Windows XP hidden text file that contains information needed to build the boot loader menu.

boot loader menu A startup menu that gives users the choice of which operating system to load, such as Windows Vista or Windows XP, which are both installed on the same system, creating a dual-boot system.

boot partition The hard drive partition where the Windows Vista/XP OS is stored. The system partition and boot partition can be different partitions.

boot record The first sector of a floppy disk or logical drive in a partition; it contains information about the disk or logical drive. On a hard drive, if the boot record is in the active partition, it's used to boot the OS. *Also called* boot sector.

boot sector *See* boot record.

boot sector virus An infected program that can replace the boot program with a modified, infected version of the boot command utilities, often causing boot and data retrieval problems.

bootstrap loader A small program at the end of the boot record that can be used to boot an OS from the disk or logical drive.

broadband A transmission technique that carries more than one type of transmission on the same medium, such as cable modem or DSL.

brownouts Temporary reductions in voltage, which can sometimes cause data loss. *Also called* sags.

BTX (Balanced Technology Extended) A form factor used by motherboards and computer cases that was expected to replace ATX. It has higher-quality fans, is designed for better air flow, and has improved structural support for the motherboard. The BTX form factor has not been widely adopted.

buffer A temporary memory area where data is kept before being written to a hard drive or sent to a printer, thus reducing the number of writes to devices.

bus The paths, or lines, on the motherboard on which data, instructions, and electrical power move from component to component.

bus speed The speed, or frequency, at which the data on the motherboard moves.

byte A collection of eight bits that's equivalent to a single character. When referring to system memory, an additional error-checking bit might be added, making the total nine bits.

cabinet file A file with a .cab extension that contains one or more compressed files and is often used to distribute software on disk. The Extract command is used to extract files from a cabinet file.

cable modem A technology that uses cable TV lines for data transmission, requiring a modem at each end. From the modem, a network cable connects to a NIC in the user's PC.

capacitor An electronic device that can maintain an electrical charge for a period of time and is used to smooth out the flow of electrical current. Capacitors are often found in computer power supplies.

CardBus The latest PCMCIA specification. It improves I/O speed, increases the bus width to 32 bits, and supports lower-voltage PC Cards, while maintaining backward compatibility with earlier standards.

cards Adapter boards or interface cards placed into expansion slots to expand the functions of a computer, allowing it to communicate with external devices, such as monitors or speakers.

CAT A rating for UTP cable. CAT-5 or higher cabling is required for Fast Ethernet.

CCITT (Comité Consultatif International Télégraphique et Téléphonique) An international organization that was responsible for developing standards for international communications. This organization has been incorporated into the ITU. *See also* ITU (International Telecommunications Union).

CD (compact disc) An optical disc technology that uses a red laser beam and can hold up to 700 MB of data.

CD (change directory) command A command given at the command prompt that changes the default directory, such as CD\Windows.

CDFS (Compact Disk File System) The 32-bit file system for CDs and some CD-Rs and CD-RWs that replaced the older 16-bit mscdex file system used by DOS. *See also* UDF (Universal Disk Format) file system.

CD-R (CD-recordable) A CD drive that can record or write data to a CD. The drive may or may not be multisession, but the data can't be erased after it's written.

CD-RW (CD-rewritable) A CD drive that can record or write data to a CD. The data can be erased and overwritten. The drive may or may not be multisession.

chain A group of clusters used to hold a single file.

child directory *See* subdirectory.

chip creep A condition in which chips loosen because of thermal changes.

chipset A group of chips on the motherboard that control the timing and flow of data and instructions to and from the CPU.

CHS (cylinder, head, sector) mode The traditional method by which BIOS reads from and writes to hard drives by addressing the correct cylinder, head, and sector. *Also called* normal mode.

circuit board A computer component, such as the main motherboard or an adapter board, that has electronic circuits and chips.

clean install An installation of an OS on a new hard drive or a hard drive that has a previous OS installed, but it's performed without carrying forward any settings kept by the old OS, including information about hardware, software, or user preferences. *Also called* fresh installation.

client/server A computer concept whereby one computer (the client) requests information from another computer (the server).

client/server application An application that has two components. The client software requests data from the server software on the same or another computer.

clock speed The speed, or frequency, expressed in MHz or GHz, that controls activity on the motherboard and is generated by a crystal or oscillator located on the motherboard.

clone A computer that's a no-name Intel- and Microsoft-compatible PC.

cluster One or more sectors that constitute the smallest unit of space on a disk for storing data. Files are written to a disk as groups of whole clusters. *Also called* file allocation unit.

CMOS (complementary metal-oxide semiconductor) The technology used to manufacture microchips. CMOS chips require less electricity, hold data longer after the electricity is turned off, are slower, and produce less heat than TTL chips. The configuration, or setup, chip is a CMOS chip.

CMOS configuration chip A chip on the motherboard that contains a very small amount of memory, or RAM, enough to hold configuration, or setup, information about the computer. The chip is powered by a battery when the PC is turned off. *Also called* CMOS setup chip *or* CMOS RAM chip.

CMOS setup The CMOS configuration chip, or the program in system BIOS that can change the values in the CMOS RAM.

CMOS setup chip *See* CMOS configuration chip.

cold boot *See* hard boot.

combo card An Ethernet card that contains more than one transceiver, each with a different port on the back of the card, to accommodate different cabling media.

command prompt window A Windows utility that is used to enter multiple commands to perform a variety of tasks.

compact case A type of case used in low-end desktop systems. Compact cases follow the NLX, LPX, or Mini LPX form factor. They are likely to have fewer drive bays, but they generally still provide for some expansion. *Also called* low-profile *or* slimline cases.

compressed drive A drive whose format has been reorganized to store more data. A compressed drive is really not a drive at all; it's actually a type of file, typically with a host drive called H.

computer name Character-based host name or NetBIOS name assigned to a computer.

console A centralized location from which to run commonly used tools.

continuity A continuous, unbroken path for the flow of electricity. A continuity test can determine whether internal wiring is still intact or whether a fuse is good or bad.

conventional memory Memory addresses between 0 and 640K. *Also called* base memory.

cooler A combination cooling fan and heat sink mounted on the top or side of a processor to keep it cool.

(CPU) central processing unit The heart and brain of the computer, which receives data input, processes information, and carries out instructions. *Also called* microprocessor or processor.

C-RIMM (Continuity RIMM) A placeholder RIMM module that provides continuity so that every RIMM slot is filled.

cross-linked clusters Errors caused when more than one file points to a cluster and the files appear to share the same disk space, according to the file allocation table.

crossover cable A cable used to connect two PCs into the simplest network possible. Also used to connect two hubs.

CVF (compressed volume file) The file on the host drive of a compressed drive that holds all compressed data.

data bus The lines on the system bus that the CPU uses to send and receive data.

data cartridge A type of tape medium typically used for backups. Full-sized data cartridges are 4 x 6 x ⅝ inches. A minicartridge is only 3¼ x 2½ x ⅗ inches.

data line protector A surge protector designed to work with the telephone line to a modem.

data path size The number of lines on a bus that can hold data, for example, 8, 16, 32, and 64 lines, which can accommodate 8, 16, 32, and 64 bits at a time.

data throughput *See* bandwidth.

DC (direct current) Current that travels in only one direction (the type of electricity provided by batteries). Computer power supplies transform AC to low DC.

DC controller A card inside a notebook that converts voltage to CPU voltage. Some notebook manufacturers consider the card to be a field replaceable unit (FRU).

DCE (data communications equipment) The hardware, usually a dial-up modem, that provides the connection between a data terminal and a communications line. *See also* DTE (data terminal equipment).

DDR (Double Data Rate) A type of memory technology used on DIMMs that runs at twice the speed of the system clock.

DDR2 A version of SDRAM that's faster than DDR and uses less power.

DDR3 A version of SDRAM that is faster than DDR2 memory and that can use triple channels.

default gateway The gateway a computer on a network uses to access another network unless it knows to specifically use another gateway for quicker access to that network.

default printer The printer Windows prints to unless another printer is selected.

defragment To "optimize" or rewrite a file to a disk in one contiguous chain of clusters, thus speeding up data retrieval.

desktop The initial screen displayed when an OS has a GUI interface loaded.

device driver A program stored on the hard drive that tells the computer how to communicate with an I/O device, such as a printer or modem.

DHCP (Dynamic Host Configuration Protocol) server A service that assigns dynamic IP addresses to computers on a network when they first access the network.

diagnostic cards Adapter cards designed to discover and report computer errors and conflicts at POST time (before the computer boots up), often by displaying a number on the card.

diagnostic software Utility programs that help troubleshoot computer systems. Some Windows diagnostic utilities are Chkdsk and Scandisk. PC-Technician is an example of a third-party diagnostic program.

differential cable A SCSI cable in which a signal is carried on two wires, each carrying voltage, and the signal is the difference between the two. Differential signaling provides for error checking and improved data integrity. *Compare to* SE (single-ended) cable.

digital certificate A code used to authenticate the source of a file or document or to identify and authenticate a person or organization sending data over the Internet. The code is assigned by a certificate authority, such as VeriSign, and includes a public key for encryption. *Also called* digital ID or digital signature.

digital ID *See* digital certificate.

digital signature *See* digital certificate.

DIMM (dual inline memory module) A miniature circuit board used in newer computers to hold memory. DIMMs can hold up to 2 GB RAM on a single module.

DIP (dual inline package) switch A switch on a circuit board or other device that can be set on or off to hold configuration or setup information.

directory table An OS table that contains file information such as the name, size, time, and date of last modification, and cluster number of the file's beginning location.

Direct Rambus DRAM A memory technology by Rambus and Intel that uses a narrow, very fast network-type system bus. Memory is stored on a RIMM module. *Also called* RDRAM or Direct RDRAM.

Direct RDRAM *See* Direct Rambus DRAM.

disk cache A method whereby recently retrieved data and adjacent data are read into memory in advance, anticipating the next CPU request.

disk cloning *See* drive imaging.

disk compression Compressing data on a hard drive to allow more data to be written to the drive.

disk imaging *See* drive imaging.

Disk Management A Windows utility used to display, create, and format partitions on basic disks and volumes on dynamic disks.

disk quota A limit placed on the amount of disk space that's available to users. Requires a Windows NTFS volume.

disk thrashing A condition that results when the hard drive is excessively used for virtual memory because RAM is full. It dramatically slows down processing and can cause premature hard drive failure.

DMA (direct memory access) channel A number identifying a channel whereby a device can pass data to memory without involving the CPU. Think of a DMA channel as a shortcut for data moving to and from the device and memory.

DMA transfer mode A transfer mode used by devices, including the hard drive, to transfer data to memory without involving the CPU.

DNS server A computer that can find an IP address for another computer when only the domain name is known.

docking station A device that receives a notebook computer and provides additional secondary storage and easy connection to peripheral devices.

domain In Windows, a logical group of networked computers, such as those on a college campus, that share a centralized directory database of user account information and security for the entire domain.

domain name A unique text-based name that identifies a network.

DOS box A command window.

dot pitch The distance between the dots that the electronic beam hits on a monitor screen.

doze time The time before an Energy Star® or "green" system reduces 80 percent of its activity.

DPMS (Display Power Management Signaling) Energy Star® standard specifications that allow for the video card and monitor to go into sleep mode simultaneously. *See also* Energy Star®.

DRAM (dynamic RAM) The most common type of system memory, it requires refreshing every few milliseconds.

drive imaging Making an exact image of a hard drive, including partition information, boot sectors, operating system installation, and application software, to replicate the hard drive on another system or recover from a hard drive crash. *Also called* disk cloning and disk imaging.

drop height The height from which a manufacturer states that its drive can be dropped without making the drive unusable.

DSL (Digital Subscriber Line) A telephone line that carries digital data from end to end and can be leased from the telephone company for individual use. DSL lines are rated at 5 Mbps, about 50 times faster than regular telephone lines.

DTE (data terminal equipment) Both the computer and a remote terminal or other computer to which it's attached. *See also* DCE (data communications equipment).

dual boot The ability to boot using either of two different OSs, such as Windows Vista and Windows XP.

dual channel A motherboard feature that improves memory performance by providing two 64-bit channels between memory and the chipset. DDR, DDR2, and DDR3 DIMMS can use dual channels.

dual core A processor package that contains two core processors, thus supporting four instructions at once.

dual-scan passive matrix A type of video display that's less expensive than an active-matrix display and does not provide as high-quality an image. With dual-scan display, two columns of electrodes are activated at the same time.

dual-voltage CPU A CPU that requires two different voltages, one for internal processing and the other for I/O processing.

DVD (digital video disk or digital versatile disk) A faster, larger CD format that can read older

CDs, store more than 8 GB of data, and hold full-length motion picture videos.

dynamic disk A way to partition one or more hard drives, introduced with Windows 2000, in which information about the drive is stored in a database at the end of the drive. *Compare to* basic disk.

dynamic IP address An assigned IP address used for the current session only. When the session is terminated, the IP address is returned to the list of available addresses.

dynamic volume A volume type used with dynamic disks for which you can change the size of the volume after you have created it.

ECC (error-correcting code) A chipset feature on a motherboard that checks the integrity of data stored on DIMMs or RIMMs and can correct single-bit errors in a byte. More advanced ECC schemas can detect, but not correct, double-bit errors in a byte.

ECHS (extended CHS) mode *See* large mode.

ECP (Extended Capabilities Port) A bidirectional parallel port mode that uses a DMA channel to speed up data flow.

EDO (extended data out) A type of RAM that can be 10 percent to 20 percent faster than conventional RAM because it eliminates the delay before it issues the next memory address.

EEPROM (electrically erasable programmable ROM) A type of chip in which higher voltage can be applied to one of the pins to erase its previous memory before a new instruction set is electronically written.

EFS (Encrypted File System) A way to use a key to encode a file or folder on an NTFS volume to protect sensitive data. Because it's an integrated system service, EFS is transparent to users and applications and difficult to attack.

EIDE (Enhanced IDE) A standard for managing the interface between secondary storage devices and a computer system. A system can support up to six serial ATA and parallel ATA EIDE devices or up to four parallel ATA IDE devices, such as hard drives, CD-ROM drives, and Zip drives.

emergency startup disk (ESD) *See* rescue disk.

EMI (electromagnetic interference) A magnetic field produced as a side effect from the flow of electricity. EMI can cause corrupted data in data lines that aren't properly shielded.

encryption The process of putting readable data into an encoded form that can be decoded (or decrypted) only through use of a key.

Energy Star® "Green" systems that satisfy the EPA requirements to decrease the overall consumption of electricity. *See also* Green Standards.

enhanced BIOS A system BIOS that has been written to accommodate large-capacity drives (more than 504 MB, usually in the gigabyte range).

EPP (Enhanced Parallel Port) A parallel port that allows data to flow in both directions (bidirectional port) and is faster than original parallel ports on PCs that allowed communication only in one direction.

EPROM (erasable programmable ROM) A type of chip with a special window that allows the current memory contents to be erased with special ultraviolet light so that the chip can be reprogrammed. Many BIOS chips are EPROMs.

error correction The capability of a modem to identify transmission errors and then automatically request another transmission.

escalate When a technician passes a customer's problem to higher organizational levels because he or she cannot solve the problem.

ESD (electrostatic discharge) Another name for static electricity, which can damage chips and destroy motherboards, even though it might not be felt or seen with the naked eye.

ESD (emergency startup disk) *See* rescue disk.

Ethernet The most popular LAN architecture that can run at 10 Mbps (ThinNet or ThickNet), 100 Mbps (Fast Ethernet), or 1 Gbps (Gigabit Ethernet).

Event Viewer (Eventvwr.msc) A Windows tool useful for troubleshooting problems with Windows, applications, and hardware. It displays logs of significant events.

expansion bus A bus that doesn't run in sync with the system clock.

expansion card A circuit board inserted into a slot on the motherboard to enhance the computer's capability.

expansion slot A narrow slot on the motherboard where an expansion card can be inserted. Expansion slots connect to a bus on the motherboard.

extended partition The only partition on a hard drive that can contain more than one logical drive.

external SATA (eSATA) A standard for external drives based on SATA that uses a special external shielded SATA cable up to two meters long.

faceplate A metal plate that comes with the motherboard and fits over the ports to create a well-fitted enclosure around them.

Fast Ethernet *See* 100BaseT.

FAT (file allocation table) A table on a hard drive or floppy disk that tracks the clusters used to contain a file.

FAT12 The 12-bit-wide, one-column file allocation table for a floppy disk, containing information about how each cluster or file allocation unit on the disk is currently used.

fault tolerance The degree to which a system can tolerate failures. Adding redundant components, such as disk mirroring or disk duplexing, is a way to build in fault tolerance.

file allocation unit *See* cluster.

file extension A three-character portion of the filename used to identify the file type. In command lines, the file extension follows the filename and is separated from it by a period, such as Msd.exe, with exe being the file extension.

filename The first part of the name assigned to a file. In DOS, the filename can be no more than eight characters and is followed by the file extension. In Windows, a filename can be up to 255 characters.

file system The overall structure that an OS uses to name, store, and organize files on a